Indigenous
Research
Methodologies

Indigenous Research Methodologies

Bagele Chilisa

University of Botswana

Los Angeles | London | New Delhi
Singapore | Washington DC

Los Angeles | London | New Delhi
Singapore | Washington DC

FOR INFORMATION:

SAGE Publications, Inc.

2455 Teller Road

Thousand Oaks, California 91320

E-mail: order@sagepub.com

SAGE Publications Ltd.

1 Oliver's Yard

55 City Road

London, EC1Y 1SP

United Kingdom

SAGE Publications India Pvt. Ltd.

B 1/I 1 Mohan Cooperative Industrial Area

Mathura Road, New Delhi 110 044

India

SAGE Publications Asia-Pacific Pte. Ltd.

33 Pekin Street #02-01

Far East Square

Singapore 048763

Acquisitions Editor: Vicki Knight

Associate Editor: Lauren Habib

Editorial Assistant: Kalie Koscielak

Production Editor: Astrid Virding

Copy Editor: Jackie Tasch

Typesetter: Hurix Systems Pvt. Ltd.

Proofreader: Ellen Brink

Indexer: Will Ragsdale

Cover Designers: Anupama Krishnan and
            Candice Harman

Marketing Manager: Helen Salmon

Permissions Editor: Adele Hutchinson

Printed in the United States of America.

Library of Congress Cataloging-in-Publication Data

Chilisa, Bagele.
Indigenous research methodologies / Bagele Chilisa.
     p. cm.
Includes bibliographical references and index.
ISBN 978-1-4129-5882-0 (pbk.)
1. Indigenous peoples–Research–Methodology.
2. Postcolonialism–Research–Methodology. I. Title.
GN380.C494 2012
305.80072'1–dc22   2011005039
This book is printed on acid-free paper.

11 12 13 14 15 10 9 8 7 6 5 4 3 2 1

BRIEF CONTENTS

DETAILED CONTENTS

PREFACE

The community of social science researchers is experiencing a struggle as it comes to terms with social justice issues that arise from the research process itself, as well as from the findings that are produced by their efforts. While more and more non-Western researchers from the third world and from indigenous societies are expressing criticism about what is viewed as colonizing epistemologies and methodologies, we (speaking as one of them) are also cognizant of the need to bring indigenous methodologies into the research arena as a means of addressing the goals of enhanced human rights and social justice. There is an increasing emphasis on the need to sensitize researchers and students to diverse epistemologies, methods, and methodologies, especially those of women, minority groups, former colonized societies, indigenous people, historically oppressed communities, economically oppressed groups, and people with disabilities, who have been excluded from dominant epistemologies.

However, there are questions about the nature of these marginalized epistemologies, their philosophical base, the standards by which they are to be validated, and the direction in which they move the scholarship of research methodologies. This book addresses some of these concerns by bringing together postcolonial indigenous epistemologies and methodologies from across the globe and creating a platform to discuss them, along with other emergent methods and methodologies in the social sciences. It is a single-authored research methods book that situates research in a larger historical, cultural, and global context and provides case studies through which students can see for themselves the dominance of Euro-Western research methodologies and hence appreciate the call for decolonizing research methodologies. The major focus of the book is on extending the theoretical and philosophical critique of decolonizing methodologies by making visible specific methodologies that are commensurate with a postcolonial indigenous paradigm. These methodologies are discussed within a postcolonial indigenous paradigm, which puts forward relational ontology, epistemology, and axiology as a philosophical framework to bring together methods, techniques, and methodologies by global postcolonial and indigenous scholars and emergent methods in Euro-Western research.

Goals of the Book

The goals of the book are to do the following:

- Promote the recovering, valuing, and internationalizing of postcolonial indigenous epistemologies, methodologies, and methods
- Explore and critique some of the dominant paradigms, using arguments based on the philsophies of the researched, as well as their ways of knowing and their experiences with colonization, imperialism, and globalization
- Present a postcolonial indigenous research paradigm as an overarching framework to explore the philosophical assumptions that undergird the use of postcolonial indigenous methodologies
- Theorize postcolonial indigenous ways of doing research, explore the application of these methodologies through case studies, and give illustrative examples
- Foreground interconnectedness and relational epistemologies as a framework within which to discuss postcolonial indigenous methodologies from across the globe
- Illustrate power relations in the research process

The first chapter introduces the debates on current Euro-Western research paradigms and the philosophical assumptions that inform these methodologies. The main thrust of the chapter is that current dominant academic research traditions are founded on the culture, history, and philosophies of Euro-Western thought and are therefore indigenous to Western societies and their academic institutions. These methodologies exclude from knowledge production the knowledge systems of the researched colonized Other. Three approaches in postcolonial indigenous research methodologies are discussed: (1) decolonization and indigenization of Euro-Western research approaches, (2) research approaches informed by a postcolonial indigenous research paradigm, and (3) third-space methodologies.

Chapter 2 presents case studies that demonstrate how colonial research served the interests of the colonizers, how globalization continues to serve the interests of former and present-day colonizers, and how postcolonial theorizing and critical race theory can be used to conduct research. Chapter 3 highlights how mainstream research in postcolonial societies still ignores, marginalizes, and suppresses other knowledge systems and ways of knowing. The chapter demonstrates how HIV/AIDS prevention has been highly compromised by employing language and categories of thinking that are alien to the infected and affected communities. It also shows how a dichotomous hierarchy informed by colonization, imperialism, and globalization privileges the first world position as knower and relegates the third world to the position of an Other who are learners; it also reflects the people's resistance to imposed frameworks and its consequences. Chapter 4 explores the meaning of postcolonial indigenous research methodologies and the philosophies and worldviews that inform these methodologies. The meaning of indigenous knowledge and its role in research are also discussed.

Chapter 5 emphasizes the role of language, oral literature, and storytelling as foundations and sources of the literature, philosophies, theories, and methods of data collection, analysis, and interpretation regarding the researched, who constitute a two thirds majority of the world population. Chapter 6 underscores the relationship between methodology, methods, and philosophical assumptions on the nature of reality, knowledge, and values. The chapter presents examples of culturally responsive indigenous methodologies and discusses how rigor and credibility are addressed in these methodologies. Chapter 7 critiques the conventional interview method from a postcolonial indigenous research perspective and offers alternative interview strategies suited to the worldviews of the researched.

In Chapter 8, participatory research approaches that enable oppressed and disempowered groups to collectively share and analyze their knowledge, life experiences, and conditions and to use indigenous knowledge as a basis to plan and to act are discussed. Two types of participatory action research are presented, one with an emphasis on participants as co-researchers and another with an emphasis on personal and social transformation. Chapter 9 highlights attempts to decolonize Euro-Western methodologies from the perspective of non-Western marginalized feminisms. The argument is that women in postcolonial and indigenous societies have been silenced by Western feminist theory, in addition to Western patriarchies, third world patriarchies, colonialism, imperialism, and globalization. The chapter is devoted to defining postcolonial indigenous feminist methodologies and articulating the worldviews, perspectives, and epistemologies that inform these methodologies, as well as research methods that privilege non-Western women. Chapter 10 draws from discussions in the book to synthesize working relations and partnerships between researchers and the researched and between institutions and communities, as well as ways of integrating knowledge systems such that indigenous knowledge, methods, and techniques are integrated into the global knowledge economy. The chapter further outlines a matrix for planning research from a postcolonial indigenous research perspective.

Audiences for the Book

Indigenous research methods and decolonizing research are relatively new areas. This book fills a gap in research methods and should find a ready market in the academy as it addresses the rising need to engage students in multiple epistemologies. It also provides the increasing number of transnational and international scholars carrying out research in third and fourth world countries, among indigenous peoples, and among historically oppressed groups with an introduction to methodologies that communicate the experiences of the researched. I would recommend this as a primary textbook for advanced undergraduate, master's, and beginning doctoral students taking research methods courses in education and the social and behavioral sciences. With the limited number of books that synthesize postcolonial indigenous methodologies, this volume can serve as a research methods book for students enrolled in postcolonial studies and cultural studies programs, indigenous education programs, and international education programs and for students and scholars conducting ethnoscience and ethnomathematics research. There is a growing interest in indigenous knowledge systems and postcolonial studies in general. There is, for instance, a move to create interdisciplinary postcolonial studies in most nation-states and within the United Nations University. A methodology book that focuses on postcolonial indigenous philosophies and methodologies becomes a useful resource for the growing disciplines in indigenous knowledge systems and postcolonial studies. Researchers and evaluators working in culturally complex societies and with postcolonial indigenous societies will find the book useful if they wish to conduct research that brings about positive change to the lives of the researched people. The book is appropriate for international and professional markets because it brings together voices of postcolonial indigenous scholars with specific reference to epistemologies, methodology, and method and creates a common platform through which these are addressed, together with other emergent research methods. Researchers from across disciplines addressing issues of power from the perspective of colonizer/colonized, self/Other, gender, ethnicity, race, and disability will find the book useful.

Features of the Book

• Provides a comprehensive overview and synthesis of indigenous research methodologies and indigenous feminist methodologies and illustrates their application through a fascinating array of global case studies

- Provides an overview and critique of predominant research paradigms and their methodologies; gives a clear justification for an indigenous paradigm; explores the theoretical and philosophical foundations of indigenous paradigms by clarifying their ontological, epistemological, and axiological assumptions and methodologies; and moves the decolonization of research agenda beyond theory to practice.

- Demonstrates the application of postcolonial theory, critical race theory, postcolonial indigenous feminist theory, indigenous knowledge, and indigenous theorizing to planning and conducting research by showcasing global examples and case studies illustrating these theories from Canada, Australia, New Zealand, the United States, Africa, Asia, and the United Kingdom.

- Presents conceptual and practical descriptions and suggestions on social justice partnerships and working relationships between the researchers and the researched; between communities and research institutions; between funding agencies, researchers, and communities; between indigenous researchers and international or transnational researchers; and between Western and non-Western researchers from developed and developing countries

- Offers suggestions on integrating knowledge systems in such a way that indigenous knowledge, philosophies, methodologies, and techniques become integrated in the global knowledge economy

- Begins each chapter with cutting-edge and thought-provoking quotations from eminent international scholars and a "before you start activity"; each chapter includes activities and suggested readings that stimulate critical thinking and a transformation of the mind

My Identity

I am a woman born in a small village in Botswana, a former British colony situated in southern Africa. My parents are subsistence farmers who worked hard to pay my school fees. At the age of 5 years, before I started school, my father taught me the vowels and letters of the alphabet; our classroom was behind the granary that stored all the produce from the fields. By the time I started school, I could count and recite the vowels and letters of the alphabet. As I was growing up, my father introduced me to the concept of decolonization of the mind, even though he never termed it such. At that time, it was common for women and men to apply skin lightening creams to their faces. My father often talked to me and my other siblings at length about why it was important always to be who we are and not to wish to be light in complexion. I was fortunate to pass my primary leaving-school examination and proceed to secondary school. While at school, I decided to convert to Christianity in the Roman Catholic denomination. I was requested to ask my parents to give me an English Christian name. My father made it clear that my name, Bagele, had a meaning to which the family and the community could connect and relate. He could not authorize any new name. He explained that he was called Tabagele and my mother Mmabagele and therefore were known in the community through the names that connected them to their daughter. My change of name would start a chain of other changes of names and would require the community to figure out new relationships with him and with me. This early lesson from my father gave me the courage to explore ways in which indigenous practices and values on connectedness and relational ways of knowing of the colonized Other could be valorized in research.

Writing this book has hence been a personal project that has enabled me to draw together my interests and training in research methodology at the University of Pittsburgh in the United States, my 20 years of experience conducting collaborative research in southern and eastern Africa with scholars from the United Kingdom and the United States, and my knowledge of the culture of my people in the village of Nshakashogwe, Botswana. Throughout my research journey, I noticed there were two knowledge systems in operation, one that resonated with the researched and another that was academic and informed by Western disciplines. The survivance of the nonacademic knowledge system of the researched inspired me to write this book.

Acknowledgments

Many people contributed to my ability to complete this book, including my family, students, colleagues, and the reviewers of the manuscript. From the University of Botswana, my special thanks to Frank Youngman for his valuable comments and encouragement to finish the book. Many thanks to A. A. Adeyinka, M. Dube, M. Sekgwa, L. Chisiyanwa, M. Sekgwa, D. Pule, and Sukhjinder Kaur for their contributions. I am indebted to Paul Bennel, Mairead Dunne, and Fiona Leach from Sussex University, United Kingdom; Martin Carnoy of Stanford University, United States; and John Jemmott and Loretta Jemmott of University of Pennsylvania, United States; for our research together. My special thanks to Donna Mertens from Gallaudet University, United States, and Michelle Commeyras from the University of Georgia, United States, who gave me important advice and practical support. From Sage, I am indebted to the editors, Lisa Cuevas and Vicki Knight, for their patience, the encouragement to start and finish the book, and their valuable support. To the following reviewers, thanks for the wealth of knowledge in the area and your willingness to share it: Tony E. Adams, Northeastern Illinois University; Alison Jones, University of Auckland, New Zealand; Peter J. Mataira, University of Hawai'i at Manoa; and Wenona Victor, Simon Fraser University.

I also wish to thank my parents, Motlalepula and Zwambele Kenosi, and my grandmother, Ponya Kenosi, for the oral literature they passed on to me. To my husband, Ernest thanks for enduring my long hours of writing. Special thanks to Wanano, Rapelang, Mboki, Kushatha, Simisami, Chedu, Nlakidzi, and Allysa for their support.

ABOUT THE AUTHOR

Bagele Chilisa is an Associate Professor at the University of Botswana where she teaches Research Methods and Evaluation courses to graduate and undergraduate students. One of her main areas of research is on research methodologies that are relevant, context specific and appropriate in African contexts, culturally complex communities and methodologies that make visible voices of those who continue to suffer oppression and discrimination be it because of their sex, race/ethnicity, disability, sexual orientation or social class. These are methods inclusive of other ways of knowing, perceiving reality and value systems and methods that empower communities to produce knowledge that they can own and use to improve their standards of living. She is first author to two books in this area: *Educational Research: Towards Sustainable Development* and *Research Methods for Adult Educators in Africa*.

Other publications include journal articles: "Educational Research Within Postcolonial Africa: A Critique of HIV/AIDS Research in Botswana (International Journal of Qualitative Studies; "Resisting Dominant Discourses: Implications of Indigenous African Feminist Theory and Methods for Gender and Education Research (Gender and Education Journal); "Mbizi: Empowerment and HIV/AIDS Prevention for Adolescents Girls in Botswana (The Journal of Specialists in Group Work); as well as book chapters: "Indigenous Researchers: Contrasting Western and Indigenous Perspectives," (in D. M. Mertens and P. E. Ginsberg, Handbook for Social Research Ethics); "Indigenous Knowledge, HIV and AIDS Education and Research: Implications for Health Educators" (in E. Taylor and P. Cranton, The Handbook of Transformative Learning); and "'Sex' Education: Subjugated Voices and Adolescent Voices" (in C. Skelton, B. Francis, and L. Smulyan, Gender and Education).

She has received numerous grants to carry out evaluation research on HIV/AIDS, gender, education, sexuality and assessment from the following International Organizations: DFID (Department for International Development); FAWE (Forum for African Women in Education); UNICEF;

UNDP; UNESCO; Economic Commission for Africa; World Bank; ILO; the National Institute of Health (NIH) USA and Spencer Foundation (USA). Most of the research involved partnerships between universities and collaboration with international scholars. She has conducted collaborative research with University of Pennsylvania, Stanford University and Harvard School of Public Health and University of Sussex. She recently won an NIH grant to build research capacity using culturally sensitive methodologies that can inform the design of cultural-specific and age-appropriate interventions that can reduce HIV/AIDS infection in adolescents in Botswana.

She has organized sessions in International Conferences to advocate for postcolonial indigenous research and evaluation methodologies and African rooted evaluation approaches. She has also made presentations at the meetings of International Sociological Association Research Committee on Logic and Methodology; African Evaluation Association; World Congress of Comparative Education Societies; and the American Psychological Association.

CHAPTER **1**

SITUATING KNOWLEDGE SYSTEMS

How is it possible to decolonize (social) research in/on the non-Western developing countries to ensure that the people's human condition is not constructed through Western hegemony and ideology?

Patience Elabor-Idemudia (2002, p. 231)

Our current range of research epistemologies—positivism to postmodernisms, poststructuralisms—arise out of the social history and culture of the dominant race, . . . these epistemologies reflect and reinforce that social history and that social group and this has negative results for the people of color in general and scholars of color in particular.

James J. Scheurich (1997, p. 141)

OVERVIEW

The main thrust of this chapter is that current academic research traditions are founded on the culture, history, and philosophies of Euro-Western thought and are therefore indigenous to the Western academy and its institutions. These methodologies exclude from knowledge production the knowledge systems of formerly colonized, historically marginalized, and oppressed groups, which today are most often represented as Other and fall under broad categories of non-Western, third world, developing, underdeveloped,

First Nations, indigenous peoples, third world women, African American women, and so on. The chapter commences with discussion of some of the concepts and terms used in the book and an outline of the process and strategies for decolonizing Western-based research. I discuss two approaches in postcolonial-indigenous research methodologies—(1) decolonization and indigenization of dominant research approaches and (2) research approaches informed by a postcolonial-indigenous research paradigm— along with third space methodologies. Western research paradigms, the positivist/postpositivist, interpretive, and transformative, are discussed. The chapter will demonstrate that a paradigm implies a methodological approach with a philosophical base that informs assumptions about perceptions of reality, what counts as knowledge and ways of knowing and values. The researcher's perceptions of reality, what counts as knowledge and values, have an impact on the way research questions are conceived, research approaches, data-gathering instruments, analysis, and interpretation and dissemination of research findings. The dominant Western research paradigms are critiqued from a postcolonial-indigenous research perspective. A case study that shows how methodologies can silence and exclude the views of non-Western, formerly colonized societies is presented, as well as a case study that shows an approach based on decolonization and indigenization of Euro-Western methodologies.

LEARNING OBJECTIVES

By the end of this chapter, you should be able to:

1. Explain the decolonization of research process and the strategies for decolonization
2. Appreciate the need for researchers to interrogate the "captive" or "colonized mind" and engage in multiple epistemologies that are inclusive of voices of those who suffered colonization, the disenfranchised, and dispossessed, often represented as the Other, non-Western, third world, developing, underdeveloped, First Nations, indigenous peoples, third world women, African American women, and historically marginalized groups
3. Critically appreciate the influence of Euro-Western history, culture, philosophy, and theoretical perspectives on research
4. Compare and contrast postcolonial-indigenous paradigms and Euro-Western paradigm assumptions about the nature of reality, what counts as knowledge and ways of knowing, and value systems in research

Before You Start

Read the introductory quotations. Make a list of studies that have been conducted in your communities by yourself or other scholars. List and discuss the research approaches, methods of collecting data and methods of analysis, and dissemination of research findings in these studies, as well as their impact on policy, practice, development change, and the standard of living of the people in these communities in general.

INTRODUCTION

There is growing evidence that social science research "needs emancipation from hearing only the voices of Western Europe, emancipation from generations of silence, and emancipation from seeing the world in one color" (Guba & Lincoln, 2005, p. 212). Social science research needs to involve spirituality in research, respecting communal forms of living that are not Western and creating space for inquiries based on relational realities and forms of knowing that are predominant among the non-Western Other/s still being colonized. I have always been disturbed by the way in which the Euro-Western research process disconnects me from the multiple relations that I have with my community, the living and the nonliving. I belong to the Bantu people of Africa, who live a communal life based on a connectedness that stretches from birth to death, continues beyond death, and extends to the living and the nonliving. I am known and communicate in relational terms that connect me to all my relations, living and the nonliving. It is common for people to refer to each other using totems as well as relational terms such as *uncle, aunt, brother,* and so on. For instance, my totem is a crocodile, and depending on who is talking to me and on what occasion, I can be referred to using my totem.

The importance of connectedness and relationships is not unique to the Bantu people of southern Africa. Shawn Wilson (2008) notes that in the speech of the Aboriginal Australians, other indigenous people are referred to as cousin, brother, or auntie. Ideally, the multiple connections that indigenous scholars have with those around them and with the living and the nonliving should form part of their social history and should inform how they see the world and how they relate with the researched. Euro-Western hegemonic methodologies, however, continue to dominate how we think and conduct research.

Recently, the United Nations Development Program (UNDP) approved a proposal from the Centre for Scientific Research, Indigenous and Innovative

Knowledge (CESRIK) at the University of Botswana to conduct a survey on indigenous knowledge systems. The CESRIK committee, of which I am a member, met to discuss the approach to the survey. First, there was brainstorming on the different categories of indigenous knowledge. The next step was to discuss the approach that would be used for a survey on a given category of indigenous knowledge. Some suggested that we should conduct a workshop where academic experts on indigenous knowledge systems would give keynote presentations to an audience made up of community elders, experts in indigenous knowledge such as herbalists, members of the association of traditional healers, storytellers, and traditional leaders. Others warned that the process of knowledge production—the naming, concepts, thought analysis, sources of knowledge, and what is accepted as evidence by indigenous knowledge experts—could be different from what academic keynote speakers accept; others pointed out that the translation from English, the official language, to local languages could distort the communication even further. Still, others noted that Indigenous experts from the communities could choose not to participate in the discussion unless they were assured of a copyright on the knowledge they brought into the discussions.

These discussions point to the operation of two knowledge systems. One is Euro-Western and indigenous to the Western academy and its institutions; the other knowledge is non-Western and peripheral, and it operates with the values and belief systems of the historically colonized. This peripheral knowledge system values relationships and is suspicious of Western academic discourse and its colonizing tendencies. Paddy Ladd (2003) notes that academic discourse systems

> contain [their] own unspoken rules as to what can or cannot be said and how, when and where. Each therefore, constructs cannons of truth around whatever its participants decide is "admissible evidence," a process that in the case of certain prestigious discourses, such as those found in universities, medical establishments and communication media, can be seen as particularly dangerous when unexamined, for these then come to determine what counts as knowledge. (p. 76)

As more and more scholars begin to engage with imperialism and colonialism in research, make choices on what they research, and delve into areas that colonial epistemologies dismissed as sorcery, they are confronted by the real limitations of Western hegemonic research practices, for example, ethical standards such as the principle of informed consent of the researched.

Batshi Tshireletso's study (2001) on the Mazenge cult is an example of challenges that confront researchers. Mazenge is a cult of affliction (hereditary spirits of the bush or spirits). Its membership is entirely women. In this study, Tshireletso wanted to show how the concepts of sacred space in the Mazenge cult are constructed and to establish the meanings of sacredness in the Mazenge cult. In doing this research, he was confronted by several challenges. Talking about the Mazenge cult is a public taboo. The word *Mazenge* is not supposed to be mentioned in public. Access to the Mazenge spirit medium in connection with the Mazenge cult is impossible when the medium is not in a state of being possessed. As a result, Tshireletso observes, he was unable to interview the Mazenge spirit medium. The impression one gets is that he would have talked to the spirit, even if she were possessed. The ethical principles that arise are:

1. Is it ethical to seek consent from one who is being possessed?
2. If the principal informant, the Mazenge medium, cannot be interviewed while not possessed, how can data collection about the spirit be validated?
3. Is it ethical to write about the researched on the basis of what others say about them?
4. What is the message behind the community sanction against communication with Mazenge spirit mediums?
5. Is there a possibility that in researching Mazenge, Tshireletso was violating Mazenge community copyrights to their knowledge?

Tshireletso's study shows how mainstream practice and interpretations of informed consent and copyright are not inclusive of the knowledge stored in rituals and practices like Mazenge. Such examples demonstrate the need for the research community to expand the boundaries of knowledge production and research practices in order to stop further abuses of fundamental human rights of the researched in historically colonized societies. These rights should include the opportunity to have a say on whether they can be written about, what can be written about them, and how it can be written and disseminated; they should also have the option of being trained to conduct the research themselves. Currently, scholars debate the following questions:

• Is the knowledge production process espoused by mainstream methodologies respectful and inclusive of all knowledge systems? Are the following inclusive of all knowledge systems:

1. the philosophies that underpin the research approach,
2. methods of collecting data,

3. sources of evidence, and

4. the analysis, reporting, and dissemination process?

- Are First Nation peoples, indigenous peoples, peoples of all worlds— that is, first world, second world, third, and fourth world, developed and developing countries, disenfranchised and dispossessed peoples—given equal rights through the research process to know, to name, to talk, and be heard?
- What are the concerns about current research methodologies?
- What challenges arise in using Western-based theory when research is carried out among those who suffered European colonial rule and slavery and are continuously being marginalized by the current research tradition?
- What are the challenges that researchers encounter in the literature that informs research on these communities?
- What do the multiple voices of scholars from across the globe say about Euro-Western research methodologies?
- How can we carry out research so that it is respectful and beneficial to the researched communities?

Most of the concerns and questions raised above are addressed in this book. It will demonstrate how scholars continue to critique Euro-Western research paradigms and advance ways of transforming them so that they are inclusive of the indigenous knowledge systems and life experiences of the historically colonized, disenfranchised, and dispossessed communities. A postcolonial indigenous research paradigm and its methods and methodologies are discussed.

TERMINOLOGY IN POSTCOLONIAL INDIGENOUS RESEARCH METHODOLOGIES

A variety of terms are used in this chapter and throughout the book. Although most of them are commonplace terms, it is important to spell out their precise meaning in this work.

Research: It is systematic, that is, it is the adoption of a strategy or a set of principles to study an issue of interest. The systematic strategy usually starts with the identification of an area of interest to study; a review of the literature to develop further understanding of the issue to be investigated; and choice of a research design or strategy that will inform the way the sampling of respondents is performed, the instruments for data collection, the analysis, interpretation, and reporting of the findings. You should in addition problematize research as a power struggle between researchers and the researched. Michel Foucault (1977), for example, observes that

> what we know and how we know [are] grounded in shifting and diverse historical human practices, politics, and power. There are in the production of knowledge multiple centres of power in constant struggle; [through] conflict, compromise, and negotiation … whichever group is strongest establishes its own rules on what can be known and how it can be known. A non-power related truth game is not possible, thus humanity installs each of its violences in a system of rules and thus proceeds from domination to domination. (p. 151)

The research you do will have the power to label, name, condemn, describe, or prescribe solutions to challenges in former colonized, indigenous peoples and historically oppressed groups. You are encouraged to conduct research without perpetuating self-serving Western research paradigms that construct Western ways of knowing as superior to the Other's ways of knowing. The book draws your attention to the emphasis on the role of the researcher as a provocateur (Mertens, 2010a) and a transformative healer (Chilisa, 2009; Chilisa & Ntseane 2010; Dillard, 2008; Ramsey, 2006) guided by the four Rs: accountable responsibility, respect, reciprocity, and rights and regulations of the researched (Ellis & Earley, 2006; Louis, 2007; Weber-Pillwax, 2001; Wilson, 2008), as well as roles and responsibilities of researchers as articulated in ethics guidelines and protocols of the former colonized, indigenous peoples and the historically oppressed. The position taken in this book is that postcolonial indigenous research methodologies should stand on an equal footing with Western research paradigms and should be an essential and integral part of any research methodology course. You are invited to problematize a "captive or colonized mind" on the entire systematic set of principles to study an issue.

The captive mind. Partha N. Mukherji (2004) challenges all researchers to debate whether the social science methodologies that originated in the West and are indigenous to the West are necessarily universal for the rest of the world. What is your reaction to the challenge? The Malaysian sociologist Syed Hussein Alatas (2004) developed the concept "the captive mind" to refer to an uncritical imitation of Western research paradigms within scientific intellectual activity. Others (Fanon, 1967; Ngungi wa Thiong'o, 1986 a, b) discuss a process they call colonization of the mind. This is a process that involves stripping the formerly colonized and historically marginalized groups of their ancestral culture and replacing it with Euro-Western culture. The process occurs through the education system, where learners are taught in languages of the colonizers to reject their heritage and embrace Euro-Western worldviews and lifestyles as the human norm. The rejection of the historically colonized and marginalized groups' heritage and the adoption of Euro-Western norms occur throughout all the stages in the research process. For instance, the conceptual framework, development of the research questions, and methods of data collection in most studies emanate from the developed world literature, which is predominantly Euro-Western. In addition, the language in the construction of research instruments and the dissemination of research findings is in most cases that of the colonizers. You are invited to problematize research and doing research "as a significant site of the struggle between the interest and knowing of the West and the interest and knowing of the 'Other'" (Smith, 1999, p. 2). What follows is a discussion of imperialism and colonialism with special attention to the power imbalance that exists between the Euro-Western research paradigm and non-Western societies that suffered European colonial rule, indigenous peoples, and historically marginalized communities.

Imperialism, Colonialism, and Othering Ideologies

One of the shortfalls of Euro-Western research paradigms is that they ignore the role of imperialism, colonization, and globalization in the construction of knowledge. An understanding of the values and assumptions about imperialism, colonization, and globalization that inform Euro-Western research paradigms will enable you to appreciate and understand how Euro-Western methodologies carry with them an imperial power and how they are colonizing. Let us begin with a description of imperialism and the values and assumptions that inform Euro-Western methodologies.

Imperialism. Imperialism, in the more recent sense in which the term is used, refers to the acquisition of an empire of overseas colonies and the Europeanization of the globe (Ashcroft, Griffiths, & Tiffin, 2000). The term is also used to describe the "practice, theory, and the attitudes of a dominating metropolitan centre ruling a distant territory" (Said, 1993, p. 8). The theory, practice, and attitudes of the metropolitan created an idea about the West and the Other that explains the dominance of Euro-Western research paradigms and the empire of deficit literature on the formerly colonized and historically oppressed. The term Othering was coined by Gayatri Spivak to denote a process through which Western knowledge creates differences between itself as the norm and other knowledge systems as inferior (Ashcroft et al., 2000). Stuart Hall (1992) explains the West as a concept describing a set of ideas, historical events, and social relationships. The concept functions in ways that allow the characterization and classification of societies into binary opposites of colonizer/colonized or first world/third world. The concept also condenses complex descriptions of other societies into a sameness image judged against the West idea. Chapter 3 illustrates how the Othering and sameness ideologies work to marginalize and suppress knowledge systems and ways of knowing of the historically colonized and those disadvantaged on the basis of gender, ethnicity, and social class.

Colonization. Colonization, defined as the subjugation of one group by another (Young, 2001), was a brutal process through which two thirds of the world experienced invasion and loss of territory accompanied by the destruction of political, social, and economic systems, leading to external political control and economic dependence on the West: France, Britain, Germany, Spain, Italy, Russia, and the United States. It also involved loss of control and ownership of their knowledge systems, beliefs, and behaviors and subjection to overt racism, resulting in the captive or colonized mind. One can distinguish between different but intertwined types of colonialism—namely, political colonialism, which refers to occupation and external control of the colonies, and scientific colonialism, which refers to the imposition of the colonizers' ways of knowing—and the control of all knowledge produced in the colonies. In Africa, colonial occupation occurred in 1884 when Britain, Belgium, France, Germany, Italy, Portugal, and Spain met at the Berlin Conference and divided Africa among themselves. African states became colonies of European powers and assumed names related to the colonial power and its the settlers, explorers, or missionaries. For example, present-day Zimbabwe was named Southern Rhodesia and Zambia was named Northern Rhodesia after the explorer Cecil John Rhodes. European explorers, travelers, and hunters were notorious for claiming discovery of African lands, rivers, lakes, waterfalls, and many other of Africa's natural showcases and renaming them. This was a violent way of dismissing the indigenous people's knowledge as irrelevant and a way of disconnecting them from what they knew and how they knew it (Chilisa & Preece, 2005). Scientific colonialism speaks directly to the production of knowledge and ethics in social science research and has been described as the imposition of the positivist paradigm approach to research on the colonies and other historical oppressed groups. Under the guise of scientific colonialism, researchers travelled to distant colonized lands, where they turned the resident people into objects of research. The ideology of scientific colonization carried with it the belief that the researchers had unlimited rights of access to any data source and information belonging to the population and the right to export data from the colonies for purposes of processing into books and articles (Cram, 2004a, 2004b). With these unlimited powers, researchers went out to collect data and write about the one reality that they understood. In the disciplines of psychology, anthropology, and history, operating on the positivist assumption of generating and discovering laws and theories that are generalizable, researchers mapped theories, formulae, and practices that continue to dictate how former colonized societies can be studied and written about. Psychology, for instance, developed standard conceptions and formulations by which all people of the world are to be understood; today, researchers molded to accept oppressive perspectives as the norm find it difficult to operate differently (Ramsey, 2006).

Scientific colonization has implications for the decolonization process. Reading and conducting research responsibly should involve reflecting on the following questions:

1. Does the research approach have a clear stance against scientific colonization?
2. Is the research approach of travelers moving to distant lands to acquire data to process them into books and journal articles ethical?
3. Where is the center of knowledge and information about a people or community located?

Globalization. Globalization is an extension of colonization. Spivak (1988) analyzes the contemporary relationship between colonial societies and the former colonizers and notes that we are witnessing a distinct phase in the way the world is ordered. She notes that, in the current phase of globalization, a mere extension of colonization,

> the contemporary international division of labor is a displacement of the field of nineteenth-century territorial imperialism. Put simply, a group of countries, generally first world, are in the position of investing capital; another group, generally third world, provide[s] the fields for investment both through the comprador indigenous capitalists and through their ill-protected and shifting labor force. (p. 287)

Current attempts by researchers to find the cure for HIV and AIDS are an example of how people in former colonized societies provide the fields as objects/subjects for research by multinational corporations. Recently, there has been conflict over a trial of the drug Tenofovir, which researchers allege may eventually serve as an effective chemical vaccine against the human immunodeficiency virus that causes AIDS. In Cambodia, efforts to test the drug among prostitutes were unsuccessful. The sex workers wanted more pay, more information, and a promise of health insurance for 40 years. Although the researchers agreed to provide more information for the sex workers, they said they could not promise long-term insurance; it was not something that is typically provided in studies and would be prohibitively expensive, they argued (Cha, 2006). The question one asks is what research benefits can accrue to poor countries, where the drug may not be affordable to the HIV and AIDS at-risk groups like sex workers? The conflict between the researchers and sex workers arose when the sex workers demanded the right to define the benefits they wanted as research subjects. The conflict between the researchers and the researched, and the determination of the researched to speak out about their rights, are indicative of local resistance against colonization and its new form, globalization.

Elsewhere, Bagele Chilisa and Julia Preece (2005) noted how the stealing of African indigenous knowledge of local resources such as plants and herbs by Western-trained researchers and Western companies is a contemporary instance of how African indigenous knowledge systems continue to be marginalized. The authors give an example of the San and their knowledge of the hoodia cactus plant, which grows in the Kalahari Desert. The original home of the San, it is a vast area of land that cuts across Botswana, Namibia, and South Africa. Through observation and experiments, the San discovered that the hoodia cactus has medicinal properties that stave off hunger. Members of generation after generation of the San have thus chewed the plant on long hunting trips. According to Pusch Commey (2003), Phytopharm, a United Kingdom-based company working with the South African Council for Scientific and Industrial Research, isolated the active ingredients in the cactus that makes this possible. The company has renamed this property, long known by the San, P57, and it has been manufactured into a diet pill that fetches large amounts of money for pharmaceutical companies. The San had to fight to reclaim their intellectual property of the qualities of the hoodia cactus plant.

Postcolonial Indigenous Research

Postcolonial indigenous research methodologies must be informed by the resistance to Euro-Western thought and the further appropriation of their knowledge.

Postcolonial. The word *postcolonial* is highly contested and at the same time popular (Mutua & Swadener, 2004; Swadener & Mutua, 2008). The bone of contention is that some can read the post to mean that colonialism has ended, while others can interpret postcolonialism to include people with diverse and qualitatively different experiences with colonialism. For instance, the United States began as a British colony, but the white settlers ended up imposing colonization on Native Americans. The word postcolonial is used in the research context to denote the continuous struggle of non-Western societies that suffered European colonization, indigenous peoples, and historically marginalized groups to resist suppression of their ways of knowing and the globalization of knowledge, reaffirming that Western knowledge is the only legitimate knowledge. Part of the project in this book is to envisage a space where those who suffered European colonial rule and slavery, the disenfranchised and dispossessed, can reclaim their languages, cultures, and "see with their own eyes" the history of colonization, imperialism, and their new form, globalization and, with that gaze, create new research methodologies that take into account the past and the present as a continuum of the future. This is the in-between space where Euro-Western research methodologies steeped in the culture, histories, philosophies, and the social condition of the Westerners can collaborate with the non-Western colonized's lived experiences and indigenous knowledge to produce research indigenous to their communities and cultural, integrative research frameworks with balanced lending and borrowing from the West.

Throughout the book, I will use the term colonized Other to refer to those who suffered European colonization, the disenfranchised and dispossessed, often represented as the non-Western Other. These people live in what has been labelled the third world, developing countries, or underdeveloped countries. Included among the *colonized Other* are indigenous populations in countries such as Canada, the United States, New Zealand, and Australia. Ethno-specific groups who have lived in some Western countries, such as African Americans in the United States and Caribbean-born people in the United Kingdom, also fall under the category of Other. Immigrants, refugees fleeing war-torn countries, and the poor are also being colonized and marginalized by Eurocentric research paradigms and thus fall under the category of the Other referred to in this book. The term colonized Other emphasizes the fact that the communities described still suffer scientific colonization as well as colonization of the mind. Part of the project in this book is to show how the colonized Other resists scientific colonization and colonization of the mind. The book illustrates some of the methodologies informed by the worldviews and ways of knowing of the colonized Other.

Indigenous. The term indigenous has been used in different ways in third-world, fourth-world, and marginalized people's struggles against invasion, political domination, and oppression. In this book, the focus is on a cultural group's ways of perceiving reality, ways of knowing, and the value systems that inform research processes. Euro-Western research paradigms are, for instance, indigenous to Euro-Western societies. This is not to say that the other has not shaped the development of these methods. The questions we ask are: what is indigenous to the other two-thirds majority of people colonized and marginalized by Eurocentric research paradigms? What is real to the diverse cultural groups of the two-thirds majority? How can this reality be studied? How would those colonized in the third world, indigenous peoples, women, and marginalized communities define their reality and ways of knowing? Their ways of seeing reality, ways of knowing, and values systems are informed by their indigenous knowledge systems and shaped by the struggle to resist and survive the assault on their culture. That is what makes the methodologies indigenous.

Indigenous research has four dimensions: (1) It targets a local phenomenon instead of using extant theory from the West to identify and define a research issue; (2) it is context-sensitive and creates locally relevant constructs, methods, and theories derived from local experiences and indigenous knowledge; (3) it can be integrative, that is, combining Western and indigenous theories; and (4) in its most advanced form, its assumptions about what counts as reality, knowledge, and values in research are informed by an indigenous research paradigm. The assumptions in an indigenous paradigm guide the research process. The book also makes reference to indigenous peoples. Linda T. Smith (1999, p. 7) says *indigenous peoples* is a relatively recent term, that emerged in the 1970s out of the struggles of the American Indian Movement and the Canadian Brotherhood Movement; it is used to internationalize the experiences and struggles of some of the world's colonized peoples.

DECOLONIZATION OF WESTERN RESEARCH METHODOLOGIES

A number of scholars (Bishop, 2008a, 2008b; Chilisa, 2005; Chilisa & Ntseane 2010; Cram, 2009; Liamputtong, 2010; Mutua & Swadener, 2004; Smith, 1999, 2008; Swadener & Mutua 2008; Wilson, 2008) articulate resistance to Euro-Western research methodologies by discussing a process called decolonization and strategies for decolonization. Decolonization is a process of centering the concerns and worldviews of the colonized Other so that they understand themselves through their own assumptions and perspectives. It is an event and a process that involves:

1. Creating and consciously using various strategies to liberate the "captive mind" from oppressive conditions that continue to silence and marginalize the voices of subordinated, colonized, non-Western societies that encountered European colonization.
2. It involves the restoration and development of cultural practices, thinking patterns, beliefs, and values that were suppressed but are still relevant and necessary to the survival and birth of new ideas, thinking, techniques, and lifestyles that contribute to the advancement and empowerment of the historically oppressed and former colonized non-Western societies (Smith, 1999, 2008).

Decolonization is thus a process of conducting research in such a way that the worldviews of those who have suffered a long history of oppression and marginalization are given space to communicate from their frames of reference. It is a process that involves "researching back" to question how the disciplines—psychology, education, history, anthropology, sociology, or science—through an ideology of Othering have described and theorized about the colonized Other, and refused to let the colonized Other name and know from their frame of reference. It includes a critical analysis of dominant literatures written by historians, psychologists, anthropologists, and social science researchers in general, aimed at exposing the problematic influence of the Western eyes (Mohanty, 1991) and how they legitimize "the positional superiority of Western knowledge" (Said, 1993). Vine Deloria (1988), reflecting on the role of anthropologist researchers, notes:

> An anthropologist comes out to the Indian reservation to make OBSERVATIONS. During the winter period, these observations will become books by which future anthropologists will be trained, so that they can come out to reservations years from now and verify the observations they have studied. (cited in Louis, 2007, p. 132)

This quotation is important in showing how knowledge about the formerly colonized and historically oppressed communities is constructed and how this knowledge accumulates into a body of literature that informs future research activities. There is also the disturbing role of theory in framing research objectives and research questions. David W. Gegeo and Karen A. Watson-Gegeo (2001) note:

> Anthropologists' accounts of other people's cultures are not indigenous accounts of those cultures, even though they may be based on interviews with and observations of indigenous community's

individuals and societies. All of the foregoing activities, while they draw on indigenous cultural knowledge, are imagined, conceptualised, and carried out within the theoretical and methodological frameworks of Anglo-European forms of research, reasoning and interpreting. (p. 58)

In Aoteroa/New Zealand, Russell Bishop (2008b) notes how the colonizers, using colonial paradigms, have developed a social pathology approach that dominates research on Maori. These observations about the role of literature and theory in the design of research studies remind us that we have to be critical readers of the research studies from which we draw and design future studies.

The Decolonization Process

Poka Laenui (2000) suggests five phases in the process of decolonization: (1) rediscovery and recovery, (2) mourning, (3) dreaming, (4) commitment, and (5) action.

Rediscovery and recovery. This refers to the process where the colonized Other rediscover and recover their own history, culture, language, and identity. It involves a process of interrogating the captive mind so that the colonized Other and the historically oppressed—for instance, women, the deaf, the disabled, children, and the elderly—can come to define in their own terms what is real to them. They can also define their own rules on what can be known and what can be spoken, written about, how, when, and where.

Mourning. This refers to the process of lamenting the continued assault on the historically oppressed and former colonized Other's identities and social realities. Mourning forms an important part of healing and moving to dreaming. As a researcher educated in the United States, my initial research uncritically used the dominant research methodologies. With time, I began to ask myself why the research was not making a difference in the lives of the people. I started asking myself if I could recognize myself in the people and communities described in the studies I and other scholars conducted. Imagine reading some of the research that distorts the life experiences of the peoples and communities you know. The first reaction to reading such texts would most likely be frustration and mourning. In Chapter 3, I relate my journey to the United States and back to conduct research in my country, Botswana. Decolonization requires going further than mourning to dreaming.

Dreaming. During this phase, the colonized Other explore their cultures and invoke their histories, worldviews, and indigenous knowledge systems to theorize and imagine other possibilities. My journey to learn methodologies indigenous to the Western culture and going back to my country, a former British colony experiencing a plethora of research-driven interventions to address social problems such as poverty and HIV/AIDS infections, took me to a phase beyond frustration and mourning to that of dreaming and imagining other ways of doing research. You are invited throughout this book to dream and imagine other ways of conducting research, employing methodologies that are indigenous to the communities you study. Imagine, for example, that there are other literatures indigenous to the communities you study that have not found their way into the global communities of knowledge and practice. Imagine that in the lived experiences, oral traditions, language, metaphorical sayings, and proverbs of the communities that you research are concepts and theoretical frameworks that can inform the research process. Imagine that in the communities where you conduct research there are researchers and that they, too, can theorize and conduct research and that they, too, have the right to ownership of the knowledge they produce. Imagine the research questions, methods, literature reviewed, ways of disseminating data, and the language used if research was by the formerly colonized and historically silenced. To dream is to invoke indigenous knowledge systems, literatures, languages, worldviews, and collective experiences of the colonized Other to theorize and facilitate a research process that gives voice and is indigenous to the communities you research.

Commitment. Dreaming is followed by commitment where researchers, for example, define the role of research in community development and their roles and responsibilities to the communities and scholarship of research. Researchers become political activists demonstrating commitment to addressing the challenge of including the voices of the colonized Other in all the stages of the research process and conducting research that translates into changes in the material conditions of the local peoples as well as their control over produced knowledge. There is a growing concern, for instance, that researchers feel compelled for career reasons to conduct research that they are ill equipped to carry out and that their passive dissemination of research findings through professional journals hardly results in meaningful changes in the lives of the researched. The third world mourns, for example, that the "massive landing of experts, each in charge of investigating, measuring, and theorizing about this or that little aspect of Third World Societies" (Escobar, 1995, p. 45) has resulted in a situation where "our own history, culture and practices, good or bad, are rediscovered and translated into the journals of the North and come back to us re-conceptualized, couched in languages and paradigms which make it all sound new and novel" (Namuddu, 1989, p. 28).

Action. The last phase is action when dreams and commitment translate into strategies for social transformation. Researchers at this phase embrace participatory research methods that give voice to the colonized Other and promote empowerment, inclusivity, and respect for all involved in the research process. The key aspect of participatory research is that the researched are actively involved in analyzing their situations, finding solutions, and taking action to address their concerns and to work for the betterment of their communities. The researcher has a moral responsibility to support the colonized Other in their belief that their collective experiences, indigenous knowledge, and history are valuable. The moral stance of the researcher as an activist committed to social transformation, indigenizing mainstream research methodologies to include other knowledge systems, is necessary to address concerns about the captive mind and the undervaluing, belittling, and marginalization of the practices, values, and worldviews of the colonized Other.

Strategies for Decolonization

Linda Smith (1999) has identified strategies for decolonization as follows:

Deconstruction and reconstruction. This refers to destroying what has wrongly been written—for instance, interrogating distortions of people's life experiences, negative labeling, deficit theorizing, genetically deficient or culturally deficient models that pathologized the colonized Other—and retelling the stories of the past and envisioning the future. These strategies facilitate the process of recovery and discovery.

Self-determination and social justice. For scholars, academics, and the overresearched former colonized and historically oppressed peoples disempowered by Western research hegemony, issues in research should be addressed within the wider framework of self-determination and social justice. Self-determination in research refers to the struggle by those marginalized by Western research hegemony to seek legitimacy for methodologies embedded in the histories, experiences, ways of perceiving realities, and value systems. Social justice in research is achieved when research gives voice to the researched and moves from a deficit-based orientation, where research was based on perceived deficits in the researched, to reinforcing practices that have sustained the lives of the researched. Social justice is addressed by ensuring that those historically oppressed groups, marginalized and labeled, former colonies, descendants of slaves, indigenous peoples, those people in the third world, fourth world and developing countries, or those pushed to the margins on the basis of their gender, race/ethnicity, disability, socioeconomic status, age, religion, or sexual orientation, and immigrants and refugees are given space to decenter dominant Western research paradigms and to place at the center of analysis the realities, knowledges, values, and methodologies that give meaning to their life experiences. Chapter 8 discusses research strategies that counter deficit-based research and reveal the researched's positive aspects, resilience, and acts of resistance to Western research hegemony, which is needed for social change.

Ethics. There is a need to recognize—and where none exists, formulate, legislate, disseminate, and make known and understood internationally— ethical issues and legislation that protect indigenous knowledge systems and ways of knowing of the colonized Other. The international community of researchers is increasingly aware of the researcher's responsibility. The American Psychological Association (2002) describe the researcher's ethical responsibilities working with Asian American/Pacific Islander populations, people of African descent, Hispanics, and American Indians:

> As an agent of prosocial change, the culturally competent psychologist carries the responsibility of combating the damaging effects of racism, prejudice, bias and oppression in all their forms, including all of the methods we use to understand the population we serve . . . A consistent theme. . . . relates to the interpretation and dissemination of research findings that are meaningful and relevant to each of the four populations. (p. 1)

Developing countries and indigenous communities have come up with their own ethics review boards and ethical guidelines. The Maori of New Zealand, for instance, have Guidelines for Research and Evaluation with Maori (Ministry of Social Development, 2004); in Australia, the aborigines have the Mi'kinaw Research Principles and Protocols (Aboriginal Research Centre, 2005). Elsewhere, Chilisa (2009) notes how the plethora of ethics review boards, each operating with its own ethics guidelines, has given rise to conflict over which ethics guidelines should be used, especially where there is partnership or collaborative research between researchers from developed countries and those from former colonized societies. Some researchers from developed countries, still operating with colonial tools of manipulation and power to access, control, and own all types of data from the former colonies, invoke contract agreements to rewrite, write over, erase, and relegate to marginal and irrelevant the ethical guideline from former colonized societies. Still, others are compelled by research funding agencies, many of them international corporations based in developed countries, to enter into contract agreements that privilege Euro-Western ethical frameworks. (See Chapter 3 for these malpractices). Committed researchers define their responsibilities and are consistently engaged in self-reflection and self-questioning that promotes and privileges the right of the disempowered to be heard.

Language. Ngugi wa Thiong'o (1986a, 1986b, 1993) and Ali Mazrui (1990) advocate for writing in indigenous languages as part and parcel of the anti-imperialist struggle. Chapter 3 discusses how language mediates the research process, recovering and revitalizing, validating indigenous knowledge and cultures of the historically marginalized, and thus creating space to decenter hegemonic Western research paradigms.

Internationalization of indigenous experiences. Indigenous scholars internationalize their experiences, issues, and struggles of the colonized people by coming together in global and local spaces to plan, organize, and struggle collectively for self-determination.

History. People must study the past to recover their history, culture, and language to enable a reconstruction of what was lost that is useful to inform the present.

Critique. There is a need to critique the imperial model of research, which continues to deny the colonized and historically marginalized other space to communicate from their own frames of reference.

A POSTCOLONIAL INDIGENOUS RESEARCH PARADIGM

In this book, I discuss a postcolonial indigenous research paradigm as a framework of belief systems that emanate from the lived experiences, values, and history of those belittled and marginalized by Euro-Western research paradigms. The term *paradigm* was first used by Thomas Kuhn (1962) to represent a particular way of thinking and seeing the world that is shared by a community of scholars, researchers, or scientists, and also one that is used to represent commitments, worldviews, beliefs, values, methods, and approaches that are shared across a discipline. A research paradigm is a way of describing a worldview that is informed by philosophical assumptions about the nature of social reality (ontology), ways of knowing (epistemology), and ethics and value systems (axiology). A paradigm also has theoretical assumptions about the research process and the appropriate approach to systematic inquiry (methodology). A postcolonial indigenous research paradigm articulates the shared aspects of ontology, epistemology, axiology, and research methodologies of the colonized Other discussed by scholars who conduct research in former colonized societies in Africa, Asia, and Latin America; among indigenous peoples in Australia, Canada, the United States, and other parts of the world, and among the disempowered, historically marginalized social groups that encounter the colonizing effect of Eurocentric research paradigms. The main argument is that ethics and value beliefs that define relations and responsibilities of researchers to the researched should be addressed before ontological and epistemological questions and should drive the research process from formulation of research proposal to dissemination of findings. A common thread that cuts across the beliefs of the colonized Other is that people are spiritual beings with multiple relationships that should be nurtured throughout the research process. A postcolonial indigenous research paradigm is thus informed by relational ontologies, relational epistemologies, and relational axiology. In his book, *Research Is Ceremony: Indigenous Research Methods,* Wilson (2008) describes a research paradigm shared by indigenous scholars in Canada and Australia as a paradigm informed by relational ontologies, relational epistemologies, and relational accountability. Philosophical assumptions on the nature of reality, knowledge, and values guide research in a postcolonial indigenous paradigm.

▐ ASSUMPTIONS ABOUT THE NATURE OF REALITY, KNOWLEDGE, AND VALUES

Ontology. Ontology is the body of knowledge that deals with the essential characteristics of what it means to exist. In a relational ontology, the social reality that is investigated can be understood in relation to the connections that human beings have with the living and the nonliving. The thrust of the discussion is that among indigenous people, in the colonized and former colonized societies, people are beings with many relations and many connections. They have connections with the living and the nonliving, with land, with the earth, with animals, and with other beings. There is an emphasis on an I/We relationship as opposed to the Western I/You relationship with its emphasis on the individual. Among the Bantu people of southern Africa, this principle is captured under the philosophy of *ubuntu*, in which one view of being is the conception that *nthu, nthu ne banwe* (Ikalanaga/Shona version). An English translation that comes close to the principle is: "I am we; I am because we are; we are because I am" or "a person is because of others" (Goduka, 2000). Communality, collectivity, social justice, human unity, and pluralism are implicit in this principle. Reality implies a set of relationships. *Ubuntu* is further elaborated in Chapter 6.

Epistemology. Epistemology inquires into the nature of knowledge and truth. It asks the following questions: What are the sources of knowledge? How reliable are these sources? What can one know? How does one know if something is true? For instance, some people think that the notion that witches exist is just a belief. Epistemology asks further questions: Is a belief true knowledge? Or is knowledge only that which can be proven using concrete data? If we say witches exist, what is the source of evidence? What methods can we use to find out about their existence? A *relational epistemology* is all the "systems of knowledge built on relationships" (Wilson, 2008, p. 74). Wilson explains the difference between an indigenous and a dominant research paradigm:

> The major difference between those dominant paradigms and an indigenous paradigm is that those dominant paradigms are built on the fundamental belief that knowledge is an individual entity: the researcher is an individual in search of knowledge, knowledge is something that is gained and therefore knowledge may be owned by an individual. An indigenous paradigm comes from the fundamental belief that knowledge is relational. Knowledge is shared with all of creation. It is not just interpersonal relationships, or just with the research subjects I may be working with, but it is a relationship with all of creation. It is with the cosmos; it is with the animals, with plants, with the earth that we share this knowledge. It goes beyond the individual's knowledge to the concept of relational knowledge. . . . you are answerable to all your relations when you are doing research. (p. 56)

Axiology. Axiology refers to the analysis of values to better understand their meanings, characteristics, their origins, their purpose, their acceptance as true knowledge, and their influence on people's daily experiences. It is the branch of philosophy that deals with the nature of ethics, aesthetics, and religion, where religion encompasses spirituality (Guba & Lincoln, 2005), and their role in the construction of knowledge. A *relational axiology* is built on the concept of relational accountability. The four Rs—relational accountability, respectful representation, reciprocal appropriation, and rights and regulations during the research process (Louis, 2007)—embrace a relational axiology. Relational accountability refers to the fact that all parts of the research process are related and that the researcher is accountable to all relations. Respectful representation is about how the researcher listens, pays attention, acknowledges, and creates space for the voices and knowledge systems of the Other. Reciprocal appropriation refers to the fact that all research is appropriation and should thus be conducted so that benefits accrue to both the communities researched and the researcher. Rights and regulations refers to the need for ethical protocols that accord the colonized and the marginalized ownership of the research process and the knowledge produced. The *ubuntu* worldview, "I am because we are," is an example of a framework that calls on the researcher to see "self" as a reflection of the researched Other, to honor and respect the researched as one would wish for self, and to feel a belongingness to the researched community without feeling threatened or diminished. *Ubuntu* "is the very essence of being human," according to Desmond Tutu (1999):

> It is not, "I think therefore I am." It says rather: "I am human therefore I belong. I participate, I share." A person with ubuntu is open and available to others, affirming of others, does not feel threatened that others are able and good, for he [or] she belongs in a greater whole and is diminished when others are humiliated or diminished, when others are tortured or oppressed, or treated as if they were less than they are. (p. 33)

In the book, *In the Spirit of Ubuntu: Stories of Teaching and Research* (Caracciolo & Mungai, 2009), authors illustrate the application of *ubuntu* as both an ethical framework and a way of knowing in research. Swanson (2009) notes that *ubuntu* offered her ways to resist normalized positions of dominance and damage-focused and deficit discourses; it contributed to decolonizing hegemonic meanings. *Ubuntu* offers guidance with regard to the researcher's responsibilities and obligations to the researched and promotes community, belongingness, togetherness, and well-being. In a study about the role of teachers in interpreting Malawi's political and social history and Malawi's contemporary problems of structural violence, Steve Sharra (2009) used *ubuntu* as an African-centered theoretical framework. Sharra notes that the lesson learned was how to shift from the preoccupation with a gloomy analysis of how bad things are in Africa to asking how to use Africa's heritage and diverse knowledges to create new social, cultural, economic, and educational programs informed by *ubuntu* as an ethical framework and also as a way of knowing and perceiving reality. *Ubuntu* offers an example of how the researcher's ethical and moral obligation foregrounds and is intertwined with perceptions of reality and ways of knowing. This also underscores the connectedness and relatedness in the I/We relationship, where hierarchy is discouraged.

METHODOLOGY

A postcolonial indigenous paradigm is driven by decolonizing methodologies as well as third-space methodologies. The quotes at the beginning of the chapter illustrate a critique of Euro-Western research paradigms from different theoretical perspectives. bell hooks (1990) speaks to representation and voice of the researched. The questions raised on voice, representation, and rights and ownership in the knowledge production process compel researchers to engage directly with the debates on how the colonized and historically silenced researched are represented in the texts that we write. Fine (1994) reminds us, for instance, that

> traditional social sciences have stubbornly refused to interrogate how we as researchers create our texts. . . . That we are human inventors of some questions and repressors of others, shapers of the very contexts we study, co-participants in our interviews, interpreters of other's stories and narrators of our own, are sometimes rendered irrelevant to the texts we publish. (p. 14)

Postcolonial indigenous research techniques include a process of decolonizing the conventional interview technique, using indigenous interview methods such as talking circles and invoking indigenous knowledge to inform alternative research methods compatible with the worldviews of the colonized Other. Chapter 6 presents culturally responsive indigenous research methodologies.

The quote by Elabor-Idemudia (2002) at the beginning of this chapter reminds us that the social sciences are founded on the culture, history, and philosophies of Euro-Western thought and are either antagonistic to the history and cultures of non-Western societies or have no strategy to give voice to their cultures (Smith, 1999, 2008). Scheurich (1997) describes social science research methodologies as racially biased. In Chapter 2, you will learn about how critical theory—more specifically, postcolonial theory, critical indigenous theory, and critical race theory—informs approaches and research practices of discovering and recovering voices of the oppressed. In this chapter, it is important to underscore decolonizing research approaches, indigenization, and third-space methodologies as essential aspects of a post-colonial indigenous paradigm.

Decolonization and Indigenization

A decolonization research approach has been described. It is important to add to the discussion possibilities of integration of knowledge systems and indigenization. While scholars critique the dominance of Euro-Western paradigms over the rest of the world, you should take note that they also value the integration of knowledge systems. Syed H. Alatas (1974), while critical of the captive mind, also asserts that "no society can develop by inventing everything on its own. When something is found effective and useful, it is desirable that it should be adapted and assimilated, whether it be an artifact or an attitude of mind" (p. 692).

Writing about third world feminism in the book, *Methodology of the Oppressed,* Chela Sandoval (2000) articulates what she calls a *coalitional consciousness* as an approach to bring subjugated peoples who suffered colonial rule or slavery together with all the peoples of the world to work together toward social change. She calls for a mixture in the appropriation of ideas, knowledge, and theories, arguing that the mixing reflects the necessary reality of surviving as a minority or Other, which entails using every and any aspect of dominant power. Mixing is the methodology of survival for the oppressed. Decolonization and indigenization of dominant research approaches entail attempts to resist universalized knowledge, critique Euro-Western research approaches, and invoke indigenous knowledge systems of the colonized Other to inform research methodologies that are inclusive of all knowledge systems and respectful of the researched.

Complementing the coalition strategy, Beth Swadener and Agenda Mutua (2008) call for the forging of cultural partnerships "with, between and among Indigenous researchers and allied 'others.'" These partnerships should create space for working collaboratively on common goals and engaging in a multidirectional lending and borrowing from diverse cultures. It is only when researchers from multiple cultures work collaboratively to acknowledge and interrogate the theories, the literature, the methodologies, and the embedded ethical and moral issues that decolonization and indigenization can become a reality.

Third-Space Methodologies

When one discusses Euro-Western paradigms and postcolonial indigenous paradigms, these paradigms become essentialized, compelling thought along binary opposites of either/or. There is also the danger of conceptualizing indigenousness as a fixed and unchanging indigenous identity (Kinchella & Steinberg, 2009). Homi Bhabha's (1994) concept of "the space in between" has led some researchers to speak of a "third space" (Moquin, 2007). In this space, Western research paradigms are contested and declared invalid because they are based on a culture that has been made static and essentialized. There is also a recognition that essentialized views of indigenous cultures inform indigenous research paradigms and methodologies, which must be interrogated and opened up to include the voices and knowledge systems of the subgroups within indigenous essentialized cultures potentially excluded within the already marginalized indigenous cultures and research paradigms. Thus, in the third space, indigenousness is interrogated to include the voices of those disadvantaged on the basis of gender, race, ethnicity, ableness, health, socioeconomic status, sexual orientation, age, and so on. In the space in between, "all cultural statements and systems are constructed, therefore all hierarchical claims to the inherent originality or 'purity' of cultures are untenable" (Bhabha, 1994, p. 54).

The space in between involves a culture-integrative research framework. This is a tapestry, a mosaic of balanced borrowing of less hegemonic Euro-Western knowledge and its democratic and social justice elements and combining it with the best of the democratic, liberatory, and social justice essentialized indigenous knowledge and subgroups' knowledges. Postcolonial indigenous feminist methodologies present some of the examples in this category of postcolonial indigenous research methodologies. (See Chapter 9.)

EURO-WESTERN RESEARCH PARADIGMS

Knowledge of the dominant Euro-Western research paradigms is necessary to enable you to contextualize a critique of these research methodologies as well as appreciate the decolonization and indigenization of these research approaches. What follows is a brief description of each dominant research paradigm in terms of the philosophies that inform its approaches and the way questions on reality, knowledge, and values are understood, explained, and incorporated in the research processes and procedures. A description of these dominant paradigms will also enable you to draw a distinction between the philosophies and histories that distinguish postco-lonial indigenous research methodologies from the dominant Euro-Western methodologies and those that do not.

Most Euro-Western research books classify research methodologies into three paradigms: positivist-postpositivist, interpretive, and transformative. Philosophical assumptions and a long history of application and practice in each of these categories inform the methodology, data-gathering techniques, analysis approaches, and reporting and dissemination of the findings. The differences in these paradigms can be understood by looking at:

- The philosophies and theories that inform the approach
- How each approach perceives or explains the nature of reality (ontology), knowledge (epistemology), and values (axiology)
- The methodology used in the research

The Positivism/Postpositivism Paradigm

Positivism is a position or approach that holds that the scientific method is the only way to establish truth and objective reality. Can you imagine using scientific methods to carry out research on witches? The positivists would conclude that witches do not exist because the scientific method does not yield any tangible results on the nature of witches. Positivism is based on the view that natural science is the only foundation for true knowledge. It holds that the methods, techniques, and procedures used in natural science offer the best framework for investigating the social world (Hitchcock & Hughes, 1995). Many Western philosophers, among them Aristotle (383–348 BCE), Francis Bacon (1561–1626), and John Locke (1632–1704), contributed to what we know as positivism today.

Aristotle believed that the world operates on fixed natural laws that can be discovered through observation and reason. He also believed that these fixed laws can be tested and measured quantitatively, with the results verified. He is considered a realist, and his thinking typifies the philosophy of realism. Realism takes the stand that reality is viewed in material terms. Realism assumes an external reality that can be objectively investigated. The basic tenet of this philosophy is that if something exists, it exists in a quantity, and we can measure it. The realist maintains that truth exists in nature, that is, the physical world, and it is discoverable by people through the use of sci-entific method. Knowing begins with sensory intake, which is then ordered and organized by means of intellect.

Francis Bacon (1561–1626) and John Locke (1632–1704) also added to our understanding of positivism as we know it today. Their thinking has been labeled *empiricism*. Empiricists believe that the senses and empirical data are the most important sources of knowledge. According to the empiricists, we know from seeing, hearing, touching, smelling, and observing. The empiricist uses deductive methods to generate generalizations from specific sensory data. Augustine Comte (1798–1857), a 19th-century French philosopher, summed up these related ideas by different philosophers as positivism. Like the empiricists and realists, he believed that genuine knowledge is based on sense experience and can be advanced only by means of observation and measurement.

The middle part of the 20th century saw a shift from positivism to postpositivism. It is influenced by a philosophy called critical realism. The postpositivists, like the positivists, believe that there is a reality independent of our thinking that can be studied through the scientific method. They recognize, however, that all observation is fallible and has error and that all theory is revisable. Reality cannot be known with certainty. Observations are theory laden and influenced by the researcher's biases and worldviews. Objectivity can nevertheless be achieved by using multiple measures and observations and triangulating the data to get closer to what is happening in reality. It is important to note that the postpositivists share a lot in common with positivists. Most of the research approaches and practices in social science today would fit better into the postpositivist category. The two will therefore be treated as belonging to the same family. It is important to note that a number of philosophers working over a long period of time contributed toward the thinking and the body of knowledge and worldviews embodied in each paradigm.

Assumptions About the Nature of Reality, Knowledge, and Values

Let us look closely at the positivist/postpositivist assumptions about the nature of reality (ontology), knowledge (epistemology), and values (axiology).

Ontology. On the question of what is the nature of reality, the positivists hold that there is a single, tangible reality that is relatively constant across time and setting. Part of the researcher's duty is to discover this reality. Reality is objective and is independent of the researcher's interest in it. It is measurable and can be broken into variables. Postpositivists concur that reality exists but argue that it can be known only imperfectly because of the researcher's human limitations. The researcher can discover reality within a certain realm of probability (Mertens, 2010a).

Epistemology. For the positivist, the nature of knowledge is inherent in the natural science paradigm. Knowledge is those statements of belief or fact that can be tested empirically, confirmed or verified, or disconfirmed; they are stable and can be generalized (Eichelberger, 1989). Knowledge constitutes hard data, is objective, and therefore is independent of the values, interests, and feelings of the researcher. Researchers need only the right data-gathering instruments or tools to produce absolute truth for a given inquiry. The research designs are quantitative and include experimental, quasi-experimental, correlational, causal, comparative, and survey designs. The techniques of gathering data are mainly questionnaires, observations, tests, and experiments. Within this context, the purpose of research is to discover laws and principles that govern the universe and to predict behaviors and situations. Postpositivists believe that perfect objectivity cannot be achieved but is approachable.

Axiology. For the positivist, all inquiries should be value free. Researchers should use scientific methods of gathering data to achieve objectivity and neutrality during the inquiry process. Postpositivists modified the belief that the researcher and the subject of study were independent by recognizing that the investigator's theories, hypothesis, and background knowledge can strongly influence what is observed, how it is observed, and the outcome of what is observed.

Methodology. In positivism and postpositivism, the purpose of research is to predict, test a theory, and find the strength of relationships between variables or a cause-effect relationship. Quantitative researchers begin with ideas, theories, or concepts that are operationally defined to point to the variables in the study. The problem statement at minimum specifies variables to be studied and the relationship among them. Variables are operationally defined to enable replication, verification, and confirmation by different researchers. Operationally defining a variable means that the trait to be measured is defined according to the way it is used or measured or observed in the study.

In Activity 1.1, a sample survey design was adopted, and variables, for instance, *literacy* and *ability*, were operationally defined. Research questions, research objectives, or hypotheses were constructed to further clarify the research problem. The researcher, independent of the participants, constructed these. The variables are therefore predetermined and fixed. Research objectives and procedures were built around the definition of literacy used by UNESCO. Tests were used to measure reading and numeracy. Skills measured in numeracy and readings are clearly delineated and are again limited

Activity 1.1

Read the study extract included here and answer the following questions:

1. Discuss how the methodological features of this study reflect positivist or postpositivist ontology, epistemology, and axiology.

2. Refer back to the concept of the "captive mind." In what ways are the researchers captives of the dominant literature on literacy and methodologies in the postpositivist research paradigm?

Source: Adapted from Central Statistics Office (1997), *Literacy Survey Report*, Gaborone, Botswana: Government Printer.

Background to study

Statement of the problem

The survey was designed to measure the country's literacy not only by the number of years spent at school (formal school), but also through the testing of objective literacy skills. In this survey, *objective literacy* was defined as the ability to read and write in Setswana, English, or both and the ability to carry out simple mathematical computations. *Ability* was ascertained through results of literacy tests in Setswana, English, and mathematics.

Specific objectives were:

To assess gender and age literacy differentials
To assess factors influencing school attendance
To assess the impact of literacy programs and factors relating to accessibility of educational facilities
To identify the most pressing needs in terms of educational policies and provision in order that the priorities can be set for the future direction of adult literacy programs in Botswana
To assess socioeconomic and cultural factors that may be associated with literacy problems in the adult population

Research design: Sample survey

Sampling procedures

Enumeration areas (EA) were identified. These are small geographic areas, which represent an average workload for an enumerator. The

(Continued)

(Continued)

average EA was 120 to 150 dwellings. EAs were subdivided into blocks. An average block was 50 households. Blocks were organized according to type of area. Urban blocks were grouped into a stratum of their own. Rural areas were organized into the following strata: villages, lands, cattle posts, and freehold farms. Probability sampling was carried out at block level, type of dwelling, and household and individual levels. Total sample size was 46,129 households.

Instruments and procedure

Questionnaires and tests were used.

An individual questionnaire was administered only to Botswana citizens in the age group 12 to 65 with an educational attainment of Standard 4 or lower and not currently attending school.

In this study, the process of decoding was assessed through tasks that required respondents to read orally some words and sentences and those that required them to identify and match words with pictures, in both Setswana and English. The process of writing was assessed through tasks that required respondents to write down dictated sentences in both languages.

The numeracy tests covered the skill of number naming, in which the respondents were required to read given numbers aloud; number writing, in which respondents were required to write down dictated numbers; and solution of written arithmetic problems. In the latter task, respondents were given written problems to read and solve. The problems involved addition of a number of cattle to that of donkeys; the numbers were embedded in the prose text. Other numeracy skills tested in this study included the ability to solve arithmetic equations involving the concepts of addition and subtraction ($50 - 20 =$; $10 + 40 =$) and that of reading time. The survey came up with a pass mark of 50% to determine the literate and illiterate, basing on a 2-point scale of correct and incorrect answers to test items.

Results

The survey found out that 68.9% of adults are literate in either Setswana or English. Females had a higher literacy rate: 70.3% compared to males, 66.9%. Also, 193,662 persons aged 12 years and over never attended formal school.

by the definition of literacy. How relevant do you think the study's definition of life is to the life experiences of people? Do you think the researched people would have a similar meaning of what it is to be literate? In most cases, research within the positivist/postpositivist paradigm is more about what researchers want to know, and what knowledge and what theory they want to legitimize. For instance, the researchers in the literacy study noted, "The narrow definition of literacy currently held by the Botswana National Literacy Programme may, to some extent, have influenced the development of tests for this survey.... Advanced functional literacy skills were not tested" (CSO, 1997, p. 9).

Commeyras and Chilisa (2001) have questioned the value of this research in providing information on the development of literacy in Botswana. They argue that the survey results reveal very little about the actual literacy of Botswana's people and the variety of literacies that exist. William L. Neuman (2010) notes that researchers in the positivist-postpositivist research paradigm adopt a technocratic approach where they ignore questions on relevancy, ethics, and morality to follow orders and thus satisfy a sponsor or a government. The paradigm is thus generally viewed as a "legitimating ideology of dominant groups" (Neuman, 1997, p. 45).

Postcolonial indigenous research methodologies challenge the ideologies embedded in these methods and propose ways of decolonizing and indigenizing the research methods so that the methods are inclusive of local and indigenous knowledges that are relevant and responsive to the experiences and needs of researched communities. How can one, for instance, carry out a literacy survey that uses local and indigenous knowledge on literacy as a conceptual or theoretical framework to inform the variables in the study? Postcolonial indigenous research methodologies propose ways in which researchers can invoke indigenous knowledge systems to decolonize dominant research methodologies and offer complementary new methods and approaches that are informed by postcolonial indigenous philosophies, histories, and indigenous knowledge systems. *Indigenous Beliefs and Attitudes to AIDS Precautions in a Rural South African Community: An Empirical Study* (Liddell, Barrett, & Bydawell, 2006) demonstrates ways in which researchers indigenize quantitative research methodologies. See Chapter 3.

The Interpretive Paradigm

The interpretivists differ with the positivists on assumptions about the nature of reality, what counts as knowledge and its sources, and the values they hold and their role in the research process. The interpretive approach can be traced back to Edmund Husserl's philosophy of phenomenology and to the German philosopher Wilhelm Dilthey's philosophy of hermeneutics (Eichelberger 1989; Neuman, 2010). Let us examine each one of these. We will also examine assumptions on ontology, epistemology, axiology, and methodologies used in the interpretive paradigm.

Phenomenology. Phenomenologists use human thinking, perceiving, and other mental or physiological acts and spirituality to describe and understand human experience. From the phenomenologist's perspective, truth lies within the human experience and is therefore multiple and bound by time, space, and context. Under these assumptions, a belief or claim coming from a culture one does not understand is consistent and correct. In contrast to the positivist/post-positivist paradigm, phenomenologists or interpretivists believe that research should produce individualized conceptions of social phenomena and personal assertions rather than generalizations and verifications.

Hermeneutics. The term comes from the name Hermes, a god in Greek mythology who had the power to communicate the desires of the gods to mortals (Neuman, 2010). Hermeneutics involves a reading and an interpretation of some kind of human text. The text of our social world is complex. Hermeneutics is therefore the process whereby we come to an understanding of a given social text and choose between two or more competing interpretations of the same text. In reading and interpreting the text, we look at the relation of parts to the whole, and we do it in a dynamic and interactive way that will lead us to a fuller and newer understanding of the actual life situation (Eichelberger, 1989). Interpretations occur within a tradition, space, time, and a situation. They are also dependent on the identity of the researcher, that is, gender, age, race/ethnicity, and socioeconomic background. Phenomenology and hermeneutics thus largely inform assumptions on the nature of reality, knowledge, and values in the interpretive paradigm: Let us examine these assumptions.

Assumptions About the Nature of Reality, Knowledge, and Values

Ontology. On the question of what is reality, the interpretivists believe that it is socially constructed (Creswell, 2009; Creswell & Clark, 2011; Mertens, 2010a) and that there are as many intangible realities as there are people constructing them. Reality is therefore mind-dependent and a personal or social construct. Do you believe, for instance, that witches exist? If you do, it is your personal reality, a way in which you try to make sense of the world around you. Reality is, in this sense, limited to context, space, time, and individuals or group in a given situation and cannot be generalized into one common reality. These assumptions are a direct challenge to the positivist's assumption about the existence of a tangible external reality. The assumptions legitimize conceptions of realities from all cultures. The question, however, is how many of the realities as viewed by formerly colonized, historically marginalized groups have been considered valid in the academic construction of knowledge. In Botswana, for example, the understanding of reality in most communities is influenced by their connectedness to earth (*lefatshe*) and the spirits (*Badimo*) (Chilisa, 2005). There are individual realities as well as group-shared realities. Of interest is how these assumptions about the nature of reality are built into the research process. In Chapter 4, I will explore possible ways in which assumptions about the nature of reality in postcolonial indigenous contexts can be built into the research process.

Epistemology. Interpretivists believe that knowledge is subjective because it is socially constructed and mind-dependent. Truth lies within the human experience. Statements on what is true and false are therefore culture bound and historically and context dependent, although some may be universal. Within this context, communities' stories, belief systems, and claims of spiritual and earth connections should find space as legitimate knowledge. Often, however, even interpretivist research operates within the mode of a Western historical and cultural-bound research framework and treats indigenous ways of knowing as "barriers to research or exotic customs with which researchers need to be familiar in order to carry out their work without causing offence" (Smith, 1999, p. 15).

Axiology. Interpretivists assert that since reality is mind constructed, mind dependent, and knowledge subjective, social inquiry is in turn value bound and value laden. The researcher is inevitably influenced by the investigator's values, which inform the paradigm chosen for inquiry, the choice of issue, methods chosen to collect and analyze data, interpretation of the findings, and the way the findings are reported. The researcher, therefore, admits the value-laden nature of the study and reports values and biases.

Methodology

The purpose of interpretive research is to understand people's experiences. The research takes place in a natural setting where the participants make their living. The purpose of study expresses the assumptions of the interpretivist to understand human experiences. Assumptions on the multiplicity of realities also inform the research process. For instance, the research questions cannot be established before the study begins but rather evolve as the study progresses (Mertens, 2010a). The research questions are generally open-ended, descriptive, and nondirectional (Creswell, 2009). A model of a *grand tour question* followed by a small number of subquestions is used. The grand tour question is a statement of the problem that is examined in the study in its broadest form, posed as a general issue not to limit the inquiry (Creswell, 2009).

The researcher gathers most of the data. In recognition of the assumption about the subjective nature of research, researchers describe themselves, their values, ideological biases, relationship to the participants, and closeness to the research topic. Access and entry to the study site are important, and sensitive issues need to be addressed. Researchers have to establish trust, rapport, and authentic communication patterns with the participants so that they can capture the subtle differences and meanings from their voices (Denzin & Lincoln, 2005). Ethics is an important issue that the researcher addresses throughout the study whenever it arises.

Common designs include ethnography, phenomenology, biography, case study, and grounded theory (Creswell, 2009). Data-gathering techniques are selected depending on the choice of design, the nature of the respondents, and the research problem. They include interviews, observations, visual aids, personal and official documents, photographs, drawings, informal conversations, and artifacts.

Imagine that you are carrying out research with and on colonized Others. What are some of the issues that might limit the inquiry process? Colonial rule created a dichotomy of the colonizer as knower and colonized as ignorant. It also created a midway space of the educated as better than those who did not go to school, although still lesser than the colonizers. Within this context, the position of the researcher as more educated than the majority of the researched still limits the inquiry process, as the researched are most likely to suppress indigenous knowledge in favor of knowledge acquired from the media and Euro-Western paradigms. Postcolonial indigenous research methodologies challenge the interpretivists to interrogate power relations between Western-educated researchers, as colonizers using dominant methodologies that legitimize ideologies of dominant groups, and the researched, as colonized and relegated to the position of an ignorant subject. Postcolonial indigenous methodologies propose ethics protocols that are informed by the value systems of the researched. These are value systems that promote, in the research process, the incorporation of spirituality, respect for the researched, cooperation between researchers and the researched, and a holistic approach to problem solving. The main argument from a postcolonial indigenous perspective is that knowledge production from the interpretive paradigm has been socially constructed using Euro-Western philosophies, cultures, and a long history of an application and practice of knowledge production that exclude the worldviews and practices of former colonized societies. *The Four Seasons of Ethnography: A Creation-Centered Ontology for Ethnography* (Gonzalez, 2000) illustrates ways of indigenizing ethnography. See Chapter 4.

The Transformative Paradigm

There are scholars who criticize both the positivist/postpositivist and the interpretive paradigms. Some scholars, for example, Carol Gilligan (1982), argue that most research studies that inform sociological and psychological theories were developed by white male intellectuals on the basis of studying male subjects. In the United States, for example, African Americans argue that research-driven policies and projects have not benefited them because they were racially biased (Mertens 2010a). In Africa, scholars, for example Robert Chambers (1997), and Arturo Escobar (1995), argue that the dominant research paradigms have marginalized African communities' ways of knowing and have thus led to the design of research-driven development projects that are irrelevant to the needs of the people. A third paradigm, labeled critical social science research (Neuman, 2010), action participatory and feminist designs (Merriam & Simpson, 2000), research with the aim to emancipate (Lather, 1991), or transformative paradigm (Mertens, 2010a) has emerged. The term *transformative paradigm* is adopted in this book to denote a family of research designs influenced by various philosophies and theories with a common theme of emancipating and transforming communities through group action (Mertens, 2010a). One of the influential theories is Marxism, originated by the German philosopher, Karl Marx. He believed that those who controlled the means of production, that is, the ruling class, also controlled the mental production of knowledge and ideas. Inevitably, the knowledge produced perpetuates the domination of other social classes by the ruling class, he said. The theory also helps to explain the dominance of Western-based research paradigms and the marginalization of knowledge produced in other cultures. Other theories include critical theory, feminist theories, Freirian theory, critical race theories, and postcolonial and indigenous theories.

Assumptions About the Nature of Reality, Knowledge, and Values

Ontology. The transformative paradigm adopts the stance that social reality is historically bound and is constantly changing depending on social, political, cultural, and power-based factors (Neuman, 2010). Scholars within this paradigm adopt the stance that reality is constructed based on social location and that different versions of reality are privileged over others (Mertens, 2009). Reality has multiple layers, the surface reality and the deep structures that are unobservable. Theories and a historical orientation help to unmask the deep structures.

Epistemology. On the question of what is truth, the researchers within this paradigm maintain that knowledge is true if it can be turned into practice that empowers and transforms the lives of the people. Theory is the basic tool that helps the researcher to find new facts. The facts are built into theory that is consistently improved by relating it to practice (Neuman, 2010). True knowledge in this context lies in the collective meaning making by the people that can inform individual and group action that improves the lives of the people. Knowledge is constructed from the participants' frame of reference. The relationship between the researcher and the researched is not based on a power hierarchy, as in the interpretive paradigm, but involves a transformation and emancipation of both the participant and the researcher.

Axiology. Researchers who adopt the transformative paradigm view research as a moral and political activity that requires them to choose and commit themselves to the values of social justice, furthering human rights and respect of cultural norms. Researchers achieve objectivity by reflecting and examining their values to ensure that they are appropriate for carrying out the research study. Whereas in the interpretive paradigm, in which every viewpoint is correct, some views will facilitate an increase in social justice while others will sustain oppressive systems (Mertens, 2009).

Methodology. In the transformative paradigm, the purpose of research is to destroy myths, illusions, and false knowledge and therefore empower people to act to transform society. Quantitative as well as qualitative methods are used in the research process. Techniques of collecting data and sampling procedures suitable to quantitative and qualitative studies are used. Participants are involved in identifying and defining the problem, collecting and analyzing the data, disseminating the findings, and using the findings to inform practice. Common designs are the participatory rural appraisal approach and action research. Refer to Chapter 8.

In the study by Michael Omolewa et al. (1998), survey methods were used along with oral texts, focus group interviews, and individual interviews. The meanings of literacy evolved from the people's experiences and eventually informed the changes in the literacy program.

Activity 1.2

Read the study extract included here and answer the following questions:

1. Discuss how the methodological features of the study reflect the transformative research paradigm ontology, epistemology, and axiology.

2. Discuss the concept of integration of knowledge systems and give your own evaluation of its application in the study.

Source: Adapted from Michael Omolewa, Olukemi Anthony Adeola, Gbolagade Adekanmbi, Michael B. M. Avoseh, & Dele Braimoh (1998), *Literacy, Tradition and Progress: Enrollment and Retention in an African Rural Literacy Programme.*

Research problem

While there has been an increasing involvement of government in literacy promotion activities, it is observed that literacy has been constrained by the problem of non-growth, which includes an inability to replicate activities, an increasing pattern of wastage, the problem of learner reluctance and rejection, and the neglect of the ultimate objective of asking learners to take over the literacy venture. All the agencies involved in literacy promotion have had their share of these problems, thus making necessary the search for an alternative.

Research objectives

Identify alternative strategies for the promotion of literacy in Nigeria, especially in rural settings
Provide a solution to the intractable problem of non-growth
Improve the replicability of literacy programs
Reduce the pattern of wastage and learner apathy
Promote learner empowerment as literacy's ultimate goal

Method

Using elements of both qualitative and quantitative research designs, combining a survey of the village with a historical analysis and a qualitative approach.

Instruments and procedures

Questionnaires; oral texts such as stories, language, proverbs, and sayings; interviews

(Continued)

(Continued)

Results

During the research, it was established that the indigenous apprenticeship system offered an attractive, alternative training program. First, the system demanded that people should begin to serve as guides (teachers) soon after a smattering of skill had been acquired. The guides, however, continue to serve under others who themselves continue their own learning.

There is a need to use aspects of the indigenous culture and practices to attract learners and to consolidate their interest. It is not enough to attract learners; it is even more important to retain learners in the program and to use them to publicize the value of the program to the hitherto unreached. Tradition encourages the cultivation of the virtues of tact, sympathy, understanding, courtesy, patience, punctuality, doing by example, and practicability, all of which seek to enhance adult learners' commitment.

Discussion

The learners have cultivated an attitude that restores learning to its status in precolonial times, when education was continuing and lifelong and promoted even beyond death in stories and songs. The suspicion of learning, resulting from intervention of Islamic traders and Christian teachers, has given place to a revival of learning for learning's sake. Thus, the participants in our project contend that learning is by no means a once-and-for-all affair, found only in pages of books and ending with the award of certificates. Rather, they contend that even the songs of birds teach lessons, and the color of the sky conveys a message to one who is eager to learn. The pride in learning is thus a return to the roots of the indigenous society, which took pride in the art of learning. It is also a rejection of the wrong ideas about Western education. For in the West, one is told, even in a village school, the truly educated person knows how little he or she knows and understands that there is no end to learning.

The postcolonial indigenous research methodologies have assumptions similar to those in the transformative paradigm. Postcolonial indigenous research methodologies adopting a decolonization and indigenization approach, however, emphasize how indigenous knowledges can be used to transform conventional ways of producing knowledge so that colonial and imperial impositions are eliminated, and knowledge production is inclusive of multiple knowledge systems. Decolonization and indigenization research methodological approaches require, for instance, that theory does not necessarily come out of written texts but can be inferred by the researcher from oral traditions, stories, legends, language, and artifacts. In postcolonial indigenous methodologies, the researcher has a duty to retrieve from the oral texts perspectives, concepts, and theories that form conceptual and theoretical frameworks for research studies, rationale, and justification for selected data-gathering techniques, data analysis, and research finding dissemination strategies. In the study on literacy in Nigeria by Omolewa et al. (1998), the researcher relinquishes conventional concepts of literacy for those based on the indigenous knowledge systems. The participants undergo a transformation and are empowered through a realization of their potential as teachers, as well as renewed confidence in their culture, its values, and what they already know. Knowledge is built through practice as it unfolds in the practice of the people and the researchers.

SUMMARY

Postcolonial indigenous research methodologies consist of approaches to decolonize and indigenize dominant research methodologies. They include the articulation of a postcolonial indigenous research paradigm informed by a relational ontology, epistemology, and axiology. The framework adopted in this chapter and throughout the book is that current dominant methodologies should be decolonized to legitimize and enable the inclusion of knowledge production processes that accommodate shared knowledge and wisdoms of those suffering from the oppressive colonial research tradition. There is also recognition that integrating indigenous perspectives in dominant research paradigms may not be the most effective strategy to legitimize the histories, worldviews, ways of knowing, and experiences of the colonized and historically oppressed. A postcolonial indigenous research paradigm is discussed as an alternative to indigenizing approaches and Western research paradigms. As a researcher, you can make a choice of the paradigm or approach that will inform your research, taking into consideration the nature of the problem you are investigating and your worldview. You will have a responsibility to critically assess the research process and procedures to see if they allow the researched to communicate their experiences from their frames of reference. Chapters 2 and 4 will illustrate further some of the ways that research can be carried out in ways that privilege the colonized's ways of knowing. For a summary of the characteristics of each paradigm, refer to Table 1.1.

Table 1.1 Beliefs Associated With the Four Paradigms

	Positivist Paradigm	Interpretive Paradigm	Transformative Paradigm	Indigenous Research Paradigm
Reason for doing the research	To discover laws that are generalizable and govern the universe	To understand and describe human nature	To destroy myths and empower people to change society radically	To challenge deficit thinking and pathological descriptions of the formerly colonized and reconstruct a body of knowledge that carries hope and promotes transformation and social change among the historically oppressed
Philosophical underpinnings	Informed mainly by realism, idealism, and critical realism	Informed by hermeneutics and phenomenology	Informed by critical theory, postcolonial discourses, feminist theories, race-specific theories, and neo-Marxist theories	Informed by indigenous knowledge systems, critical theory, postcolonial discourses, feminist theories, critical race-specific theories, and neo-Marxist theories
Ontological assumptions	One reality, knowable within probability	Multiple socially constructed realities	Multiple realities shaped by human rights values, democratic and social justice values, and political, cultural, economic, race, ethnic, gender, and disability values	Socially constructed multiple realities shaped by the set of multiple connections that human beings have with the environment, the cosmos, the living, and the nonliving
Place of values in the research process	Science is value free, and values have no place except when choosing a topic	Values are an integral part of social life; no group's values are wrong, only different	Researchers prioritize the value of furthering social justice and human rights.	All research must be guided by a relational accountability that promotes respectful representation, reciprocity, and rights of the researched. The ethics theory is informed by appreciative inquiry and desire-based perspectives

40

Nature of knowledge	Objective	Subjective; idiographic	Dialectical understanding aimed at critical praxis	Knowledge is relational, as is all the indigenous knowledge systems built on relations
What counts as truth	Based on precise observation and measurement that is verifiable	Truth is context dependent	It is informed by a theory that unveils illusions	It is informed by the set of multiple relations that one has with the universe
Methodology	Research designs: quantitative, correlational, quasi-experimental, experimental, causal comparative, survey	Research designs: qualitative, phenomenology, ethnographic, symbolic interaction, naturalistic	Research designs: combination of quantitative and qualitative action research; participatory research	Participatory, liberatory, and transformative research approaches and methodologies that draw from indigenous knowledge systems
Techniques of gathering data	Mainly questionnaires, observations, tests, and experiments	Mainly interviews, participant observation, pictures, photographs, diaries, and documents	Culturally responsive techniques of data collection	Techniques based on philosophic sagacity, ethnophilosophy, language frameworks, indigenous knowledge systems, talk stories, and talk circles; adapted techniques from the other three paradigms

KEY POINTS

- Research methods are dominated by Western modes of thinking.
- Research is value laden, and the choice of a methodology used in a study implies a worldview or way of thinking about the topic of research, the community researched, the data collection procedures, analysis, and reporting.
- The range of research approaches and designs, from surveys to ethnography, should open space for the inclusion of indigenous knowledge systems.
- Postcolonial indigenous methodologies interrogate imperial and colonial power in research and invoke indigenous knowledge systems to envision other ways of doing research that are informed by the worldviews of the colonized and historically marginalized groups.

Activity 1.3

1. Debate the main points from this chapter and use research studies to support your views.
2. Select a journal in your discipline and analyze studies done within a 5-year period for visibility of the colonized and historically marginalized groups' worldviews, ways of knowing, and indigenous knowledge.

SUGGESTED READINGS

Creswell J., & Clark P. (2011). *Designing and conducting mixed methods research.* Thousand Oaks, CA: Sage.

Deloria, V. (1969). *Custer died for your sins: An Indian Manifesto.* Norman: University of Oklahoma Press.

Fixico, D. L. (Ed.). (2003). *The American Indian mind in a linear world: American Indian studies and traditional knowledge.* New York: Routledge.

Liamputtong P. (2010). *Qualitative cross cultural research.* Cambridge, UK: Cambridge University Press.

Mertens, D. M. (2010). *Research and evaluation in education and psychology: Integrating with quantitative, qualitative, and mixed methods.* Thousand Oaks, CA: Sage.

Scheurich, J. J., & Young M. D. (1997). Coloring methodologies: Are our research epistemologies racially biased? *Educational Researcher, 26*(4), 4-16.

Smith, L. T. (1999). *Decolonizing methodologies: Research and indigenous peoples.* London: Zed Books.

Wilson, S. (2008). *Research is ceremony: Indigenous research methods.* Manitoba, Canada: Fernwood.

CHAPTER **2**

DISCOVERY AND RECOVERY

Reading and Conducting Research Responsibly

When any group within a large, complex civilisation significantly dom-
inates other groups for hundreds of years, the ways of the dominant
group (its epistemologies, ontologies and axiologies), not only become
the dominant ways of that civilisation, but also these ways become so
deeply embedded that they typically are seen as "natural" or appropri-
ate norms rather than as historically evolved social constructions.

James J. Scheurich and Michelle D. Young (1997, p. 7)

The range of contemporary critical theories suggests that it is from
those who have suffered the sentence of history-subjugation, domina-
tion, diaspora, displacement that we learn our most enduring lessons
for living and thinking.

Homi Bhabha, 1994, p. 172

OVERVIEW

This chapter extends the discussion on paradigms to show the relationship
between methodology, methods, and philosophical assumptions about the
nature of reality, knowledge and values, and theory. Postcolonial indigenous

theory and critical race theory are discussed as potential decolonizing tools that rupture the hegemonic Euro-Western methods that see "the world in one color" (Guba & Lincoln, 2005, p. 212). This chapter presents case studies that will enable you to understand how colonial research served the interests of the colonizers and how critical theoretical frameworks are used to inform the design, analysis, and reporting in a study with a postcolonial indigenous research perspective.

LEARNING OBJECTIVES

By the end of this chapter, you should be able to:
1. Discuss the role of postcolonial indigenous theory and critical race theory in indigenous research.
2. Critique the universal application of mainstream research methods from the perspective of postcolonial indigenous theory and critical race theory.
3. Understand the resistance of the researched communities to imposed knowledge systems and the implications of that resistance for research.
4. Acquire skills that will enable you to be a critical reader of research studies.

Before You Start

Discuss the quotations at the start of this chapter in relation to the experiences of the colonized and those historically marginalized by the colonizing Western-based research tradition. Do you think there is any suppressed knowledge or value systems belonging to the colonized that could inform the construction of research knowledge? Think of the colonized as all those hurt by the colonizing Euro-Western research tradition, for instance, the formerly colonized, indigenous peoples, the deaf, the immigrants, women, and girls in these societies.

▌ INTRODUCTION

An anticolonial critique framework, using critical theory, postcolonial discourses, and critical race-based theories, is challenging every discipline to assess how knowledge production and theories of the past and the present have been shaped by ideas and power relations of imperialism, colonialism, neocolonialism, globalization, and racism. Postcolonial studies have shown that no subject area or theory, be it biology, physics, language, mathematics, Marxism, or feminism, has escaped Eurocentric colonialism and modern imperialism or globalization (Said, 1993). In Chapter 1, you learned that scholars are expressing their criticism about what they view as the dominance of Euro-Western methodologies, which marginalize indigenous knowledge of the colonized and historically oppressed. Evidence is mounting about the failures of research-driven interventions that draw from mainstream research epistemologies. Arturo Escobar (1995), in *Encountering Development: The Making and Unmaking of the Third World,* documents the failures of research-driven development projects in the third world, while Robert Chambers (1997), in *Whose Reality Counts: Putting the First Last,* documents the errors in research-driven development projects that arise when mainstream research methodologies are used among communities in developing countries. Aaron M. Pallas (2001, p. 7), in a discussion of educational research, proposes that to prevent a recurring pattern of "epistemological single-mindedness, educational researchers should engage with multiple epistemologies" that include beliefs about what counts as knowledge. Lauren J. Young (2001), Pallas (2001), Reba N. Page (2001), and Mary Haywood Metz (2001) argue that novice researchers and graduate students should be prepared to deal with epistemological diversity.

It is important to give space and listen to the voices from these historically silenced groups and those who sympathize with them to learn about other epistemologies and other ways of knowing. For many reasons, this is a noble undertaking at this point in time.

- Indigenous knowledge and local knowledge have become important in the emerging global economy, with observers noting that "the basic component of any country's knowledge system is its indigenous knowledge" (Economic and Social Development Department, 2006, p. 9).
- An increased volume of research on the colonized Other is funded by international organizations, amid a growing realization that Euro-Western-based research methodologies fail to capture the experiences of these colonized Others (Chambers, 1997; Chilisa, 2005; Chilisa & Ntseane 2010; Escobar, 1995; Nitza, Chilisa, & Makwinja-Morara, 2010).
- An increased number of international and transnational researchers are committed to writing on methodologies and carrying out research that promotes social justice, human rights, and democracy (Mertens, 2009, 2010a, 2010b).
- The emerging trend where "the knowledge paradigms of the future are beginning to develop by reaching out to those excluded to move together towards a new synthesis" (Fatnowna & Pickett, 2002, p. 260) shows the growing need to hear from multiple voices, including those who critique mainstream research and those write on postcolonial/indigenous epistemologies.

- Indigenous knowledge and local knowledge systems are already part of the global dialogue with regard to ethics, copyrights, and the production of knowledge, increasing the need to internationalize postcolonial indigenous research epistemologies and methodologies.

In Chapter 1, you learned about the following strategies for decolonization:

- Deconstruction and reconstruction as strategies for discovering and recovering the past to inform the present and future
- Self-determination and social justice in research
- Implementation of ethical frameworks that promote rights and ownership to knowledge produced
- Implementation of research using indigenous languages
- Excavation of the past to know our history and thus promote self-determination and social justice in research
- Mobilization of communities to internationalize indigenous knowledge systems
- Critique
- Paradigms and their philosophical and theoretical underpinnings, methodologies, and techniques of gathering data

In this chapter, I expand the discussion on decolonization as a process that engages with imperialism, colonialism, and globalization to understand the assumptions and values that continue to inform research practices that privilege Western thought and the resistance of the majority two-thirds of the world's population to this privileged knowledge. Postcolonial theories and critical race feminist theories provide a framework with which we can discuss imperialism, colonialism, and globalization as processes with assumptions and values that legitimized Euro-Western methodologies and further build deficit literatures communicated in dominant languages, such as English, about the colonized Other. The contribution of feminist theory to indigenous research is discussed in Chapter 9. Let us commence with a discussion of postcolonial theories.

❧ POSTCOLONIAL AND INDIGENOUS THEORIES

Postcolonial theories discuss the role of imperialism, colonization, globalization and their literature and language in the construction of knowledge and people's resistance to imposed frameworks of knowing. It takes a poststructural view of the world with the aim of deconstructing truths, beliefs, values, and norms that are presented as normal and natural and presenting them as politically and socially constructed. Postcolonial theory engages with issues of power. In the context of research, it enables scholars to interrogate power relations that arise between researchers and the researched, for example, when choices are made about the literature to be reviewed, the theoretical frameworks, research questions, techniques of gathering data (for example, tests). These power relations come with "Othering" ideologies, which see the world in binary opposites of colonizer/colonized Other, first world/third and fourth world. Postcolonial theory pays attention to how race and ethnicity interact with class, gender, age, and ableness in interlocking forms of oppression. (Chapter 9 discusses postcolonial indigenous feminist theories and methodologies). In addition, it exposes how academic discourse uses Othering ideologies to make sense of the world along binary opposites, which devalue indigenous knowledge and marginalize the voices of the colonized Other.

Postcolonial discourses also look at the resistance to the colonizing methodologies by researchers who chart other ways of doing research that are culturally sensitive to those colonized by the Euro-Western research tradition. Postcolonial theorizing is useful in indicating a general process of colonization and counterattempts by the colonized Other to disengage from the colonial syndrome. The resistance is a challenge to Western-educated indigenous researchers, demanding that they begin to interrogate their multiple identities as colonizers participating in the Othering of their people through the use of Western research methodologies and as peripheral Others marginalized by the global network of first-world research elites and by global markets that continue to define and determine knowledge discourses on the basis of global market prices. It is in this context that a relational ethical framework in indigenous research is essential.

Postcolonial Theory Critique

Indigenous scholars (Grande, 2000; Smith, 2000) have argued that postcolonial theory can easily become a strategy for Western researchers to perpetuate control over research related to indigenous peoples and the colonized Other in general, while at the same time ignoring their concerns and ways of knowing. The argument is that postcolonial theory is a version of critical theory and thus born of a Western tradition that emphasizes individuality, secularization, and mind-body duality (Grande, 2000). Values of the colonized Other, such as concepts of family, spirituality, humility, and sovereignty, are most likely to be missed in a postcolonial research approach that draws from critical theory. Gerald Vizenor (1994) calls for the inclusion of *survivance* in postcolonial theory. The concept of survivance goes beyond survival, endurance, and resistance to colonial domination, calling for the colonizers and the colonized to learn from each other. The postcolonial indigenous theory envisioned in this book includes the concept of survivance and the recognition of indigenous knowledge as a rich source from which to theorize postcolonial indigenous research methodologies.

Augmenting the debate, Eve Tuck (2009, p. 413) notes that research based on postcolonial theory has a tendency to look to historical exploitation, domination, and colonization to explain contemporary brokenness, such as poverty, poor health, and so on. This is a pathologizing view that focuses on damage, ignoring the wisdom and hope of the researched. The alternative, he proposes, is a desire-based research framework, where desire "is about longing for a present that is enriched by both the past and the future" (Tuck, 2009, p. 417). Here, Tuck invokes the space in between, also termed the "third space" in postcolonial theory, to explain desire-based research frameworks. I have used the term *postcolonial indigenous theory* to emphasize indigenous theorizing and indigenous knowledge as essential ingredients in postcolonial theory. Postcolonial indigenous theory thus gives researchers the tools to theorize indigenous research, indigenous research paradigms, and culturally integrative research approaches. What follows are aims of research informed by postcolonial indigenous theory.

Research Aims

Catriona Macleod and Sunil Bhatia (2008) have identified three aims of research informed by postcolonial theory:

1. *Researching back.* This process examines our history, deconstructing how postcolonial subjects have been theorized, produced, and reproduced and reconstructing the present and the future, which carries some hope for the oppressed. Researching back involves

   > interrogating colonial discourses, imploding their political partisanship by introducing in strategic points of their critiques subaltern texts that see the colonial moment differently, that use other knowledges—as distinct from western—to articulate another view of the self, of history, of knowledge–power formations, resisting in the process the burden of colonialist epistemology and in fact mounting a counterassault by enabling previously disabled languages, histories, [and] modes of seeing the world. (Mishra, 2000, p. 1086)

2. *Theory-driven research.* The second aim is conducting contextually relevant and theory-driven studies that emphasize how the oppressed, in the struggle against the assault on their identities by Western methodologies, borrow theories from across cultures and academic disciplines and adopt a mixed method research approach. The mixed method research approach can range from a design that imposes indigenous worldviews on a predominantly Euro-Western paradigm or a design that uses a postcolonial indigenous paradigm, but borrows some Euro-Western methods to a culturally integrative approach with a balanced borrowing from Euro-Western paradigms and postcolonial indigenous paradigms.

3. *Liberatory and transformative intent.* The third aim is to produce knowledge that has a liberatory and transformative intention. In Chapter 8, you will learn how the development of action research impacted research methodologies, leading to indigenous struggles for voice, representation, and the transformative intent of research with the historically oppressed. Chapter 8 discusses change-focused research based on appreciative inquiry (Ludema, Cooperrider, & Barrett, 2006) and desire (Tuck, 2009). You will learn about contemporary research practices that place greater importance on people's existential realities, lived experiences, discursive practices, emotions, and cultural sensitivities and examine how these elements can contribute to community development and ongoing community action.

In what follows, I go back to history to interrogate and question the Euro-Western archives of methods to enable an appreciation and revaluing of the indigenous knowledge, languages, and ways of knowing devalued in Euro-Western research tradition. I will present the Porteus Maze tests as an example of methodological imperialism in colonial research, showing how methods were manipulated to create binaries of the knowers and the ignorant.

RESEARCHING BACK: METHODOLOGICAL IMPERIALISM

There is a debate over whether methods and their rules are sometimes allowed to claim methodological hegemony, so that methods tell researchers how they must see and what they must do when they investigate. The rules imposed on the researchers, it is argued, carry with them "a set of contingent and historically specific Euro-American assumptions" (Law, 2004, p. 5). Colonial research, it is argued, contains incontestable evidence of the manipulative ability of research to prove and perpetuate the dominance of one race over another (Ramsey, 2006). A case study that shows the use of a test as a method of collecting data is presented to illustrate methodological imperialism. As a researcher, you can revisit some of the research studies carried out in former colonies to review the use of research techniques in those studies. The assumption is that when we know about the past, we can deconstruct it and rupture the myth of the superiority of data-gathering techniques such as tests, questionnaires, and observation as neutral instruments in the construction of general knowledge and theories on formerly colonized societies.

One of the main techniques of gathering data during the colonial period was observation. So powerful was the sense of seeing that, for those who could not be there to see, ethnography became a discipline of "culture collecting" (Smith, 1999, p. 61), displaying collections of both human remains and animals. The Other was seen as an object of study through observation and public display. Thus, Richard A. Oliver (1934), writing on the mentality of the African, observed:

> The main method up until now has necessarily been observation—observation of the behaviour of Africans in natural, everyday situations; and the result of this method has been the description of such behaviour. To this method, we owe almost all our present knowledge of the mentality of the African; and it seems likely that this must for a long time remain the chief source of knowledge. (p. 41)

Using the observation method, anthropologists in Africa transformed descriptions of daily life of Africans into theories about the mental ability of Africans, about the child-like race, the impulsive Africans, and the passive onlookers (Blaut, 1993; Schumaker, 2001). In such cases, the colonizers through their research established themselves as the authorities of African cultures. Africans were not consulted on the researchers' interpretation of the observed data. Consequently, Africans are always shocked to read these anthropological collections, which depict their cultures as barbaric or inhuman. Obviously, such research was a powerful instrument for legitimizing colonialism since it justified the agenda of the colonizer, whose mission was defined as the duty to civilize.

Researchers need to be familiar with these debates on methods and techniques, as well as the evidence of how methods and techniques were manipulated to perpetuate the dominance of one race over the other. The Porteus Maze, which was used as test of intelligence among Africans in the 20th century, is an example of how techniques could be manipulated to privilege the dominance of one race over another, or the colonizer over the colonized. Following is Oliver's (1934) description of the Porteus Maze.

The Porteous Maze Tests as Tests of Intelligence

In these tests, the subject is presented with printed plan of a maze, and he has to trace with pencil the path he would follow in getting to the centre of the maze. If he enters blind alleys, he fails. The mazes form a series, graded in difficulty, and constituting an age scale of intelligence. A European child, when he reaches a maze beyond his mental age, tends to enter a blind alley and explore it to the end, and then to retrace his path to the entrance of the blind alley and go on again. He penetrates the centre of the maze quickly enough, but with many errors. The typical procedure of the African tested was different. The subject would study the maze for many minutes without making a move: then he would trace his path to the centre without hesitation or error. The test had to be abandoned as a test of intelligence, for even the most difficult mazes in the series were solved in this way by too many of the subjects. But this experience made me wonder about the African's alleged impulsiveness. (Oliver 1934, p. 44)

In the above tests, the results were at odds with colonial ideology that labelled Africans as ignorant and Europeans as intelligent, hence the tests were abandoned. The colonial research practice was dualistic, hierarchical, and dependent on maintaining patterns that always privileged one race. Researchers observed, saw, and then named. All other research approaches sought to reproduce the "Other from a Euro-Western eye." The questionnaires, interviews, and tests sought to create the Euro-Western white male as the norm against which the Other was judged. When attributes allocated to the Euro-Western white male appeared more frequently in the Other who was judged primitive, then the instruments were declared unreliable and lacking validity. This was methodological imperialism—a strategy to build a collection of methods, techniques, and rules calculated to market only that knowledge that promoted and profited Eurocentrism.

The questions we ask are:

1. What is our role as researchers when we come across such literature on techniques?
2. Have research methods changed, or have they maintained Euro-Western perspective?
3. How can we as researchers use the Porteus Maze test to reconstruct the past and modify the body of literature on the tests on intelligence for example?

Resistance to Methodological Imperialism

Methodological imperialism, it should be noted, was not without resistance. There are many ways in which the researched in former colonized societies continue to resist imposed knowledge production frameworks. Chapter 3 presents case studies of former colonized societies' resistance to imposed Western-informed ways of knowing. In *Africanising Anthropology,* Schumaker (2001) shows how local research assistants in today's Zimbabwe mediated the anthropologist's initial exposure to the societies they studied, through their translation work, introductions to potential informants, smoothing of the way for the researcher's questions, and general management of the researcher's interactions with local people. She argues that research assistants interpreted for the researchers, who did not speak the local languages, while at the same time protecting the local society and the interests of some of its members. In addition, local interpreters came to the anthropologist through local channels of power rather than through the researcher's choosing. African royals or educated elites controlled the researcher through handpicked interpreters of their choice. The researched could, when they wanted to protect themselves, give unreliable data to the researchers. In one instance, a researcher noted, for instance, that in a village where she had collected demographic data, the researched confessed how they had lied, making the figures collected unreliable. Schumaker (2001) notes, "In all cases, the relationship between the researcher, the assistants, and the informants had to some degree, an antagonistic character" (p. 94).

In some parts of Africa, entry into a research site, for instance, a village, is sanctioned by the chief. The researcher first obtains consent to do research from the chief, who then informs the people about the research. The relationship between the researcher and the research assistants, where the researcher might not know the local language and the researched, still remains a matter of concern and raises many questions about validity and reliability of research findings in former colonies. The relationship is also a reminder that research is not always an initiative of the researched and that it is at times regarded as an intrusion into their lives. Indigenous research methodologies, therefore, explore ways of making research a partnership between the researcher and the researched.

Academic Imperialism

The current global political economy still features overt domination over who can know, who can create knowledge, and whose knowledge can be bought. The term *academic imperialism* refers to the unjustified and ultimately counterproductive tendency in intellectual and scholarly circles to denigrate, dismiss, and attempt to quash alternative theories, perspectives, or methodologies. Lee Jussim (2002) notes that within American psychology, behaviorism in the period 1920 to the 1960s is one of the best examples of intellectual imperialism. Behaviorists, he notes, often characterized researchers taking nonbehaviorist approaches to psychology as nonscientific. For colonized, historically oppressed, and marginalized groups, intellectual imperialism speaks to the tendency to exclude and dismiss as irrelevant knowledge embedded in the cultural experiences of the people and the tendency to appropriate indigenous knowledge systems in these societies without acknowledging copyrights of the producers of this knowledge. Most colonized societies were thought of as primitive, barbaric, and incapable of producing useful knowledge.

In Africa, for example, Levy Buhl denied Africans south of the Sahara "properties of ratiocination and its cognates" (Kaphagawani, 2000, p. 86). The consequence of Buhl's theses was to deny that there could be an African philosophy or African philosophers and to claim that philosophy is Greek or European (Oruka, 1998). Those dismissing the existence of African philosophy claim that philosophy must be a written enterprise, and accordingly, a tradition without writing is incapable of generating philosophy. This denial of the existence of other knowledge systems is not unique to philosophy. It is still current practice in academic debates to invoke Euro-Western belief systems and methodologies to dismiss as irrelevant knowledge from former colonized societies, indigenous peoples, and historically oppressed groups. Susan Easterbrooks, Brenda Stephenson, and Donna Mertens (2006) note, for instance, that research in the field of deaf people focuses on the abilities that the deaf people lack rather than the abilities they have; viewing deafness as a deficiency is a way for the people in power to keep control of academic knowledge and power in their hands.

In some cases, the conflict is with publishers, reviewers of manuscripts, and other gatekeepers of knowledge over what can be said. My experience as a writer theorizing on postcolonial indigenous methodologies is another testimony to monopolies on knowledge production. In a book project, one of the reviewers of my manuscript had difficulties in opening space for research methodologies informed by African worldviews. The reviewer noted,

> There are difficulties in getting Africans involved in the theorising and building of knowledge on ways of conducting research. You have to address questions such as how do you test the validity of your findings . . . by African or Western standards. What language do you use to

build a research community and how do you research, store, and transmit the accumulated knowledge? Arguably, the whole idea of research belongs to the north/western paradigm, so probably some Africanness will have to be sacrificed in the process.

The argument in this book is that the colonized should be the center for the production and storage of information and knowledge produced about its people. The indigenous knowledge systems of these communities should provide answers on how knowledge is validated, sources of evidence and credibility of interpretation of research findings, and methods of dissemination of the research results. Postcolonial indigenous theories and critical indigenous theories offer tools to expand the borders and boundaries of Euro-Western methodologies to include subjugated knowledges and to empower the colonized majority.

Analytical Tool: Blaut's Theory

James M. Blaut's theory on the colonizer's model of the world offers a useful analytical tool that researchers can use to expose misconceptions, prejudices, racism, and stereotypes in the review of literature. In *The Coloniser's Model of the World,* Blaut (1993) reveals the role of European diffusionism ideology in constructing dichotomies of colonizer/colonized. He defines diffusionism as the claim that the rise of Europe to modernity and world dominance is due to some unique European quality of race, environment, culture, mind, or spirit. Blaut (1993) distinguishes two historical epochs in his theorization of diffusionism and the rise of Europe to dominance. The first period was marked by an inside/outside relationship constructed on the basis of a world with a permanent center from which all ideas and technology tended to originate and a periphery that must borrow from the center for change and development to occur. The inside/outside relationship begins with colonization, when Westerners propagated the myth that those living in the colonies-to-be lacked intellectual creativity, spiritual values, and rationality, thus justifying the displacement of natives from their lands. The diffusionism ideology enabled the division of the world into binary opposites of inside/outside, center/periphery, colonizer/colonized, and first world/third world. The colonizer/colonized binary had evolved over time, and at each historical point, it scripts the social license by which its ideas gain currency and hegemony. Table 2.1 captures Blaut's binary opposites on Western/European and non-European/Other.

Table 2.1 Binary Opposites on Western/European and non-European/Other

Characteristics of Western/European	Characteristics of non-European/Other
Inventiveness	Imitativeness
Rationality, intellect	Irrationality, emotion, instinct
Abstract thought	Concrete thought
Theoretical reasoning	Empirical, practical reasoning
Mind	Body matter
Discipline	Spontaneity
Adulthood	Childhood
Sanity	Insanity
Science	Sorcery
Progress	Stagnation

Source: Blaut, J. M. (1993). *The colonizer's model of the world: Geographical diffusionism and Eurocentric history.* New York: Guilford Press. Used by permission.

Blaut's construction of the colonizer's model of the world can be used as an analytical tool to interrogate the literature we read and the way we conduct research. The researcher can use these binary opposites to identify deficit theorizing, damage-focused assumptions, prejudices, and stereotypes in the literature reviewed, the methodology, the analysis, and interpretation in a study.

POSTCOLONIAL THEORY AND LANGUAGE

Postcolonial theories critique the dominance of Euro-Western languages in the construction of knowledge and argue that indigenous languages can play a significant role in contributing to the advancement of new knowledge, new concepts, new theories, and new rules, methods, and techniques in research that are rooted in former colonized societies' ways of knowing and perceiving reality. Language plays an important role in the research process (1) as a medium of communication, (2) as a vehicle through which indigenous knowledge can be preserved during fieldwork, and (3) as a symbol of objects, events, and experiences a community considers worth naming. It is widely accepted that communities use language to develop conceptual frameworks and ways of thinking about their lived realities and everyday lives (Hoppers, 2002; Mazrui 1990). Language holds people captive, and their way of talking reflects their thinking and who they are. Despite its important role in knowledge construction, research knowledge continues to be produced, communicated, and disseminated in dominant languages.

In his book, *Decolonizing the Mind: The Politics of Language in African Literature,* Ngugi wa Thiong'o (1986a, pp. 1–30) discusses language as a colonizing instrument. Recalling his own educational formation, how English-language use was enforced, and how African literature in English continues the legacy of colonization, he shows that the content and the arrangement of English literature in many African universities privileges the Western canons and, more fundamentally, alienates students from their cultures, worldview, environment, and continent. Ngugi wa Thiong'o discusses at length how the postcolonial intellectuals of Africa have now become the promoters of English language, hence systematically annihilating indigenous languages and continuing the legacy of colonialism.

> The biggest weapon wielded and actually daily unleashed by imperialism against that collective defiance is the cultural bomb. The effect of a cultural bomb is to annihilate a people's belief in their names, in their languages, in their environments, in their heritage of struggle, in their unity, in their capacities and ultimately in themselves. It makes them see their past as one wasteland of non-achievement and . . . it even plants serious doubts about the moral righteousness of the struggle. (p. 3)

The critique on language is an attempt to sensitize researchers about the role of language in the production of knowledge and to further challenge researchers to explore the use of the historically oppressed groups' languages in the construction of new theories, concepts, techniques, methodologies, and analysis procedures across disciplines. Easterbrooks et al. (2006) argue, for instance, that research for the deaf with the deaf has to explore the use of deaf language because dominant hegemonic methods have a tendency "to filter out any potentially deaf-centric stance" (quoted in Lane, 1999, p. 71). The abstract below shows current attempts in research to construct new concepts derived from the use of indigenous languages of the oppressed.

Indigenous Economic Concepts (T. Tsuruta, 2006)

Examining four well-known Swahili words, *utani, chama, ujamaa,* and *ujanja,* Tsuruta offers some tentative and exploratory comments on "indigenous" moral-economic concepts in Tanzania. These terms convey not only notions about social relations but also relations, which one could consider economic, along with unique cultural connotations. Various things Westerners consider separate are impossible to disentangle in these concepts; joking and mutual aid, dance and politics, wit and cunning, all related to people's subsistence economy. These phenomena cannot easily be put into pre-arranged Western categories nor should they be disregarded from a modernist perspective because these concepts and practices reflect a rich tradition of self-help solutions in Africa, thereby serving as a source of imagination for alternative visions of economic development. (Tsuruta, 2006)

Literature and Deficit Theorizing

Colonialism—in the form of the universal application of Western-based research methodologies and techniques of gathering data across cultures— and the subjectivity of researchers are among the factors that have created a body of literature that disseminates theories and knowledge unfavorable to the colonized Other. This body of literature threatens to perpetuate research that constructs the researched colonized Other as the problem. The challenge for researchers is how to manage the literature that informs our research studies, where the literature that is available on the colonized Other is written by outsiders and the literature by the colonized Other is predominantly oral.

In research, the literature review plays an important role in conceptualizing research topics, choosing the research designs for the study, and analyzing and interpreting the results. The golden rule for novice researchers is that they should always read the literature to help them choose a researchable topic, focus the research questions, provide theoretical basis for analyzing findings, legitimize their own assumptions, and give credit to and acknowledge the strength of previous findings. One major limitation of this approach is that the concepts, the theories, and the research studies conducted and the literature on former colonized societies have been written by missionaries, travellers, navigators, historians, anthropologists, and so on, who in most cases looked on the researched as objects with no voice in how they were described and discussed. This literature and body of knowledge continues to inform our research practices. The theories and literature have not been favorable to historically oppressed and former colonized societies. Noting these assaults by the literature and the theories, Linda T. Smith (1999) observes:

Indigenous people have been in many ways oppressed by theory. Any considerations of the ways our origins have been examined, our histories recounted, our arts analyzed, our cultures dissected, measured, torn apart and distorted back to us will suggest that theories have not looked ethically at us. (p. 38)

Western-educated scholars need to investigate the psychological harm, humiliation, embarrassment, and other losses that these theories and body of knowledge caused to the researched colonized Other. They also need to use the body of indigenous knowledge about the researched to counter theories and other misinformation that may cause communities humiliation and embarrassment.

Resistance to Dominant Literature

Postcolonial indigenous research methodologies provide an important framework through which Western-educated researchers can explore the possible biases in the literature we read, identify the knowledge gaps that have been created because of the unidirectional borrowing of Euro-Western literature, and bring to a halt the continuing marginalization of other knowledge systems that occurs because of the dominant Euro-Western research paradigms and their discourses on what can be researched and how it can be researched. Applying indigenous research methodologies to research with and about the colonized Other should involve going back and forth to retrieve marginalized and suppressed literatures to review, analyze, and challenge colonizing and deficit theorizing and interpretation, to create counternarratives that see the past differently, and to envision a transformative agenda with the researched. It also involves defining what literature and theorizing in the context of former colonized societies is. Postcolonial indigenous research methodologies perceive literature as language, cultural artifacts, legends, stories, practices, songs, rituals poems, dances, tattoos, lived experiences such as the people's fight against HIV/AIDS, personal stories, and community stories told in weddings, funerals, celebrations and wars. When I speak about songs as literature, this song by O. Mutukudzi always comes to my mind because, in my view, it captures the realities of HIV/AIDS beyond what the academic discourse can manage:

Senzeni What shall we do?
Ooooh toddii?
What shall we do? Senzi njani X3

Verse 2

How painful it is to nurse death in the/your hands!
What shall we do?

How......
What shall we do....?
(Verse 1 repeat)

Source: Excerpt from Mutukudzi, O. *Greatest Hits: The Tuku Years 1998–2002.*
  Harare: Frontline Promotions.

In the song, the artist resists co-option into the dominant discourse
on HIV and AIDS that insists on using a standardized science laboratory
language that is constructed on the basis of a cause-effect relationship to
describe people's experiences. The artist does not mention the word HIV/
AIDS. He sings about the realities seen through another lens, and we know
it is about what has been named by the Westerners HIV/AIDS. Mainstream
discourse about HIV/AIDS usually involves statistics on infection and the
number of condoms sold, a Western measure of profits made in Western capital markets masquerading as genuine concern for the spread of HIV/AIDS
and the problem with the historical colonized Africans. In the song, the pain
of nursing death resonates with people's experiences. People in Africa have
come up with many labels and names that describe their daily experiences
with HIV/AIDS. These have been invariably labeled irrelevance, ignorance,
beliefs in sorcery, barbaric cultural beliefs, simplistic and uncivilized thinking, belief in witchcraft, and so on. Such songs and the daily descriptions of
people's experiences of what happens in their families and communities
provide arguments to discursive regimes of representations that seek to construct Africans as the problem. What seems to be the problem is an attempt
to standardize the language that describes people's experiences with HIV/
AIDS and to insist on communicating in a science laboratory language that is
constructed on the basis of a cause-effect relationship. Consequently, former
colonies continue to operate two knowledge systems on HIV/AIDS, a global
knowledge system marketed by the West and a knowledge system that is
built on the experiences of the people and the values that inform the practices. The resilience of the people's knowledge challenges the single-mindedness of Western-driven interventions directed toward halting the spread of
HIV/AIDS in Africa and in the third and fourth world in general. This makes
urgent an expansion of the boundary of what it means to review literature
from the perspective of the historically colonized, the marginalized, and the
oppressed. Researchers should not delude themselves that literature constitutes only the written text. Rather, they should ask how each society produces
and stores knowledge. In most indigenous societies, knowledge is stored
in songs, sayings, rituals, jokes, and stories surrounding an issue of community concern.

Activity 2.1

Read the study extract included here and answer the following questions:

1. Discuss the features of a study that reflect a postcolonial framework.

2. What reasons does the researcher give for using an eclectic theoretical framework as well as eclectic interpretive methods?

3. List the data sources and the methods used in the study and their appropriateness in achieving the aims of research with a postcolonial framework.

Source: J. Kaomea (2003), "Reading Erasures and Making the Familiar Strange: Defamiliarising Methods for Research in Formerly Colonized and Historically Oppressed Communities," *Educational Researcher, 32*(2), 14–25. Used by permission.

Background to study

Since the first pilot kupuna program in 1980–1981, Native Hawai'ian elders have become a pivotal part of the Hawai'ian studies curriculum. According to students, teachers, principals, and district specialists who speak highly of the program, the kupuna are "invaluable resources" in the teaching of the Hawai'ian culture and language and also bring a special feeling of "warmth and aloha" to the elementary school classrooms. The kupuna epitomize Hawai'ian cultural values and the aloba spirit and provide positive intergenerational exchanges for those children who do not have grandparents of their own (Afaga & Lai, 1994).

On the surface it looks and sounds like a wonderfully conceived program, one whose virtues are acknowledged by teachers, children, and administrators alike. Personally, as a Native Hawai'ian who has been raised to honor the wisdom of my elders, it initially brought me great joy to see Hawai'ian kupuna resuming a larger role in the cultural education of Hawai'i's youth. However as my more extensive investigations into this program later revealed, there is much more (and less) going on with this kupuna program than initially appears.

Methodology

To delve beyond surface appearances, I used classroom observations and interviews with kupuna in eight elementary schools across Hawai'i, along with reviews of related program documents, to develop a critical analysis of this long-cherished program. Beginning with a look at students' artwork and written reflections on the kupuna's classroom visits, I employed various defamiliarizing interpretive techniques to look beyond the initial and overwhelmingly positive impressions of the familiar, manifest text. I also examined the subtext, or that which has been put under erasure. Through the persistent uncovering of silences and erasures in this program, I defamiliarized taken-for-granted perspectives on this much-applauded curriculum and rendered this familiar program "strange."

This defamiliarizing inquiry into the Hawai'ian studies kupuna program serves as a reply to contemporary calls for antioppressive (Kumashiro, 2000, 2001) and decolonizing (Smith, 1999) research methodologies that look beyond familiar, dominant narratives and give voice to the previously marginalized or voiceless. In response to these requests, this study employs a variety of defamiliarizing techniques drawn from literary and critical theory, in concert with Native Hawai'ian cultural traditions, to force readers into dramatic awareness of previously silenced perspectives on the lesser known aspects of this highly praised curriculum. Through a careful analysis of the kupuna program's many silences, absences, and erasures, this defamiliarizing study reveals the various ways in which numerous Hawai'ian kupuna are systematically misused and abused in Hawai'i's public elementary schools.

Theoretical framework

Consistent with the logic of postcolonialism and its suspicion of grand theories and narratives (Bhaba, 1994; Said, 1978; Spivak, 1987), my theoretical framework and interpretive methods are intentionally eclectic, mingling, combining, and synthesizing theories and techniques from disparate disciplines and paradigms. Writing as a Native Hawai'ian in the middle of the Pacific, far removed from the academic center of the metropolis, I do not have the luxury of attaching myself to any one theoretical perspective but instead "make do" (de Certeau, 1984) as an interpretive handyman or bricoleur (Levi-Strauss, 1966; see also Denzin & Lincoln, 1998).

Throughout this study, I draw widely from an assortment of structuralist and post structuralist theorists, moving within and between sometimes competing or seemingly incompatible interpretive

(Continued)

(Continued)

perspectives and paradigms. Consequently, this study has both a deconstructive playfulness as well as a Marxist earnestness. It engages with Jacques Derrida's (1976) notions of deconstruction and erasures as well as Karl Marx's (1886/1977) concern with deep structures and material effects. At the same time, it consciously and unapologetically privileges Native Hawai'ian philosophies and concerns. Although I do not deny the possible contradictions between these various theoretical perspectives, I believe that postcolonial studies require such theoretical innovation and flexibility. If we are to meet the demands of postcolonial studies for both a revision of the past and an analysis of our ever-changing present, we cannot work within closed paradigms (Loomba, 1998).

Discussion and conclusion

I do not doubt that the Hawai'ian studies kupuna program was well intended at its inception, and I have seen—and reported on elsewhere (Kaomea-Thirugnanam, 1999)—a few situations in which Hawai'ian studies kupuna have effectively contested or resisted the restrictions of this state-mandated curriculum and used their positions to function as positive agents for social change or "cultural production" (Levinson & Holland, 1996). However, after uncovering the many ways in which numerous other kupuna have been disempowered and disembodied in Hawai'i's schools, I am made aware of the many challenges of implementing a progressive, liberating Hawai'ian curriculum within a system whose goals may, in many respects, be incompatible with—or even hostile to—Hawai'ian self-determination and empowerment. For in every instance when Hawai'ian kupuna are incorporated into the school system as handmaidens of the larger state apparatus, the Hawai'ian studies kupuna program is effectively turned on its head and is ultimately made to serve ends inimical to its original, progressive intentions.

With the aid of these defamiliarizing tools, anti-oppressive researchers working in historically marginalized communities can begin to ask very different kinds of questions that will enable us to excavate layers of silences and erasures and peel back familiar hegemonic maskings. Building upon Friedrich Nietzsche's (1881/1964) "insidious questions," we can begin to ask: What does this textbook passage, classroom dialogue, interview transcript, or curricular artifact intend to show? What does it intend to draw our attention from or conceal? What does it seek to erase?

CRITICAL RACE THEORIES

In addition to postcolonial theory, critical race theory interrogates Euro-Western methodology, using race as its tool of analysis. Critical race theory reveals how race functions to construct rules, norms, standards, and assumptions that appear neutral but that systematically disadvantage or subordinate racial minorities (Vargas, 2003, p. 1). It has its roots in law and gained visibility in the 1970s and popular currency in the 1980s and early 1990s (Vargas, 2003). Critical race theory takes a transformative approach, asserting that through knowledge and critique of how race operates "to mediate and color the work we do," researchers can reconsider the practices, methods, approaches, tools of data collection, and modes of analysis and dissemination of results so that research promotes justice and is respectful and beneficial to racial minorities. Out of this critique has emerged what is termed race-based methodologies (Pillow, 2003), which insist that current Euro-Western methodologies are based on white-race colonizing ideologies. Race-based methodologies are adopted by scholars writing from the vantage of the colonized Other.

The characteristics of critical race-based research methodologies include the following:

1. A challenge to dominant ideologies
2. Importance of interdisciplinary approaches
3. Emphasis on experiential knowledge
4. The centrality of race and racism and their intersectionality with other forms of subordination and commitment to social justice
5. History as the foundation of knowledge, the body of experience, and voice from which to work
6. Rethinking language as the source of knowledge

Activity 2.2

Read the study extract included here and answer the following questions:

1. Discuss the features of a study that reflect a decolonization of mainstream methodologies.

2. Discuss the role of storytelling and counter-storytelling in privileging voices of those at the margins.

(Continued)

(Continued)

Source: D. G. Solórzano and T. J. Yosso (2001), Critical race and LatCrit theory and method: Counter-storytelling, Chicana and Chicano graduate school experiences, *International Journal of Qualitative Studies in Education, 14*(4), 471–495. Reprinted by permission of the publisher (Taylor & Francis Group, http://www.informaworld.com).

Purpose of study

This article is an attempt to inject into the race discourse the multiple forms of racism in graduate education for Chicana and Chicano students and to answer the following questions: How do the structures, processes, and discourses of graduate education and the professorate reinforce racial, gender, and class inequality? How do Chicana/o graduate students and professors respond to race, gender, and class inequality?

Methodology

In order to integrate critical race theory with the experiences of Chicanas and Chicanos in graduate education, we use a technique that has a tradition in the social sciences, humanities, and the law—storytelling. Delgado (1989) uses a method called counter-storytelling and argues that it is both a method of telling the story of those experiences that are not often told (i.e., those on the margins of society) and a tool for analyzing and challenging the stories of those in power and whose story is a natural part of the dominant discourse—the majoritarian story (Delgado, 1993). For instance, while a narrative can support the majoritarian story, a counter-narrative or counter-story, by its very nature, challenges the majoritarian story or that "bundle of presuppositions, perceived wisdoms, and shared cultural understandings persons in the dominant race bring to the discussion of race" (Delgado & Stefancic, 1993, p. 462). These counter-stories can serve at least four theoretical, methodological, and pedagogical functions: (1) they can build community among those at the margins of society by putting a human and familiar face to educational theory and practice; (2) they can challenge the perceived wisdom of those at society's center by providing a context to understand and transform established belief systems; (3) they can open new windows into the reality of those at the margins of society by showing the possibilities beyond the ones they live and demonstrating that they are not alone in their position; and (4) they can teach others that by combining elements from both the story and the current reality, one can construct another world that is richer than either the story or the reality alone (Delgado, 1989; Lawson, 1995). Storytelling has a rich and continuing tradition in African-American (Berkeley Art Center, 1982; Bell, 1987, 1992, 1996; Lawrence, 1992), Chicana/o (Paredes, 1977; Delgado, 1989, 1955a, 1966; Olivas, 1990), and Native American cultures (Deloria, 1969; Williams, 1977; Delgado, 1989, 1995a, 1996). Delgado (1989) has stated, "oppressed groups have known instinctively that stories are an essential tool to their own survival and liberation" (p. 2436). We want to add to the tradition of counter-storytelling by illuminating the lives of Chicana and Chicano graduate students, who are often at the margins of graduate education. As a way of raising various issues in critical race theory and method, we offer the following counter-story about two composite characters engaged in a dialogue. One is Professor Leticia Garcia, a junior sociology professor at a Western University (UC-Oceanview). The other is Esperanza Gonzalez, a third-year graduate student at the same university in the education department. Using our definition of critical race theory and its five elements, we ask you to suspend judgment, listen for the story's points, test them against your own version of reality (however conceived), and use the counter-story as a theoretical, conceptual, methodological, and pedagogical case study (see Barnes et al., 1994).

Discussion

Indeed, critical race and LatCrit methodology challenges traditional methodologies, because it requires us to develop "theories of social transformation, wherein knowledge is generated specifically for the purpose of addressing and ameliorating conditions of oppression, poverty, or deprivation" (Lincoln, 1993, p.33). Counter-narrative-as qualitative method, exemplified in this article as a conversation between two Chicana academics, allows us to explore the breadth of what happens through the structures, processes, and discourses of higher education, as well as the depth of how and in what ways Chicanans/os respond. We concur with Denzin & Lincoln (1994) as they describe that, "the multiple methodologies of qualitative research may be methods . . . within a single study may be viewed

(Continued)

(Continued)

as a bricologe, and the research as bricoleur . . . the combination of multiple methods . . . within a single study is best understood, then, as strategy that adds rigor, breadth, and depth to any investigation" (p. 2) This strategy has allowed us to look to the experiential and other forms of knowledge from people of color and subordinated peoples, whose knowledge has often been excluded as an official part of the academy. We believe strength of critical race and LatCrit theory and methodology is the validation and combination of the theoretical, empirical, and experiential knowledge. Through our counter-narrative, we delve into lives of human characters who experience daily the interactions of racism, sexism, and classism. We look to continue this methodological, theoretical, conceptual, and pedagogical journey as we also express our deep gratitude and dedicate this work to those both inside and outside the academy who share their stories with us.

Postcolonial theory and critical race theory share the same aim of critiquing Euro-Western methodologies and seeking to promote methodologies that privilege the disenfranchised, dispossessed, and marginalized colonized Other in the third and fourth worlds. Both have a liberatory and transformative intent, and research using these frameworks thus shares the same investigative practices and methods. Catriona Macleod and Sunil Bhatia (2008) give examples of qualitative studies using a postcolonial framework and the methods they employ. The latter include colonial discourse analysis, narrative analysis, historiography, genealogy, organizational analysis, case study, ethnography, comparative research, participatory action research, deconstruction, and visual analysis. See Table 2.2.

Table 2.2   Examples of Qualitative Research in Postcolonialism

Methods Used	Data Source	Brief Explanation
Colonial discourse	Mostly written texts and archives	Analysis of discourse (often but not always Foucauldian) Highlighting (neo)colonial construction of the other
Narrative analysis	Interviews, autobiographies	Exploring the conditions of possibility in which the colonized and colonizing subjects emerges

Histography	Archives, texts	Reading against the grain to uncover blind spots and recuperate evidence of subaltern agency
Genealogy	Texts, archives	Using Foucauldian notion of descent to trace the emergence of colonial subjects and objects
Organizational analysis	Texts, organizational records and arrangements, interviews, training videos, observation	Analysis of (neo)colonial institutional practices and power relations
Case study	Interviews, participant observation, records	In-depth study of specific case (group, organization or individual) in which (neo) colonial power relations are manifested
Ethnography	Interviews, archives, texts, observations	A decent practice that overcomes its colonial history by examining the subject position of the ethnographer, collapsing the *us* and *them* assumption and privileging local knowledge
Comparative research	Interviews, archives, texts, observations	Contextual analyses of systems (often educational) or texts in ways that undermine the West as the given
Participatory action research	Participation in individual and group dialogue and action	Accountable research that is driven by participants and focuses on change within a given (neo)colonial setting
Deconstruction	Texts, interviews	Employment of Derridean concepts such as *différance* to expose exclusions and absent traces in (neo) colonial discourse

(Continued)

Table 2.2   (Continued)

Methods Used	Data Source	Brief Explanation
Visual analysis	Images (e.g., art, films, landscapes, drawing)	Analysis of images as signifiers of (neo)colonialism

Source: C. Macleod and S. Bhatia (2007), "Postcolonialism and Psychology," in C. Willig and W. Stainton-Rogers (Eds.), *The SAGE Handbook of Qualitative Research in Psychology.* London: Sage. Used by permission.

SUMMARY

This chapter has discussed postcolonial theory and critical race theories as important analytical tools to use to interrogate the universal application of Euro-Western methodologies across cultures. Using these theories as analytical tools reveals the biases, distortions, and misconceptions about the colonized Other that are legitimized by the accumulated body of literature and the use of dominant languages in research. The chapter proposes that the researched communities' language, cultural artifacts, legends, stories, songs, rituals, poems, and dances, are important sources of literature that should inform problem identification and formulation, research theoretical frameworks, and meaning making, as well as legitimizing research findings. Chapter 5 discusses community-centered methods of knowledge production while Chapter 6 discusses the place of language in research.

KEY POINTS

- Research ignores the history of colonization and imperialism and its impact on the colonized Other.
- There is a need to critique mainstream history, colonialism, imperialism, and globalization in research methods courses so that methodologies, theories, and literatures are understood as practices seeking to see and know realities in diverse historical moments bound with politics and power.
- Scholars are engaged in an ongoing attempt to decolonize research methodologies.
- In postcolonial indigenous research, it is important to avoid damage-focused research and employ desire-based research frameworks and frameworks that include research as survivance.

Activity 2.3

1. Discuss the terms *imperialism, colonization,* and *globalization.* Explain how you can apply each of these terms to a critical review of:

    a. Methodological approaches and techniques of gathering data as neutral and applicable to people across cultures.

    b. Literature as a building block for formulation of research proposals and frameworks for discussing research findings.

    c. The role of language in research.

2. Through a search of literature, identify a research study and, using Blaut's construction of the colonizer's model of the world, review the study for assumptions, prejudices, and stereotypes, if any, that informed the choice of study, its formulation, reviewed literature, and discussion of the findings.

3. Discuss literature from the perspective of indigenous research methodologies.

4. Discuss the role of language in research.

SUGGESTED READINGS

Blaut, J. M. (1993). *The colonizer's model of the world: Geographical diffusionism and Eurocentric history.* New York: Guilford Press.

Deloria, V. (1995). *Red earth, white lies: Native Americans and the myth of scientific fact.* New York: Scribner.

Getty, G. A. (2010). The journey between Western and indigenous research paradigms. *Journal of Transcultural Nursing, 21*(1), 5-14.

Grande, S, (2000). American Indian identity and intellectualism: The quest for a new red pedagogy. *Qualitative Studies in Education, 13,* 343-359.

Henderson, J. S. Y. (2000). Ayukpachi: Empowering aboriginal thought. In M. Batiste (Ed.), *Reclaiming indigenous voice and vision* (pp. 248-278). Vancouver, Canada: University of British Columbia Press.

Kaomea, J. (2003). Reading erasures and making the familiar strange: Defamiliarizing methods for research in formerly colonized and historically oppressed communities. *Educational Researcher, 32*(2), 14-25.

Law, J. (2004). *After method: Mess in social science research.* London: Routledge.

Ngugi wa Thiong'o (1993). *Decolonizing the mind: The politics of language in African literature.* London: James Currey.

Pillow W. (2003). Race-based methodologies: Multicultural methods or epistemological shifts? In G. R. Lopez & L. Parker (Eds.), *Interrogating racism in qualitative research methodology* (pp. 181–202). New York: Peter Lang.

Said, E. W. (1993). *Culture and imperialism.* London: Vintage.

Smith, G. H. (2000). Protecting and respecting indigenous knowledge. In M. Batiste (Ed.), *Reclaiming indigenous voice and vision* (pp. 207–224), Vancouver, Canada: University of British Columbia Press.

Solórzano, D. G., & Yosso, T. J. (2001). Critical race and LatCrit theory and method: Counter-storytelling, Chicana and Chicano graduate school experiences. *International Journal of Qualitative Studies in Education, 14*(4), 471–495.

Spivak, G. C. (1988). Can the subaltern speak. In N. Cary & L. Grossberg (Eds.), *Marxism and the interpretation of culture* (pp. 271–313). Urbana: University of Illinois Press.

Tuck, E. (2009). Suspending damage: A letter to communities. *Harvard Educational Review, 79*(3), 409–427.

CHAPTER 3

WHOSE REALITY COUNTS?

Research Methods in Question

Research institutions and practitioners are called upon to commit themselves to undertaking research that is relevant, participatory; based on indigenous culture and language of the people and that would serve the needs of the local communities.

UNESCO (1996)

OVERVIEW

In Chapter 2, you looked at a critique of dominant research paradigms from two perspectives: a postcolonial-indigenous theoretical framework and a critical race-based theoretical framework. Using excerpts from studies on HIV/AIDS, this chapter highlights how mainstream research in postcolonial societies still ignores, marginalizes, and suppresses other knowledge systems and ways of knowing. The chapter demonstrates how HIV/AIDS prevention has been highly compromised by employing language and categories of thinking that are alien to the infected and affected communities; how a dichotomous hierarchy informed by colonization, imperialism, and globalization privileges the first world position as knower and relegates the third world to the position of Other who is a learner, and how peoples' resistance to imposed frameworks has consequences.

LEARNING OBJECTIVES

By the end of this chapter you should be able to:

1. Use HIV/AIDS research as an example to critically discuss how current knowledge production in postcolonial indigenous societies is still being shaped by ideas and power relations of modern imperialism
2. Illustrate how conventional research methodologies marginalize and suppress other knowledge systems and ways of knowing
3. Understand the sameness error ideology and the exceptionality myths and how they marginalize certain research agendas and promote others
4. Debate the ethics that inform research approaches in former colonized societies

Before You Start

Think of all stakeholders in the research conducted in the communities where you live. These could be funders, policymakers, or researchers themselves, some of them from within the communities where the research takes place and others from foreign countries. Discuss the different interests that the different stakeholders bring to the research agenda. Whose voice is most likely to be heard and why? What are some of the ways in which the voices of the researched communities can be heard?

COLONIZER/COLONIZED DICHOTOMIES AND THE IDEOLOGY OF THE OTHER

While contemporary Western theories have dramatically changed in the last 30 years, the universalized research methods of the so-called first world, using self-valorization and hegemonic powers, continue to construct the world along binary opposites of self/Other, colonizer/colonized, center/periphery, developed/developing, North/South, first world/third world. These constructions privilege the first world and subjugate the various knowledge formations originating in former colonies. Although these categories are useful, they are broad and run the risk of being labeled essentialist or universalistic and of homogenizing the differences among members of the category (Dube, 2002). Gillan (1991) argues that these broad categories are at times necessary as they enable a discussion that connects the "local to the national and international." For this discussion, I explain the center/periphery, self/Other dichotomies. The main actors at the center are the United States, Great Britain, France, Germany, China, and Japan. These world powers work through multiple global networks that include transnational corporations, research institutions, international research funding agencies, and donor agencies to penetrate all cultural, political, and economic structures of nation-states. It is, however, not the masses in these countries that form the center but the ruling class—a male bourgeoisie minority "predominantly Eurocentric and making up one percent or two percent of the world's population" (Skutnabb-Kangas, 2000, p. 393). This male bourgeoisie at the center constructs the periphery Other. Frantz Fanon (1967), one of the earliest postcolonial theorists, discusses the binary opposites of *self* and *Other* in the image of a Whiteman and a Blackman. His argument is that in postindependence Africa, the ruling black male inherited and worked with the hegemonic structures created by the colonizers during colonial rule. Consequently, the ruling class became alienated from the peripheral masses, their cultures, and the value systems that inform their daily activities and experiences. This argument has been picked up by other postcolonial writers, such as Ngugi wa Thiong'o (1986a) and Ali Mazrui (1990).

In the current phase of global capitalism, the periphery ruling class Blackman/Other struggles to represent the nation-state and the local communities as an equal partner in international relations dominated by global capitalism. For instance, in the emerging global economy, sub-Saharan Africa is included in the category of a "fourth world" where the majority in "the region's population has shifted from a structural position of exploitation to a structural position of irrelevance" (Castells, 1993, p. 37). That is, in the context of HIV/AIDS, for instance, local knowledge, languages, cultures, and value systems cannot be converted into a capital value in the global market and are thus excluded from the knowledge and information that circulate globally to make profits.

Worse still, the image of a Whiteman/first world/center and a Blackman/fourth world/periphery blurs all other social hierarchies that exist. The woman's image, for example, is irrelevant and subsumed under that of man. This is despite the fact that patriarchal ideologies in all worlds continue to oppress women, placing them last in the social hierarchy and constructing their experiences and bodies as handicaps or making them invisible except as sites for investment. Indeed in her article, "Can the Subaltern Speak?" Gaytri Spivak (1988) underlines that "the subaltern as female is even more deeply in shadow" or "muted," (p. 83) and she can only speak through self-erasure (pp. 101–103). This is vividly demonstrated in the HIV/AIDS zones, where women are at the center of the storm. The globally marketed knowledge on HIV/AIDS shows that the hegemonic research language on HIV/AIDS constructs women as fields of investment for research experiments on toxic drugs in Botswana. In short, the subjugation of knowledge formations from the position of the Other is further entrenched along the lines of race, ethnicity, social class, age, and gender.

To take the example of HIV/AIDS, the colonized Other particularly in sub-Saharan Africa fail to participate as equal partners in the search for solutions to the HIV/AIDS pandemic because donor agencies and research funding institutions define global research agendas, preferring to pay attention to common problems that can be addressed through uniform research methodologies. In Botswana, it is clear that the hegemony of Western knowledge entrenched in its research methodologies, systems of thought, and analysis marginalize and make irrelevant knowledge on HIV/AIDS from the perspective of the majority of the people who live there. Most Batswana (meaning the people in Botswana) cannot participate in setting the HIV/AIDS national research agenda. They also become irrelevant because what falls outside the language of HIV/AIDS research is stigmatized, made invisible, and labeled false, of less value, or a handicap to addressing the spread of HIV/AIDS. The end result is that national research agendas are decided elsewhere, and the government's efforts to respond to local communities' needs are frustrated. Local research conducted by students and independent scholars from tertiary institutions are also constrained by the hegemony of Western-informed research methodologies and fail to create space for community knowledge systems. The colonized, however, continue to resist this subjugation of their knowledge and use their experiences to build new knowledge formations.

▓ DISMISSING INDIGENOUS WAYS OF KNOWING

Global research on HIV/AIDS and its language are shaped by the concerns, relevancies, and norms of the first world/center operating through the United Nations family, for example, the World Health Organization (WHO) and the joint United Nations Programme on HIV/AIDS (UNAIDS); international agencies, for example, the Department for International Development (DFID) and Western medical research institutes, for example, the Harvard

Institute of Research. In fact, the almost universal usage of the name HIV/ AIDS at a global level speaks for itself. It indicates that many cultures were not allowed to name the disease from their own cultural perspectives and languages. Thus, language and topics of research on HIV/AIDS, based on Western perceptions of reality, continue to exclude and marginalize the third world's own perceptions of reality and what counts as knowledge in the fight against HIV/AIDS.

Botswana has been conducting annual sentinel surveillance on HIV/ AIDS since 1992. The research follows standardized procedures determined and closely supervised by the UNAIDS/WHO working group on global HIV/ AIDS and STD surveillance. The main areas of concern recommended by this group are HIV/AIDS prevalence rates, prevention indicators, and knowledge of HIV/AIDS and sexual behavior. The UNAIDS (2000) epidemiological sheet, for instance, contained statistical language on the following: prevalence rates by age and sex, AIDS cases by mode of transmission, access to health services, condom availability and knowledge, and behavior. These areas of concern and these statistics are used by the U.S. Centers for Disease Control, for instance, to create league tables that compare HIV/AIDS prevalence and mortality rates in the world. It is a naming game where those countries with the highest HIV/AIDS prevalent rates, like Botswana, increasingly come under pressure to embrace Western-prescribed norms, buy the circulating knowledge and technology on HIV/AIDS, and sacrifice the vulnerable sick to research experiments and drug trials. The research on HIV/AIDS simply works within the colonially established framework of homogeneity in the search for answers and solutions to the HIV/AIDS pandemic. This leaves out the voices of the researched colonized Other.

The Journey Into the Empire and Back

Bill Ashcroft, Gareth Griffiths, and Helen Tiffin (1989) have named their book *The Empire Writes Back: Theories and Practice in Postcolonial Literature,* capturing the literary resistance of postcolonial subjects and the formerly colonized masses. Edward Said (1993), on the other hand, speaks of the colonized populations that have taken a voyage "to the metropolitan centres of their former colonizers" (p. 244). I invoke these titles and phrases to describe my journey into the empire and back as one who has studied in the Western centers. Returning back to my own communities, cultures, and languages brings me to realize the gap between my training and my culture. I therefore wish to reflect and narrate on the lessons I learned as an indigenous Western-educated intellectual co-opted into the dominant first-world epistemologies on HIV/AIDS and participating in the naming and description of the Other. The discussion is based on a critique of research studies that I conducted, along with researchers from the so-called first world. I found myself troubled by the standard topics and language in the research on HIV/AIDS because they trivialized the core values that define my identity, such as the totem and taboos that I continue to practice without question. Worse still, the language and topics are in most cases further entrenched through data-gathering instruments such as the questionnaire survey that make it impossible to escape from Eurocentric perceptions on HIV/AIDS.

The questionnaire survey is a top-down method of collecting data that mirrors the worldview of the researchers or their perception of the topic to be covered (Mukherjee, 1997), blocking any continuity with the researched people's worldview. The questionnaire serves the dominant statistical language and is conceived within the positivist paradigm with its claim of rationality, objectivity, and knowledge as absolute truth. In a study that others and I conducted (Bennell et al., 2001) and in other studies on HIV/AIDS (Jack et al., 1999; Ramasilabele, 1999), questionnaire surveys were used. Of interest in these studies are the controlled meaning of HIV/AIDS and the modes of transmission when respondents were requested to answer questions that are indicative of their knowledge on HIV/AIDS. Table 3.1 shows questionnaire items on HIV/AIDS knowledge used in a study on knowledge attitudes and behavioral aspects of HIV/AIDS among students at the University of Botswana. The items are limited to Euro-scientific definition of the virus and the dominant modes of transmission as perceived in the first world and leaves out Batswana understanding of the disease. The consequence of such an instrument is that respondents play a passive role because knowledge on HIV/AIDS and its modes of transmission resides outside their realm. What are the implications of using first-world epistemologies in such life and death matters?

When people give their meanings of HIV/AIDS based on their life experiences and perceptions of reality, Western-trained researchers, often operating within the dominant HIV/AIDS language, label them as misconceptions or cultural ignorance. For example, during a study on the impact of HIV/AIDS (Bennell et al., 2001), I and two other independent consultants from the first world dismissed the indigenous people's definition of what HIV/AIDS is. The meanings given differed depending on the context of illness. If it was the middle aged and elderly who were sick, HIV/AIDS was called *Boswagadi*. In Tswana culture, anyone who sleeps with a widow or widower is afflicted by a disease called Boswagadi. For the majority of the young, AIDS is *Molelo wa Badimo* (fire caused by the ancestral spirits), and for others, AIDS is *Boloi* (witchcraft). For Christians, AIDS is the Fire that is described in the Bible Chapter of Revelations; nobody can stop it.

Table 3.1 HIV/AIDS Knowledge Questionnaire Items

Instructions: Circle/tick the correct response in 201–203, and all that apply in 204.

201. What is the difference between HIV and AIDS?	1. There is no difference 2. HIV is a disease while AIDS is a virus 3. HIV is a virus while AIDS is a disease 4. AIDS can occur without HIV, but HIV cannot occur without AIDS
202. Is there a vaccine for HIV infection, or a cure for AIDS?	1. _____Yes 2. _____No
203. Can preventing the spread of HIV virus prevent AIDS?	1. _____Yes 2. _____No
204. How can HIV/AIDS be transmitted? *(Tick all Applicable)*	1. _____Air or insects 2. _____Sharing needles and syringes 3. _____Blood transfusions 4. _____Heterosexual activity 5. _____Contact such as handshakes and hugging 6. _____Homosexual activity 7. _____Mother to child at birth 8. _____Sharing food and utensils 9. _____Body fluid such as saliva and sweat 10. _____Sharing toilets and bathrooms

Source: Jack et al. (1999) *A Study of Knowledge, Attitude and Behavioral Aspects of HIV/AIDS Among Students of the University of Botswana.* Gaborone: University of Botswana, Botswana Ministry of Health, and World Health Organization. Used by permission.

The people's naming is embedded in their perception of reality. In their world of reality, things don't just happen. There is always a cause. The cause may be traced back to the supernatural as, for example, the ancestral spirits or experience. This cause-effect relationship is informed by careful observation, as illustrated in the Setswana saying, *Mafoko a mathong*, literally meaning "words are from what you observe." From the people's observation, those who died from HIV/AIDS had relationships with widows or widowers; thus, the name *Boswagadi*. For the young, a distinct observation was the appearance of herpes or *Molelo wa Badimo* (fire caused by the ancestral spirits) because herpes does look like a burn. Closely connected to this meaning making is also the people's perception of health. For the Batswana and people in most African societies, illness is associated with unhealthy relations with the family, the wider community, the land, or the ancestral spirits (Dube, 2001). To us Western-trained researchers, these constructions were dismissed as a reflection of illiteracy. But suppose we pause a little on the assertion that HIV/AIDS is caused by bad social relations. Such an assertion is not radically different from saying that HIV/AIDS is caused by poverty, disempowerment of women and children, and unfaithfulness. Nonetheless, failure to work with the framework and language of the researched means that life and death matters are either not understood or take a long time before they are understood.

Similarly, modes of transmission of HIV/AIDS derive from social relations aimed, among other things, at maintaining healthy relations with the family, the community, the ancestral spirits, and the environment in general. A study on the impact of HIV/AIDS on the University of Botswana (Chilisa, Bennell, & Hyde, 2001) included focus group interviews with students, who identified the following as modes of spreading the HIV/AIDS virus: (1) caregiver practices, (2) the practice of *seya ntlong* (wife inheritance), (3) unequal power relations between men and women, and (4) religion, for example, in terms of church attitudes toward the use of condoms, which give power to men to insist on unprotected sex.

Ideally, these ways of knowing should form the basis for understanding peoples' perceptions of realities and informing education, communication, and information strategies on the prevention of HIV/AIDS. For us, the researchers, these were treated as separate from the universal definition and modes of HIV/AIDS transmission that are perceived as the sole indicators of what counts as knowledge about HIV/AIDS. As Western-educated people who use Western-defined categories of analysis, we were not in a position to acknowledge the explanations of other realities. Noting a similar trend, Smith (1999) observes that some methodologies do not treat values and belief systems of communities as an integral part of research but as "barriers to research or exotic customs with which researchers need to be familiar in order to carry out their work without causing offence" (p. 15).

Dismissing these perceived realities has resulted in a dichotomy of knowledge, where the researched refer to "their knowledge" (belonging to the researchers, mainly from the first world or educated in the Western ways) and "our knowledge," the researched people's knowledge. This is illustrated in Table 3.2. The researched use their knowledge to inform daily life practices, ignoring researcher-based knowledge aimed at combating the spread of HIV/AIDS. This competition between the two knowledge systems in part delays progress in combating the spread of HIV/AIDS.

Table 3.2   Ways of Knowing

	Western First-World Knowledge	*Indigenous Knowledge in Botswana*
Naming illness	HIV/AIDS Virus	*Boswagadi* *Molelo wa Badimo* (herpes) *Boloi* (witchcraft) *Bolwetse Jwa Makgoa* (Westerner's disease for which Westerners know the name but do not know the cure) *Bolwetse jwa radio* (The disease described in the radio)
Means of transmission	Blood transfusion Needle and syringes Heterosexual sex Mother-to-child transmission	Unequal power relations between men and women Caregiver practices Wife inheritance Religious and diviner practices

Source: Chilisa B., (2005) Educational Research Within Postcolonial Africa: A Critique of HIV/AIDS Research in Botswana. *International Journal of Qualitative Studies, 18*(6), 659–684. Used by permission from Taylor and Francis (http://www.informaworld.com).

The Error of Sameness

In this discussion, I show how the global network of international organizations that fund research work within the long-established categories of the colonized and the colonizer (although, of course, today they would identify themselves with different titles of first and third world or developed and developing) to produce a sameness error by presenting research methodologies that blur any differences in the researched Other. Colonization can be described as an attempt by the Western world to order the whole world according to Western standards of culture, politics, economic structures, and policies. It is an attempt to fashion the diversities of the earth community into same, into its own image. The error of sameness or universalism is that it can proceed only by the massive domination and silencing of the less powerful. I therefore argue that the progress in combating the spread of HIV/AIDS is tragically delayed by prescribing research methodologies that blur any demographic differences in the research and in the process committing a sameness error. I use the Botswana Annual Sentinel Surveillance Reports 1992 to 2000 to illustrate how the positional superiority of first-world knowledge systems and perceptions of reality has created a dichotomy where the remaining world is perceived as opposite and therefore the same. Africa and its inhabitants, for instance, are seen as one mass, exhibiting the same characteristics and same behavior, irrespective of geographical boundaries, diverse languages, ethnicity, and particular institutional practices (Teunis, 2001). Thus, even though context is an important factor in postpositivist research, it is context in the mirror of Eurocentric Western epistemologies and realities. Often, context is limited to those factors that can be contrasted with the standard first-world experiences and expectations of what is worth studying. Very often, however, context is ignored in preference for describing the generic Other that is the same. The sameness error is characteristic of embedded errors about the third world, which as Chambers (1997) notes, "go deeper, last longer, and do more damage. Often, they reflect widely held views, and are generalized. Often they fit what powerful people want to believe. They tend to spread, to be self-perpetuating, and to dig themselves in" (p. 15).

The damage, resilience, and permutation of the sameness error are reproduced by transnational companies and international organizations that prescribe research methodologies that ignore contextual differences.

Botswana carries out annual national sentinel surveys of pregnant women attending clinics. The purpose of the Botswana Annual Sentinel Surveillance Reports is to monitor the impact of the prevention interventions in place, determine the status and trend of HIV/AIDS, and direct further strategies of action. Noting the link between research and intervention, HIV *Sentinel Surveillance in Botswana* (Ministry of Health, 2000) asserts that "data must therefore be used to direct strategies of action and distribution of resources for the survey to be meaningful," p. ii).

Despite claims that information contributes to the distribution of resources in a country marked by diverse cultures and disparities of income (Botswana Institute for Development Policy and Analysis [BIDPA], 2000), the Botswana Annual Sentinel Surveillance Reports also treat the researched as a homogenous universal mass where occupation, education, and social class do not matter. Context-specific differential analysis is ignored, and only detailed age-specific prevalence and mortality rates are given. (Refer to Table 3.3 for age-specific prevalence rates.) Kenneth Bailey (1994) notes that it is unethical to provide partial information, present facts out of context, or provide misleading information. Augmenting this ethical perspective, Jay O'Brien (2006) contends that researchers have to ensure that "the quality of the data forecloses the possibility of it bringing harm through good efforts by planners or others who use the information" (p. 4). In the research on HIV/AIDS in Botswana, partial information is given by blocking local views on HIV/AIDS and its modes of transmission and by ignoring context and basic demographic variables such as occupation, education, and social class that count even in mainstream research. The end result is that research fails to give substantive information that can assist in addressing national concerns of equitable distribution of resources.

Table 3.3   Age-Specific Prevalence Rates Among Pregnant Women (percentages)

Year	Age Span					
	15–19	20–24	25–29	30–34	35–39	40–44
1992	16.4	20.5	19.4	16.5	13.5	9.3
1993	21.8	27.1	24.2	16.8	13.3	9.4
1994	20.7	31.5	30.2	18	11.8	8
1995	32.4	34.8	32.6	33.5	11.1	15
1996	27.2	40.9	34	32	25	20
1997	28	41.4	41	33.3	39	23.1
1998	28.6	42.8	45.2	38.2	33.3	23.9
1999	21.5	38.7	43.3	42	33.3	25.5
2000	25.3	41.0	52.6	49.6	41.9	34.9

Source: STD/AIDS Unit, Ministry of Health, HIV/AIDS Sentinel Surveillance Surveys, 1992–2000.

The Botswana Annual Sentinel Surveillance Reports (1992–2000) corresponds with the nature of information, education, and communication materials, which are mostly aimed at preventing the spread of HIV/AIDS and are insensitive to context and culture. The materials do not target the vulnerable groups and are mostly written in English. There is an assumption that everybody is middle class and can therefore read English. Yet, because the reports meet the validity and reliability criteria from the Western-based research perspective, they form part of the archival knowledge that informs policy, practice, and perceptions about the Other.

This point is illustrated by the relationship between the data collection methods in the Sentinel Surveillance Reports, the reports that solicit people's knowledge on HIV/AIDS (Jack et al., 1999), and cartoons used in educational campaigns. In Table 3.1, I demonstrated that mother-to-child transmission is an important mode of transmission in the Western mode of knowing. The Sentinel Surveillance reports use data from pregnant women as the most reliable source of information on HIV/AIDS. Similarly, some intervention programs target women, ignoring the complex networks that contribute to the spread of HIV/AIDS. Mother-to-child transmission is an important mode of transmission. The cartoon shown here focuses on women like those in the Sentinel Surveillance reports. Because of the sameness error, it assumes that men and women have equal power to negotiate for sex. The message communicated by the cartoon is that most women can choose when to have children. However, research shows that women in some cultures in Botswana do not have reproductive rights (Tlou, 2001). Furthermore, such pictures or cartoons endorse existing gender stereotypes, which have come to associate illness with women, for they seem to suggest that if a woman knows her status, the child will not contract HIV/AIDS. The picture thus ignores the fact that it might be the partner who is HIV-positive or that the partner might contract HIV/AIDS and infect the woman during pregnancy. This illustrates Spivak's argument that within the postcolonial context, the subaltern as female is even more deeply in shadow that is muted. The emphasis here is that women are further distanced from the male ruling elite periphery/Other by the male ruling elite center/first world that frames problems and solutions from the vantage of men.

Furthermore, some billboards are written from a colonizing perspective that equates the Other with lack of intelligence. Take for example, the billboards that read: "Don't Be Stupid, Condomise" or "Are you careless, ignorant, and stupid?" The messages are offensive, degrading, and written from the perspective of a superior observer who casts the recipients of the message as ignorant. The billboards also seem to suggest that condoms are the major solutions to the spread of HIV/AIDS. Such hegemonizing content does not leave space for the marginalized majority people to name other multiple solutions from their perspectives. The methodologies on HIV/AIDS further entrench the marketing of condoms. The epidemiological fact sheet on HIV/AIDS (UNAIDS, 2000), along with researchers (e.g., Bennell et al., 2001; Chilisa et al., 2001), measures change in sexual behavior by the number of condoms that are used. Government, para-state, and private institutions deposit condoms in strategic places at the workplace. Sexually active primary and secondary school students are encouraged to obtain condoms from hospitals and clinics, while in tertiary institutions, condom bins are located in numerous points. Thus, condom sales become tied up

with HIV/AIDS research and education; and a country's effort to curb the spread of HIV/AIDS is measured by condoms per capita (UNAIDS, 2000). It is a sad story of the price that the third world has to pay as knowledge becomes more and more an important profit-making mechanism in the global capitalist economy; as it clearly shows, the first world must devalue knowledge from the peripheral Other to expand its markets.

The Exceptionality and Crisis Myth

Research on HIV/AIDS informed by colonially established Otherness ideology is sustained by development narratives, which are simply legitimized stories that explain events (Sutton, 1999). The policies have created the "Except Africa" and "Crisis" myths (Roe, 1995). The exceptionality notion is that things will happen everywhere else except in Africa. Reports in South Africa (Coombe, 2000) warn that unless preventive measures are taken, school effectiveness will decline to a point where 30% to 40% of teachers, officials, and children are ill, lacking morale, and unable to concentrate on teaching and learning. In Botswana, it is predicted that up to 50% of all students will become infected during or after their education (Abt Associates, 2001, p. 4). Narratives have circulated on how teachers in Africa have the highest HIV/AIDS infection and death rates despite their higher education and greater access to information relative to other social groups. One report (Abt Associates, 2001) sums it thus:

> It is generally acknowledged that the teaching service in many African countries has been severely affected by AIDS. Death rates in excess of 3% per year have been recorded in at least two countries and some prevalence surveys indicate teachers have higher infection rates than other adults. (p. 9)

The effect of these narratives is to legitimize certain research agendas and marginalize others. Donors, for example, are quick to fund research on HIV/AIDS and teachers, schools, and universities. But these priorities are simply based on myths. Research (Chilisa et al., 2001) shows that HIV/AIDS in Botswana has a poverty dimension: The less privileged, the less educated, and poorly paid women and girls are experiencing high mortality rates. The industrial class workers of the University of Botswana, for example, who earn the lowest wages and have the lowest education in comparison to other cash income groups, had the highest mortality rates. Primary school teachers also had high mortality rates in comparison to secondary teachers and university lecturers, who earned higher wages and had higher education. Table 3.4 shows mortality rates per 1,000 for selected occupational groups.

Table 3.4   Mortality Rates for Selected Groups 2000 (deaths/000)

	Female	*Male*	*All*
Primary teachers	7.2	7.7	7.4
Junior secondary teachers	3.5	5.3	4.4
Senior secondary teachers	2.3	5.1	3.7
University lecturers			2.0
University of Botswana junior support staff			17.0
University industrial class staff			18.0
University students			1.8
Adult population			20.0

Source: Chilisa, B., Bennell, P. S., & Hyde, K. (2001). *The impact of HIV/AIDS on the University of Botswana: Developing a strategic response.* London: Department for International Development.

▌ RESEARCH ETHICS AND THE LEGITIMACY OF KNOWLEDGE

The colonially established superiority of Western epistemologies is privileged and reproduced through the research regimes of acceptable practice and conduct in research or simply research ethics. The simple definition of ethics is that it refers to regulations of conduct of a given profession or group. The questions to ask are: Can there be universal research ethics? Can they be value free and inclusive of all knowledge systems? Ethical issues in research include codes of conduct that are concerned with protection of the researched from physical, mental, or psychological harm. Here the assumption is that the researched might disclose information exposing them to psychological and physical harm, including discrimination by the community or the employer. The codes of conduct to protect the researched include ensuring anonymity of the researched and confidentiality of the responses.

This dimension of the ethical codes emphasizes the individual at the expense of the communities and society to which findings from the study can be generalized or extrapolated. Paradoxically, while in quantitative research one of the major aims is to generate laws and principles that govern the universe, the universe is not protected against harmful information about the sample researched. The assumption made is that quantitative research procedures that include sampling, validity, and reliability eliminate any respondent and researcher biases from the findings.

Activity 3.1

Read the excerpts of the study below and do the following:

1. Discuss lessons that you can draw from the study.

2. Based on the reading of this study, describe the indigenous belief in your community that you might explore to study HIV/AIDS and precautionary behavior or any other topic of interest.

3. Discuss other ways of giving voice to indigenous communities not employed in this study.

Source: Drawn from C. Liddell, L. Barrett, and M. Bydawell (2006), "Indigenous Beliefs and Attitudes to AIDS Precautions in a Rural South African Community: An Empirical Study," *Annals of Behavioral Medicine, 23*(3), 218–225. Used with kind permission from Springer Science+Business Media.

Introduction

Indigenous knowledge and beliefs take shape around a culture's unique understandings of the social and physical world. They are based on generations of folk wisdom and experience and help explain past events and predict future ones. Indigenous belief systems are based on one of variety of different worldviews, from the rational to the animistic. Whatever their foundation, they shape a culture's folklore, cosmology, rituals, childbearing practices, and patterns of social exchange between adults; for these reasons, they are thought to be deeply embedded.

The study presented here explores two aspects of indigenous thought, namely, beliefs about ancestral protection from misfortune, and traditional beliefs about illness. It examines whether the people's endorsement of these beliefs is related to their attitudes to AIDS precautions.

The study draws on theoretical insights from a variety of disciplines, including indigenous psychology, health psychology, and medical anthropology. Indigenous psychologists believe that behavior is best understood when studied in local or emic settings. They take issue with the view that health beliefs that diverge from Western biomedical hegemony are primitive or irrational. If afforded scrutiny in local sociohistorical contexts, such beliefs can often be construed as highly adaptive or at least benign. In the light of this, indigenous psychologists argue that health promotion

(Continued)

(Continued)

campaigns, which blend biomedical and indigenous messages are likely to have better outcomes than campaigns that ignore or deny the legitimacy of lay representation.

Method

It was hypothesized that indigenous systems might have a bearing on attitudes toward HIV/AIDS prevention in southern Africa. Participants ($N = 407$) lived in a remote rural area of Kwazulu Natal, South Africa, and were divided into younger (18–24 years) and older (35–45 years) cohorts. All participants completed a questionnaire measuring attitudes to AIDS precautions, indigenous knowledge, indigenous beliefs about ancestral protection, and indigenous belief about illness.

Results

Indigenous beliefs pertaining to health behavior emerged as multidimensional in both structure and effect. Among older participants, there were significant associations between indigenous belief measures and attitudes to AIDS precautions. In this group, a strong belief in ancestral protection was associated with more negative attitudes to AIDS precautions, whereas a strong belief in traditional explanations was associated with more positive attitudes to AIDS precautions. The indigenous beliefs measures were not associated with attitudes toward AIDS precautions among younger participants.

Conclusion

The data lends modest support to the hypothesis that indigenous beliefs have a measurable association with attitudes to AIDS prevention, although these associations may be diminishing across generations.

While generalization of findings is clearly an essential ethical issue to consider, disrespect and psychological harm to communities, societies, and nations to which research findings are generalized or extrapolated is another important dimension. Research knowledge authorizes views and perceptions about the researched. An accumulated body of knowledge about the researched becomes the point of reference for legitimizing new knowledge. The problem of giving legitimacy to research knowledge is that most of the accessible research was not carried out by the researched. Even in cases where there is collaborative research between first-world researchers and third-world researchers, the first-world researcher's voice is dominant and imposes foreign categories of research, hence determining what type of knowledge can be produced. Here, I will consider the power struggles that arise between first-world researchers and third-world researchers in collaborative research and the power of written sources.

First-world researchers get research funds from international donors under the pretext that they are building research capacity in the third world. One proposal for research funds, for instance, read thus:

> In both countries and at all stages of the research process, in-country researchers will play an integral part. They will also be provided with important research training opportunities, especially in the use of qualitative and ethnographic data collection tools, with which researchers in developing countries are often unfamiliar. (Department for International Development, 2001, p. 5)

Collaborative research between first- and third-world researchers invariably begins with a contract that positions each researcher within a hierarchical structure. Notably, the first-world researcher has nothing to learn! Rather, first-world researchers are invariably referred to as team leaders, lead researchers, or research coordinators. They bring certain methods to be learned and applied by the third world. As leaders, they are also assigned the responsibility of producing the final document. The assumption is that they are better researchers in comparison to the Other because their educational background is superior in comparison to the Other and also because research is communicated in their language, at which they are masters— although the Other should become masters. The framework has roots in colonial times, when the colonized were regarded as empty vessels to be filled. But it also indicates the colonial ideology that seeks to fashion the world into sameness. The draft of the contract agreement between the first-world researchers and the third-world researchers was clear on who was producing and controlling knowledge. The contract read thus: "Any and all intellectual property including copyright in the final and other reports arising from the work under this agreement will be property of the University of x" (Department for International Development, 2001).

This quote speaks for itself. The third world still gets exploited for the good of the West! Accordingly, my experience on collaborative research about the impact of HIV/AIDS on education in primary and secondary schools (Bennell et al., 2001) demonstrated these underlying notions of the Other that researchers carry into the field. The research design was quantitative but used qualitative techniques to complement the quantitative and mainly focused on teachers and students. We agreed that there should be document reviews to expand on the quantitative data. The lead researchers were responsible for producing drafts. Statements in the first draft read as follows:

> A high acceptance of multiple sexual partners both before marriage and after marriage is a feature of Botswana society.
>
> Given the high priority and status given to sexual pleasure and fathering children, condoms are not popular, especially with regular partners.

These sentences conflicted with what I considered to be the valued norms of the society. I was told that these statements were informed by a review of the literature. The first-world researchers argued they would simply quote statements from the literature to show that they were not making any value judgments about the society. But this begged the question of which literature, generated by which researchers, and using which research frameworks? Answers to these questions point to the vicious circle of power in the process of knowledge production. The following statements were quoted from a situational analysis of HIV/AIDS in the Kweneng West Sub-District in Botswana (Hope and Gaborone, 1999):

- "Sex for drink" is common.
- Botswana society is too "permissive and bordering on lawlessness."
- Sex tends to be an "important activity" for the unemployed and the poor.
- "Failure to please one's partner can lead to abandonment and loss of income (however meagre)."

But what if the researched do not own a description of the self that they are supposed to have constructed? From my perspective, the quoted statements were a Western interpretation of the Other, perfectly feeding into and relying on colonial stereotypes about African sexuality. They were selected from a variety of information because they were perceived as important in weaving a story about the Other. Becker (quoted in Denzin, 1992) notes that interpretation is always "incomplete and unfinished." Peshkin (2000) notes, "It is the work of others to reject, modify and recount the researcher's selection of fact, and the order and relationships that form the basis of interpretation and its conclusion," p. 9).

The question however is the number of the researched Others who can engage in this debate and be heard. This is precisely where Spivak's (1988) question, "Can the Subaltern Speak," remains legitimate. First-world researchers have enjoyed the privilege of the written word and have used the written text as the forum for debate and legitimizing knowledge. Unfortunately, the majority of the researched—two-thirds of the world population—are left out of the debate and do not therefore participate in legitimizing the very knowledge they are supposed to produce. The end result has been that ethics protocols of individual consent and notions of confidentiality have been misused to disrespect and make value judgments that are psychologically damaging to communities and nations at large.

Above all, the production of knowledge continues to work within the framework of colonizer/colonized. The colonizer still strives to provide ways of knowing and insists that others use these paradigms, too. Marilee J. Bresciani (2008) reports similar colonizing tendencies in a collaborative research involving principal investigators (PIs) from the United States and Mexico. The starting point for U.S. PIs was that Mexican PIs were disadvantaged with quality of research equipment. The U.S. PIs ignored Mexican PIs' efforts to persuade them that they could be equal intellectual partners. In some instances, it is clearly a case of the "captive mind," where non-Westerners feel they do not have the research skills and knowledge to collaborate with Westerners as equal partners. Another research group (Pryor, Kuupole, Kutor, Dunne, & Adu-Yeboah, 2009, p. 779) reports that in a collaborative project between UK and Ghananian researchers in Africa, Ghananian researchers looked to their UK-based counterparts to impart "relevant knowledge and research skills," which in most cases refer to banked knowledge on research methodologies. In postcolonial indigenous research methodologies, non-Westerners are called on to invoke community oral literature and indigenous knowledge to inform what is relevant methodology from the perspectives of the colonized. Postcolonial indigenous research methodologies move beyond knowledge construction by the Western first world as the knower. Resistance to this domination is attested by emerging theorizing on decolonizing research methodologies (Bishop, 2008a, b; Chilisa & Ntseane 2010; Denzin, Lincoln, & Smith, 2008; Lester-Irabinna, 1997; Liamputtong, 2010; Mutua & Swadener, 2004; Porsanger, 2004; Smith 1999, 2008). Chapter 4 explores current theorizing on methodologies that are inclusive of postcolonial-indigenous knowledge systems.

SUMMARY

This chapter illustrated ways in which research on former colonized societies continues to create stereotypes about the researched and accumulates volumes of literature that speaks only of deficits and deviance in the behaviors and cultures of former colonized societies. The chapter proposed addressing ethics from a postcolonial indigenous perspective as one of the many ways of addressing social justice in research. Chapters 4, 5, and 10 look at ethics from a postcolonial indigenous research perspective.

KEY POINTS

- Research still ignores, marginalizes, and suppresses the colonized Other's knowledge systems and ways of knowing.
- Research produces deficit theorizing that casts the Other as a peripheral homogenous group in crisis and needing help from an outsider.
- Current research ethics protocols value the individual at the expense of the community and continue to privilege the colonizer as the knower.
- The resistance of researched communities to imposed knowledge frameworks should be recognized, along with the implications of this resistance for building research-based interventions.

Activity 3.2

The extract below is from an ongoing study on designing risk reduction interventions for adolescents funded by the National Institute of Health (USA). This study shows efforts by some sponsors to support culturally relevant research. Read and do as follows:

1. Discuss the methods used to create locally-relevant constructs.

2. Discuss ways in which Western theories can be integrated with indigenous knowledge and how quantitative and qualitative methods can complement each other.

Source: Chilisa, B., Malinga, T., & Mmonadibe, P. (2009). *Predictors of abstinence among 10–18 year adolescents in Botswana: application of the theory of planned behaviour.* Paper presented at the AIDS Impact Conference 22–25 September 2009, Gaborone.

Introduction

There is a growing need to carryout research to inform the development of culturally gender and age sensitive interventions to

(Continued)

---

help curb the spread of HIV/AIDS. The Theory of Planned Behavior (TPB) is a theoretical framework for understanding the predictors of individual behavior that has been frequently applied to understanding health behaviors. The TPB incorporates a structured data-collection approach that utilizes specific, direct questions to assess behavioral, normative, and control beliefs about the behaviors of interest (in this case abstinence, condom use, and multiple partners). However, the use of this structured format may overlook the contextual information necessary to understand responses to these questions within specific cultural contexts. In predominantly oral societies, cultural knowledge, beliefs, and values are expressed and transmitted through language, stories, songs, myths, and proverbs. These modes of communicating are an important means of understanding the cultural context of behavior. The study explored the contextual and theory based factors that explain 14 to 17 year old adolescents' intentions to engage in sexually risky behaviors.

Method A: Stories and Myths: Eleven adolescent (five boys and six girls) aged 14 to 17 years, selected from two randomly sampled junior secondary schools in the city of Gaborone, were provided with verbal and written instructions asking them to write down stories, myths, sayings, proverbs that they had heard regarding the following five behaviors: abstinence, virginity, using condoms, having multiple partners. In addition, eleven focussed group interviews (five in semi-urban and six in urban schools) were held. Each focus group had ten to twelve participants. A total of 104 students participated in the focus group interviews.

Method B: Structured Interviews Based on TPB: Twenty four adolescents between the ages of 14 and 17 years, of which 12 were female and 12 were male, were recruited from four junior secondary schools in the urban area of Gaborone and the semi-urban area of Molepolole. Method B followed the TPB approach to data collection. Twenty four participants were interviewed individually and asked to respond verbally to questions assessing behavioral, normative, and control beliefs related to condom use, abstinence, and having one partner. See Chapter 6, page 213, on structured TPB questions.

(Continued)

(Continued)

Conclusion

Analysis of data revealed patterns of hedonistic, prevention, and partner reaction beliefs on abstinence, condom use, and limiting the number of partners. These views are similar to what is found in the literature. There was however an additional subcategory that we have called "adolescents local-behavioral beliefs" that emerged from the data. These local behavioral beliefs were mainly on the consequences of prolonged abstinence and multiple partners. Examples were as follows:

If girls stay virgins for a long time they will not bear children.

Those who stay virgins for a long time will be struck by the "virgin disease."

Sexual organs might become dysfunctional due to lack of sexual intercourse.

If a guy does not have sex regularly he will go crazy.

If one abstains from sex he/she will not be healthy and fit.

Breaking virginity when one is older causes a lot of pain.

Beliefs in the multiple-partner category included the following:

A man must be shared.

If I have multiple partners I will be respected.

When a man/woman sticks to one partner, it is a sign that he/she is bewitched.

The adolescents' local behavioral beliefs emerged as an important subscale under abstinence and multiple partners. In the second phase of the study, a quantitative survey will be conducted to find out if these beliefs will predict adolescents' intentions to abstain and to be monogamous. The qualitative data will also provide cultural relevant materials to use in the design of the risk reduction intervention.

SUGGESTED READINGS

Bresciani, M. (2008). Exploring misunderstanding in collaborative research between a world power and a developing country. *Research and Assessment, 2*(1), 1–11.

Castells, M. (1993). Economy and the new international division of labor. In M. Carnoy, M. Castells, S. S Cohen, & H. Cordons (Eds.), *The new global economy in the information age.* London: Macmillan.

Chambers, R. (1997). *Whose reality counts?* London: Intermediate Technology.

Mutua, K., & Swadener, B. (2004). *Decolonizing research in cross-cultural contexts.* Albany: State University of New York Press.

Peshkin, A (2000). The nature of interpretation in qualitative research. *Educational Researcher, 30*(9), 5–9.

Pryor, J., Kuupole, A., Kutor, N., Dunne, M., & Adu-Yeboah, C. (2009). Exploring the fault lines of cross-cultural collaborative research. *Compare, 39*(6), 769–782.

Roe, E. (1995). Development narratives or making the best of blueprint development. *World Development Narratives, 19*(6), 1065–1070.

CHAPTER 4

POSTCOLONIAL INDIGENOUS RESEARCH PARADIGMS

Oral forms of knowledge, such as ritualistic chants, riddles, songs, folktales, and parables, not only articulate a distinct cultural identity but also give voice to a range of cultural, social and political, aesthetic, and linguistic systems—long muted by centuries of colonialism and cultural imperialism.

Patience Elabor-Idemudia (2002, p. 103)

OVERVIEW

Chapter 3 demonstrated that deficit theorizing, the written literature on the colonized, and the use of dominant languages are implicated in the construction of knowledge that marginalizes the worldviews and indigenous knowledge of the colonized Other and historically disadvantaged groups. This chapter explores the meaning of postcolonial indigenous research methodologies and philosophies, as well as the worldviews that inform these methodologies. The meaning of indigenous knowledge and its role in research is also discussed. Two postcolonial indigenous research approaches are also discussed: (1) the indigenization of conventional research and (2) a relational indigenous research paradigm.

LEARNING OBJECTIVES

By the end of this chapter you should be able to:

1. Discuss the meaning of indigenous knowledge and its implications for research
2. Distinguish between the two postcolonial indigenous research approaches
3. Discuss the features of a relational indigenous paradigm
4. Explain an indigenization research approach and its application
5. Understand and apply postcolonial indigenous methodologies to research

Before You Start

Conduct a literature search for studies that have used indigenous knowledge to inform their research framework. Reflect on the features of indigenous research and classify the studies as either predominantly quantitative, qualitative, or a mix of both quantitative and qualitative methods. Discuss how indigenous knowledge was used and the value it added to the study.

◾ INDIGENOUS KNOWLEDGE AND RESEARCH

What is meant by indigenous knowledge and how does it inform the construction of other forms of methodologies not common in conventional research methodologies? The idea of indigenous knowledge is a relatively recent phenomenon, gaining conceptual and discursive currency in the 1970s (Smith, 1999). Indigenous knowledge can be specific to locations, regions, and groups of peoples, for instance, indigenous knowledge for women, the deaf community, the poor, and so on. Just as Euro-Western research methodologies are indigenous to the Western academy, its institutions, and the dominant group, postcolonial indigenous knowledge is connected with the colonized and the historically oppressed. Indigenous knowledges, therefore, differ from conventional knowledges in their absence of colonial and imperial power. These indigenous knowledges are also postcolonial since they arise from people who have lived colonial history and have learned to value justice through collectively fighting for their liberation. Indigenous knowledge is used synonymously with traditional and local knowledge to differentiate the knowledge developed by a given social group or community from the knowledge generated by the Western academy and its institutions (Grenier, 1998).

In reference to Africa, George J. Sefa Dei (2002) notes that indigenousness may be defined as knowledge consciousness arising locally and in association with long-term occupancy of a place. Indigenousness refers to the traditional norms, social values, and mental constructs that guide, organize, and regulate African ways of living in making sense of the world. Different forms of knowledge (e.g., knowledge as superstition, knowledge as a belief in the invisible order of things, and knowledge as "science," all build on one another to provide interpretations and understanding of society. Thus, different knowledges represent ways that people perceive the world and act on it (Sefa Dei, 2002).

Characteristics of Indigenous Knowledge

According to Adrian Grenier (1998), characteristics of indigenous knowledge can be summarized as follows:

1. Indigenous knowledge is accumulative and represents generations of experiences, careful observations, and trial and error experiments.
2. It is dynamic, with new knowledge continuously added and external knowledge adapted to suit local situations.
3. All members of the community, that is, elders, women, men, and children, have indigenous knowledge.
4. The quantity and quality of indigenous knowledge that an individual possesses will vary according to age, gender, socioeconomic status, daily experiences, roles and responsibilities in the home and the community, and so on.
5. Indigenous knowledge is stored in people's memories and activities and is expressed in stories, songs, folklore, proverbs, dances, myths, cultural values, beliefs, rituals, cultural community, laws, local language, artifacts, forms of communication, and organization.
6. Indigenous knowledge is shared and communicated orally and by specific example and through cultural practices such as dance and rituals.

The Role of Indigenous Knowledge in Research

Indigenous knowledge plays an important role in the articulation of indigenous research methodologies. Indigenous knowledge's role in framing postcolonial-indigenous research methodologies can be summarized as follows:

1. Indigenous knowledge is embodied in languages, legends, folktales, stories, and cultural experiences of the formerly colonized and historically oppressed; it is symbolized in cultural artifacts such as sculpture, weaving, and painting and embodied in music, dance, rituals, and ceremonies such as weddings and worshipping. It is the source of literature to draw from to challenge stereotypes of postcolonial societies. Instead of relying on written literature, which is often written from the Euro-American perspective, the above sources assist in giving voice to postcolonial indigenous communities.

2. Postcolonial indigenous knowledge systems can enable the researcher to use new topics, themes, processes, categories of analysis, and modes of reporting and dissemination of information not easily obtainable through conventional research methods.

3. Postcolonial indigenous knowledges enable researchers to unveil knowledge that was previously ignored, enabling the researcher to close the knowledge gap that resulted from imperialism, colonization, and the subjugation of indigenous knowledges. In Chapter 2, you saw how the use of local language enabled the researcher to bring into the development discourse other theoretical perspectives not common in the literature.

4. Researchers can draw from indigenous knowledge systems to theorize about methods and research processes from the perspective of the cultures and values of the colonized Other and those historically marginalized, either because of their race, ethnicity, age, gender, ableness, or religion. Maori culture and values have, for instance, been used to craft Kaupapa Maori and the whanaungata methodological frameworks (Bishop, 2008a, 2008b; Smith, 1999), while the African adage "I am because we are" has added to theorizing on relational ontologies, epistemologies, and axiologies.

5. Indigenous knowledge-driven research methodologies can enable reclamation of cultural or traditional heritage; a decolonization of the captive and colonized mind and thought; protection against further colonization, exploitation, and appropriation of indigenous knowledge; and a validation of indigenous practices and worldviews.

6. The colonized Other can become the source of solutions to the challenges they face.

7. Indigenous knowledge-driven research methodologies can enable research to be carried out in respectful, ethical ways, which are useful and beneficial to the people.

8. The methodologies open space for collaboration between researchers and the researched as well as community participation during all the stages of the research process.

What follows is a discussion of how to draw from indigenous knowledge systems to indigenize conventional research methodologies.

INDIGENIZING RESEARCH METHODOLOGIES

A large body of postcolonial indigenous research advocates for a process of decolonizing and indigenizing Euro-Western research methodologies. Indigenization is a process that involves a critique and resistance to Euro-Western methodological imperialism and hegemony as well as a call for the adapting of conventional methodologies by including perspectives and methods that draw from indigenous knowledges, languages, metaphors, worldviews, experiences, and philosophies of former colonized, historically oppressed, and marginalized social groups. It is a process that is informed by modern critical theory, postcolonial theory, critical race theory, feminist theory, and notions of decolonization, resistance, struggle, and emancipation (Battiste, 2000; Porsanger, 2004; Rigney, 1999; Smith, 1999). An indigenization process challenges researchers to invoke indigenous knowledge to inform ways in which concepts and new theoretical frameworks for research studies are defined, new tools of collecting data developed, and the literature base broadened, so that we depend not only on written texts but also on the largely unwritten texts of the formerly colonized and historically oppressed peoples.

Chapter 2 illustrated how academic imperialism, scientific colonialism, methodological imperialism, and Western literature marginalize worldviews and ways of knowing of the colonized Other. It also showed the use of postcolonial theory and critical race theory as theoretical frameworks to frame a decolonization of Euro-Western research methodologies. The emphasis was that researchers with an indigenization focus could combine theoretical approaches and methodologies borrowed from the literature and knowledge archives of the West with indigenous perspectives. The process requires sensitivity to the culture of the researched and promotion of their participation and ownership of the research process. Carole Sutton (1999) underscores the process of indigenization by giving an example of indigenizing local music through combining elements of one or more indigenous traditional music styles with elements of Western-style pop. For example, in Botswana, we hear folk genre music sung in vernacular languages mixed with pop, reggae, rap, gospel, disco, and other genres that use traditional instruments to make the music attractive to people of different cultures. Indigenization of conventional research methodologies can be viewed as the "blending of an imported discipline with the generation of new concepts and approaches from within that culture" (Adair et al., 1993, p. 152). In the indigenization of conventional research methodologies, the focus is on the degree to which approaches, methods, measures, the literature, and the language of the research are embedded in the culture of the researched societies.

Adair et al. (1993) has listed the following as measures of indigenization of research.

Cultural reference. It refers to the extent to which the research emanates from the culture in which it is conducted and is measured by mention of "country, its customs, norms, or behaviors not found in the West" (Adair et al., 1993, p. 152).

Culture-based justification. The rationale and justification of the research should arise from the needs and unique relevance of the research to the indigenous societies.

Conceptual bases for research. It is measured by the extent to which the conceptual framework for the study emanates from the religion, cultural traditions, norms, language, metaphors, indigenous knowledge systems, community stories, legends and folklores, social problems, rapid social change, or public policies, as opposed to conceptual frameworks from some universalistic or Western literature. In this context, specific hypotheses tested will reflect the culture-specific variables.

Methodology. An indigenized methodology refers to the extent to which the research methods and measures are tailored to the culture of the researched. Methodological indigenization can be reflected in the extent to which the local language is used in the construction of research instruments, for example, questionnaires, tests, interviews, and the research process in general, and the use of methods, concepts, and variables emanating from indigenous knowledge systems.

From Adair et al.'s (1993) criteria of indigenous research, it is clear that one can place indigenous research studies along a continuum scale that varies depending on the degree of theory, conceptual framework, values, methods, and variables emanating from the indigenous knowledge and experiences explicated from the perspective of a postcolonial indigenous framework. In its simplest form, indigenous research can entail an exploratory study that necessitates the discovery of a local phenomenon that challenges

Euro-Western theories using predominantly Euro-Western methodologies and ideologies. Timothy Church and Marcia Katigbak (2002), in their conceptualization of indigenization, have called this type of model the *encounter stage*. In this stage, researchers acknowledge the limitation of applying Western theories, categories of analysis, findings, and modes of reporting, and they attempt to address the challenge through a limited degree of adaptation of these imported concepts, models, and measures with the hope of gaining better understanding of local circumstances. Kagendo Manuelito's (2004) study on an indigenous perspective on self-determination illustrates one of the models in this category. Manuelito, a Navajo who grew up around Navajo communities in New Mexico, conducted a qualitative study in which she wanted to find out the Ramah Navajo community's understanding of the concept of self-determination. Manuelito explains that the data collection methods included participant observation, document analysis, and interviews. Throughout the study, Manuelito observes that Navajo values and respect, known as "K'" in the Navajo language, were maintained and that Navajo protocol was upheld at all times. The important contribution of this study to postcolonial indigenous knowledge production was in the operationalization of self-determination from a Navajo community perspective. Manuelito went on to note that during the study, "I was continuously aware of the context of the study, which was constructed around Navajo framework and explicated in Euro-Western ideology" (p. 241). Manuelito's observation highlights the fact that a lot could still be done in the study to embrace a context-specific and context-sensitive approach with locally relevant constructs, theories, and methods of data collection.

Another level of decolonization and indigenization of research may involve cross-context comparative research in which the aim is to identify constructs, conceptual frameworks, measures, and categories of analysis unique to a local community so as to modify or revise Euro-Western theories and research practices. Many studies with a postcolonial indigenous approach are committed to developing tests and measures that are culturally sensitive and context specific. A study based in Harare, Zimbabwe (Patel, Simunyu, Gwazura, Lewis, & Mann, 1997) in Africa serves as an example. The objective of the study was to develop an indigenous measure of common mental disorders (CMD) in a primary care setting and to examine the psychometric properties of the measure. The study was conducted out of a growing concern that the Euro-American instruments that detect and measure CMD were not adequately validated for use in diverse settings in Africa. There were several stages in the design of the study. In the first stage, a qualitative approach was adopted, and focus group interviews were held with primary caregivers to generate concepts of mental illness. Qualitative interviews were also held with patients with conspicuous psychiatric morbidity, selected on the basis of clinical assessment and screening criteria. The interviews elicited idioms of distress of mental disorder. In the next stage, the Shona idioms were collated and classified into broad domains of similar phenomena. The idioms were formed on the basis of 47 questionnaire items with forced categorical responses of *yes* or *no*. The Shona Symptom Questionnaire is the first indigenous measure of mental disorder developed in sub-Saharan Africa. What is important to note is that the study involved a qualitative measure at the beginning, complemented by a quantitative approach that involved the development of a questionnaire and a description of its psychometric properties.

A more advanced level in the conceptualization of indigenization in psychology is what Church and Katigbak (2002) have called the *immersion-emersion stage*. This stage is characterized by the rejection of Western research paradigms in favor of efforts to develop indigenous research paradigms. Church and Katigbak note that the rejection can at times be intense, leading to uncritical rejection of applicable Western ideas simply because they originate in the West or acceptance of potentially ill-judged ideas just because they were developed from within an indigenous community. In the next section, an indigenous research paradigm based on relations is presented. A relational indigenous paradigm begins with relations, love, harmony, and social justice as important aspects of a research framework and employs an inclusive approach rather than rejection. The goal of theorizing on indigenous research paradigms is to augment the academic discourse on research methods as well as to challenge academics in all cultures and the Western academy to reevaluate and enrich their perspectives so that research can best serve the interests of the researched.

Activity 4.1

Read the study extract included here and answer the following questions:

1. Discuss research principles that are indigenous in the extract.

2. List the methods of collecting data in the study, and categorize them into indigenous and conventional methods.

3. Discuss the extent to which the ethical procedures in the study are informed by a relational accountability, respectful representation, reciprocal appropriation, and rights and regulations.

4. What does the author say is the limitation of research that attempts to conflate Western and indigenous approaches?

Source: C. Lippie (2007), "Learning From the Grandmothers: Incorporating Indigenous Principles Into Qualitative Research," *Qualitative Health Research, 17*(2), 276–284. Used by permission.

Purpose of study

The purpose of the study on which this article is based was to explore the perceptions (physical, psychological, emotional, social, and spiritual) of midlife health, with particular emphasis on the menopausal transition, among midlife Mi'kmaq women in Nova Scotia.

Research design

The emergent nature of both indigenous knowledge (Castellano, 2000) and qualitative inquiry (Guba & Lincoln, 1989) necessitated the development of a research design that accommodated the multiple realities and unpredictable interactions between research partners. The flexibility of my design was evident in its emergence through collaboration and consensus building with participating communities and participants. The overall design represented an amalgamation of the principles of Indigenous and Western methodological traditions (i.e., ethnography, participatory research, and feminism).

Indigenous principles

In designing this study, I positioned myself within a prevalent indigenous epistemology by acknowledging the wisdom of elder women and inviting their partnership in storytelling as a vehicle of teaching, learning, and sharing (Battiste, 2000; Castellano, 2000). Not surprisingly, the participants of this study favored group discussions as a means of sharing their experiences and engaging in reciprocal learning and healing. My learning also came from listening to, observing, and interacting with the women who partnered in this research and not necessarily from the literature that had previously shaped my perspective, nor from Eurocentric methods that assume the inferiority of experiential pedagogy (Henderson 2000; Posey, 2004; Smith, 2000).

(Continued)

(Continued)

Many indigenous principles foreground the interconnectedness of that which Western science often seeks to separate. For example, rather than a linear process whereby each discrete step of the research process is followed by another discrete step, indigenous methods generally emphasize the ways in which interrelated constituents flow together to facilitate the goals of the research as well as the relationship between research partners and the potential service of the research process and products (Henderson, 2000; Smith, 2005). In this case, the decision to use group discussions to gather data emerged from the opportunities afforded by this method to engage in reciprocal learning and sharing of stories. Similarly, the engagement of intuition in the analysis process arose from the grandmothers' accentuation of holistic learning, which involves all of the senses not just those related to cognition. Submission of this article for academic publication represents its potential to act as a conduit through which other researchers may learn from this process and conduct future research that is respectful of and beneficial to Aboriginal peoples.

Participatory practice

Through the engagement of participatory principles, the community partners and I designed this study to reflect a deep respect for the intellectual and intuitive capacities of Aboriginal women. Full and active participation by Aboriginal women in the development of the research project, recruitment of participants, and modification of the discussion guide, as well as collection and analysis of data ensured a participatory approach of mutual benefit. Indeed through this collaborative mode of research, I attempted to honor our diverse knowledge and expertise as well as "distribute power more equitably among the various" research partners, thereby creating harmony within the group (Glesne & Peshkin, 1991, p. 100). Nevertheless, each woman was free to choose the extent to which she participated in various components of the project. For instance some chose to sit in on discussion groups, whereas others engaged more fully in reflecting on and interpreting the data.

In this research design, I incorporated feminist traditions within the context of indigenous principles of holism by focusing on the entirety of women's realities (Lather, 1991). I emphasized relationality by rejecting the separation of subject and object. Rather, data collection represented an equal two-way exchange of information. I promoted balance and harmony by continuously and reflexively considering the significance of culture and gender as well as attending to ethical concerns related to respectful and reciprocal research with Aboriginal people. Finally, I emphasized personalism and the empowerment of women by integrating participation and consciousness raising into the research process (Bowles & DuelliKlein, 1983; Cook & Fonow, 1991; Kirby & McKenna, 1989).

Forming circles

In an effort to respect various levels of literacy, I also reviewed the introduction letter and the consent form aloud. Participants were given the option of providing either written or oral consent. Finally, for those women who might not feel comfortable discussing menopause in a group setting, I offered the opportunity to participate in a one-on-one interview.

Social activities were incorporated into every group meeting. This cultural custom of including opportunities to socialize provided an opportunity for me to get to know the women and for them to become more comfortable with me.

Gathering grandmothers' stories

First Nations people are very respectful of others' opinions (Wadsworth, 2000). So these women did not query one another during discussions, making conflict within the context of group discussions rare. Some researchers might view this practice as a potential limitation of group discussions. However, many Aboriginal peoples simply express their perceptions through other more diplomatic means (Brant, 1990). . . . In these groups, a simple yet poignant story or well-placed comment later in yet another poignant story or well-placed comment later in the discussion clearly conveyed a contrary opinion without overtly disrespecting another's point of view.

Learning my lessons

In an attempt to honor Western methods, during my initial analysis, I followed a modified grounded theory approach (open, axial, and selectivity coding) in which I derived themes inductively and deductively (Patton, 1990).

A summary of my initial analysis was sent to community partners for review and discussion

The most obvious tension in research that attempts to conflate Western and indigenous approaches of inquiry begins with paradigmatic, ontological and epistemological differences which have been discussed extensively by other authors (Battiste, 2000; McIsaac, 2000; Royal Commission on Aboriginal Peoples, 1996; Simpson, 2000).

█ POSTCOLONIAL INDIGENOUS RESEARCH PARADIGMS

Shawn Wilson (2008) argues that inserting an indigenous perspective into one of the major paradigms may not be effective because it is hard to remove the underlying epistemology and ontology on which the paradigms are built. Researchers and scholars researching with and on the colonized Other are challenged to articulate their own research paradigms, their own approaches to research, and their own data collection methods. Wilson (2008), arguing for an indigenous research paradigm, notes:

> We have tried to adapt dominant system research tools by including our perspective into their views. We have tried to include our cultures, traditional protocols and practices into the research process through adapting and adopting suitable methods. The problem with that is that we can never really remove the tools from their underlying beliefs. (p. 41)

You learned in Chapter 1 that scholars articulate an indigenous research paradigm informed by a relational ontology, epistemology, and axiology. In this chapter, the discussion focuses on how indigenous knowledge in diverse historical and geographical spaces informs a relational ontology, epistemology, and axiology.

In Chapter 1, you learned that philosophical assumptions about the nature of reality (ontology), knowledge (epistemology), and values (axiology) informed the research approaches, techniques for collecting data, analysis, report writing, and dissemination of findings. What follows is a discussion of African perspectives on relational indigenous methodologies (Goduka, 2000; Kaphagawani & Malherbe, 2000) and perspectives from indigenous peoples of Canada and Australia as articulated by Shawn Wilson (2008) in the book, *Research Is Ceremony: Indigenous Research Methods.*

█ RELATIONAL ONTOLOGY IN CONTEXT: PERSPECTIVES FROM AFRICA

I am we; I am because we are; we are because I am, I am in you, you are in me.

Relational ontology addresses the nature of being and how worldviews on being are implicated in the social construction of realities. In Chapter 1, you saw that among the Africans in southern Africa, the *ubuntu* world sums up this conception of reality. The *ubuntu* worldview expresses an ontology that addresses relations among people, relations with the living and the nonliving, and a spiritual existence that promotes love and harmony among peoples and communities. *Ubuntu* and the African adage, "I am we; I am because we are; we are because I am" (Goduka, 2000), explains the web of connection of people with each other and with the living and the nonliving. The principle is in direct contrast to the Eurocentric view of humanity, "I think, therefore, I am," which was expressed by René Descartes. The latter, Ivy Goduka (2000) observes, expresses a concept of self that is individually defined and "is in tune with a monolithic and one-dimensional construction of humanity" (p. 29). In the principle of "I am because we are," "the group has priority over the individual without crushing the individual, but allowing the individual to blossom as a person" (Senghor, 1966, p. 5). Existence-in-relation and being-for-self-and-others sum up the African conception of life and reality (Onyewumi, 1998).

The I/We Obligation Versus the I/You: An Illustration

How do we construct reality in such a way that the I does not overshadow the other and the community or the We does not overshadow the I? How is reality defined from an I/We relationship, and how can indigenous knowledge shed light on how to capture and interpret this reality? How can we, for example, conceptualize an HIV/AIDS testing policy that is informed by an I/We relationship?

Kipton Jensen (2007) has argued that workers in education, development, policy making, and research have at times adopted the individualistic approach to the construction of knowledge and its application. In Botswana, the *UNAIDS/WHO Policy Statement on HIV Testing* (World Health Organization, 2004) is an example of a unidimensional construction of humanity where the rights of the individual take precedence over those of the community (Jensen, 2007). According to the policy, the conditions under which people undergo HIV testing must be anchored in a human rights approach, which protects their human rights and pays due respect to ethical principles. In practice, this has meant that the HIV-testing results can be disclosed to a second party only with the permission and consent of the person affected, except in a case where the tested individual is a minor. It has also meant that testing is voluntary; no one can be forced to go. Although this policy, in Botswana and other countries in sub-Saharan Africa underlines individual rights and privacy, community rights and many African cultural perspectives are silenced. African communities are robbed of the ability to creatively inform the HIV prevention strategies designed for them. With HIV reaching epidemic proportions in sub-Saharan Africa, an I/We-based obligation with emphasis on the well-being of the community would promote a policy that requires all members to get tested.

Relations With the Living and the Nonliving: Implications for Research

How do we capture and interpret a reality that takes into account our "being" relations with the earth, the living, and the nonliving; and how can indigenous knowledge shed light on this reality? Laara Fitznor (1998), articulating the interdependence and interconnectedness among humans living and nonliving, observes:

> Mother earth and her inhabitants, plants, animals, minerals, rocks, insects etc., are all viewed in an interactive way—they are viewed as alive, as having a spirit, as conscious and as capable of responding to people. They are our "relatives." In ceremonies and teaching circles, each of these relatives is discussed in relation to its connection and contribution to healing, wisdom, power, and teachings. (cited in Goduka, 2000, p. 69)

For example, the Bakalanga of Botswana are connected to the living and the nonliving and to each other through the sharing of totems. These totems are symbolically represented through nonliving things, for example, a heart, or through living things and animals such as elephants and lions. Figure 4.1 shows 18 totems marking the identities of the Bakalanga people. Men and women are addressed by their totems as a sign of respect for their identity. They, in turn, have an obligation to respect the living and nonliving that represent their totems. People sharing the same totem have values that they share that are celebrated through rituals. They could, for instance, observe the same rituals marking birth, passage to manhood or womanhood, and burial.

The emphasis in this chapter is that researchers can draw from indigenous knowledge systems to create methodological frameworks that capture the voices of communities who value and practice an ontology of connectedness. The ontology of connectedness poses the following challenges for indigenous research methodologies:

Figure 4.1   Totems of the Bakalanga People in Botswana

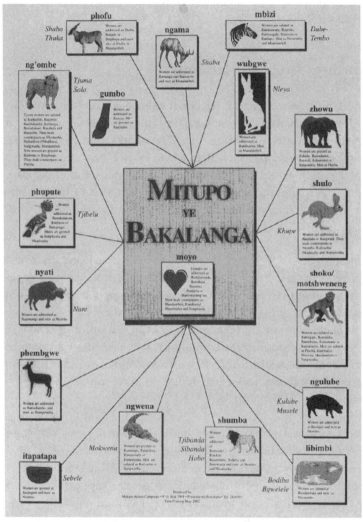

Source: Mukani Action Campaign (2002). Francistown, Botswana. Used by permission.

How can the web of connectedness inform researchers who do research among the Bakalanga community?

What are the metaphors to be drawn from these networks to inform intervention research?

Indigenous research methodologies should make use of social networks in designing studies. There is an emphasis on moving from a focus on the I of the individual to a collective We with multiple connections. What community-based intervention research would a network such as that of the Bakalanga serve?

Spirituality, Love, and Harmony

The I/We connection is a relational existence that is spiritual and promotes love and harmony. Desmond Tutu, the archbishop of the Anglican Church in South Africa, explains the I/We relationship as an organic relationship between people such that when we see one another, we should recognize ourselves and God, in whose image all people are made. We are so connected with one another that if you are in pain, so am I. It is a relationship that is guided by *agape*, a Greek principle for unselfish and altruistic love, (Goduka, 2000). King (1958) explained agape as

> disinterested love. It is love in which the individual seeks not his/her own good, but the good of his/her neighbour. Agape does not begin by discriminating between worthy and unworthy people, or any qualities people possess. It begins by loving others for their sakes . . . It springs from the need of the other person . . . It is love in action. It is love seeking to preserve and create community. It is insistent on community even when one seeks to break. It is a willingness to sacrifice in the interest of mutuality and a willingness to go to any length to restore community. (p. 87)

Chela Sandoval (2000), in her book, *Methodology of the Oppressed*, about third-world feminism, proposes love as a method made up of a set of practices that can mobilize all people regardless of race and class to work together toward meaningful change. How do we capture and interpret a reality that is spiritual and promotes love and harmony? How can indigenous knowledge shed light on how this reality is captured and interpreted? Folktales and stories can, for example, serve as valuable tools for awareness-raising on values that promote love, harmony, social justice, solidarity, and human rights. For Example, here is a well-known African story about the youth and the elderly.

> The story goes that the youth of a certain village arrived at a conclusion that old people who were past their prime economically should be stoned to death because they were an intolerable burden. Each person in the village proceeded to kill their parents. After several years of living in plenty because there were fewer mouths to feed, one of the younger

men was attacked by a python. The python had wound itself around the young man with coils that only tightened with every attempt to help him. There seemed to be no way of killing the python without endangering the young man. Eventually, a mysterious old man appeared from nowhere and helped free the young man. The old man who saved the young man turned out to be one of the fathers, who was hid in a cave by his children who did not want to kill him. The old man was rehabilitated into the village, and the village has ever since retained a wholesale veneration of all human life, even those that seem to present an intolerable economic burden to the community. (Author unknown)

The story teaches against discrimination. In the context of capturing a reality based on love and harmony, the story makes the researcher aware of the need to capture the data in such a way that our samples are inclusive of all social groups, for example, by gender, race/ethnicity, disability, socioeconomic status, age, religion, and sexual orientation. Every segment of the community has a place and a value in the community, and the omission of the voices of any one of these segments in the research process is not in the interest of the values of the community from which the story comes; it has potential to harm the welfare of that community.

RELATIONAL ONTOLOGY: PERSPECTIVES FROM SCHOLARS IN CANADA AND AUSTRALIA

According to Wilson (2008), indigenous peoples in Australia and Canada articulate a relational ontology that emphasizes relations with people, with the environment/land, with the cosmos, and with ideas. Each of these relationships has implications for how research is conducted.

Relations With People

Relation building is an essential aspect of everyday life experience for indigenous communities in Australia and Canada. To illustrate the importance of this relation building, Wilson (2008) notes that greetings among indigenous people include asking an acquaintance about their hometown, their relatives, and so forth. The person is inevitably placed in relationship, through mutual friends or through knowledge, with certain landmarks and events. The researcher becomes part of circles of relations that are connected to one another and to which the researcher is also accountable. The implication for research is that participants in a research study are able to make connections with each other when this greeting ritual is respected. Greeting becomes a way of building relationships and rapport among participants and researchers.

Relations With the Environment/Land

Indigenous people recognize a spiritual connection with the environment/land. Their relationship with the environment/land has implications for the way research is conducted. The construction of knowledge has to be done in a manner that builds and sustains relationships with the land/environment and is respectful of the environment. In this context, knowledge is held in connection with the land and the environment. When interviews are used as a technique of gathering data, it is best to conduct them in a setting familiar to the researched and relevant to the topic of research; this enables the researched to make connections with the environment and the space where the construction of knowledge takes place.

Relations With the Cosmos: The Role of Spirituality

Spirituality is "one's internal sense of connection to the universe," which may include one's personal connection to a higher being, or humanity, or the environment (Wilson, 2008, p. 91). Spirituality can be viewed as a connection to the cosmos so that any exercise that increases connection or builds relationships is spiritual and ceremonial in nature. A recognition of spirituality allows researchers to explore the interconnections between the researched's experience of the sacred and the practical aspects of research. Understanding comes through factual and oral history that connects the researched to the ancestral spirits. Knowledge is also regarded as a sacred object, and seeking knowledge is a spiritual quest that may begin with a prayer or a ceremony. Knowing can thus come through prayer as a way people connect themselves with those around them, the living, the nonliving, and the ancestral spirits. In this way, the mind, the body, and the spirit are regarded as legitimate ways of gathering information and coming to know (Pelletier, 2003).

Relations With the Cosmos: An Illustration

Jason Brent Ellis and Mark A. Earley (2006) give an example from their fieldwork of how the researched's relation with the cosmos became part of the research process that informed the construction of knowledge. The Anishambe, one of the indigenous people of North America, use *aseema* (tobacoo) as a cultural symbol for thanking people, asking for help, praying for information, and sharing stories. According to Edward Benton-Banai (1988), tobacco sharing comes from the legend about Waynaboozhoo.

> Waynaboozhoo showed the people how to smoke tobacco in the Pipe and in so doing seal peace, brotherhood and sisterhood among bands, tribes, and nations. Waynaboozhoo told the people that the smoke that came from the Pipe would carry their thoughts and prayers to the Creator just as their Tobacco offerings in the fire would. (cited in Ellis & Earley, 2006, p. 80)

Doing research on how indigenous spiritual traditions affected the process of grieving after the death of a loved one among the Anishambe, Ellis and Earley (2006) had challenges gaining entry to the setting and conducting interviews. They got advice from one of the Anishambe people:

> Go to a corner store and buy a packet of pipe tobacco, take about the size of a large gum ball and place it in the middle of the broadcloth you ripped, then tie it tight with one of the strips. When you go to speak with someone and ask them to do your interview, you need to reach them out with the aseema in your hand. If you don't do it, they won't talk. (p. 6)

Third- and fourth-world communities have resisted intrusion into their lives since the colonial period. The resistance has been largely ignored because, in essence, it questions the validity of the colonial research-built theories. Once they brought tobacco, Ellis and Earley (2006) report, key informants responded positively to the request for the interview saying, "You have shown respect for our ways by offering tobacco and smudging, your intentions seem to be good ones, let's see how we can help you." (p. 8). The lesson learned is that without offering culturally sensitive means of building reciprocity, researchers end up with empty findings. It follows that stereotyped findings also reflect resistance from the colonized because the researcher is unable to access the realities of the communities' experiences. In most postcolonial indigenous societies, building reciprocity and rapport requires a process that connects the researcher to the researched through sharing of values or through practices that recognize that both the researcher and the researched are connected to the living and the nonliving; knowledge is constructed with recognition that the living and the nonliving play a part in the outcome of the process of building it. The tobacco smudging practice places at the center stage people as spiritual beings.

RELATIONAL EPISTEMOLOGIES

A relational epistemology draws our attentions to relational forms of knowing as opposed to individual descriptions of knowing, which, according to Barbara Thayer-Bacon (2003), have dominated Euro-Western theories on ways of knowing for a long time. In this context, our understanding of reality should begin with questions of the way we are in the world (being or ontology). Whereas traditional epistemologies focus on the objects of knowledge, relational epistemologies focus on subjects or communities as knowers (Thayer-Bacon, 2003). In relational epistemology, knowledge is viewed as

> something people develop as they have experiences with each other and the world around them. People improve on the ideas that have been developed and passed to them by others. They do so by further developing their own understandings and enlarging their perspectives. With enlarged perspectives, they create new meanings from their experience. (Thayer-Bacon, 2003, p. 9)

Knowing is something that is socially constructed by people who have relationships and connections with each other, the living and the nonliving, and the environment. Knowers are seen as beings with connections to other beings, the spirits of the ancestors, and the world around them that inform what they know and how they can know it.

African perspectives view relational epistemology as knowledge that has a connection with the knowers. It is the well-established general beliefs, concepts, and theories of any particular people, which are stored in their language, practices, rituals, proverbs, revered traditions, myths, and folktales. This knowledge is practiced in various fields such as medical science, religion, child bearing, agriculture, psychology, and education. This relational epistemology has favorite ways, usually institutionalized in the society, of acquiring new knowledge and evaluating accepted fact; it has accepted authorities (whether people, institutions, or texts) in matters of knowledge and beliefs (Kaphagawani & Malherbe, 2000). Perspectives on relational epistemology from Australia and Canada focus on the researched as knowers with a web of connections that inform what they know and how it can be known. Explaining knowing informed by the multiple connections of knowers with other beings and the environment, Deloria (1995) observes, for instance, that indigenous communities gain knowledge and understanding of the world by participating in events and observing nature such as the birds, animals, rivers, and mountains. Wilson (2008) and Getty (2010) add that knowledge comes from the people's histories, stories, observation of the environment, visions, and spiritual insights. A common thread in postcolonial indigenous relational epistemologies is that knowledge arises out of the people's relationship and interaction with their particular environments. This view underscores the right of the formerly colonized and indigenous peoples to construct knowledge in accordance with the self-determined definitions of what they want to know and how they want to know it.

RELATIONAL AXIOLOGY

In Chapter 1, you learned about the basic tenets of a relational axiology. In this chapter, the discussion is expanded to include how a research with a relational axiology is carried out. The questions we need to ask are: From a relational axiology perspective, how is ethical theory and practice in research defined? How can indigenous knowledge shed light on this ethical theory and practice? In Chapter 2, we noted the following limitations of dominant research methodologies:

- The tendency to ignore the role of imperialism, colonization, and globalization in the construction of knowledge
- Academic imperialism—the tendency to denigrate, dismiss, and attempt to quash alternative theories, perspectives, or methodologies
- Methodological imperialism—a tendency to build a collection of methods, techniques, and rules that valorize the dominant culture
- The dominance of Euro-Western languages in the construction of knowledge
- The archives of literature that disseminate theories and knowledge that are unfavorable to former colonized societies and historically oppressed groups

How does a relational axiology—that is, research guided by the principles of accountable responsibility, respectful representation, reciprocal appropriation, and rights and regulations—address some of the concerns raised in the literature on research on the colonized Other?

A Relational Axiology: African Perspectives

The Bantu in southern Africa discuss a relational axiology that is embedded in the *ubuntu* relational ontology principles of (1) I am we, I am because we are; (2) relations of people with the living and the nonliving; and

(3) spirituality, love, harmony, and community building. From these principles, an ethical framework emerges that emphasizes accountable responsibilities of researchers and respectful relationships between the researchers and the researched and that takes into account the researched web of relationships with the living and the nonliving. Chapter 6 addresses this ethical framework in detail.

RELATIONAL AXIOLOGY: PERSPECTIVES FROM NORTH AMERICA AND CANADA

Wilson (2008) and Cora Weber-Pillwax (2001) discuss a relational ontology informed by four principles of accountable responsibility, respectful representation, reciprocal appropriation, and rights and regulations. These principles were defined in Chapter 1 and will be further illustrated in Chapter 6.

Weber-Pillwax (2001) suggests that researchers should interrogate their relations with the researched, paying attention to the following:

- The manner in which methods help to build respectful relationships between the topic of study and the researcher
- Ways in which methods help to build respectful relationships between the researcher and the research participants
- Ways in which a researcher can relate respectfully with participants involved in the research so that together they can form strong relationships
- The role and responsibilities of the researcher in the relationship
- The extent to which researchers are being responsible in fulfilling their role and obligations to the participants, to the topic, and to all of the indigenous relations
- The extent to which the researcher is contributing or giving back to the relationship and the extent to which the sharing, growth, and learning that are taking place are reciprocal.

Linda T. Smith (1999), writing on rights, regulations, and relations with the Maori people in New Zealand, proposes that the researcher using an indigenous framework needs to interrogate questions on ownership of research, the interests it serves, the benefits to the researched, and the role of the researched in framing the research, designing the research questions, carrying out the work, writing up the research findings, and disseminating the results. The emphasis is on respectfully involving the researched as co-participants throughout the research process. To be respectful is to build relationships with the researched. In the Maori culture, respect requires the researcher to begin the research by explaining who they are, where they are from, the purpose of the research, and their interest in the research (Bishop, 2008a, b; Smith, 1999, 2008). Such an approach enables the researcher and the researched to recognize, build, and celebrate respectful relationships and connections that they have with each other. To be respectful also involves developing long-term relationships with the researched (Lavallée, 2009; Moseley, 2007).

Anonymity, Confidentiality, and Relations With People

A relational ethical framework moves away from the concept of the researched as participants to the researched as co-researchers. The principle of relations with people also requires that the co-researchers are trained and empowered to participate in the study with the required skills to execute the study efficiently. Rather than keep co-researchers anonymous, there is emphasis on revealing their names so that the knowledge in the study can be traced to its originators. From a relations with people perspective, the information imparted, or story offered, would lose its power without knowledge of the teller; and thus, the reason why the researched do not want to be anonymous.

Activity 4.2

Read the study extract included here and answer the following questions:

1. Discuss ways in which the research conducted in the context of an indigenous paradigm differs from that conducted within the context of dominant research paradigms.

2. What are the features of storytelling that inform an indigenous research paradigm?

3. How are these features used in the study?

4. What are the ethical principles in an indigenous research paradigm that differ from those from dominant research paradigms?

5. Discuss limitations, if any, in the approaches that Wilson used in the study.

(Continued)

(Continued)

Source: Drawing from S. Wilson (2008), *Research Is Ceremony: Indigenous Research Methods,* Manitoba, Canada: Fernwood. Used by permission.

Purpose of study

There are two goals: (1) to examine how an indigenous paradigm can lead to a better understanding of and provision for the needs of indigenous people and (2) to document the differences indigenous people have in terms of their ontology, methodology, and axiology; and how these can lead to research methods that are more fully integrated with an indigenous worldview. Wilson (2008) notes "I am going to write about an indigenous research paradigm: What it is, why it is important and what it means to me" (p. 13).

Research questions

1. What are the shared aspects of the ontology, epistemology, axiology, and methodology of research conducted by indigenous scholars in Australia and,

2. How can these aspects of an Indigenous research paradigm be put into practice to support other indigenous people in their own research?

Literature review

Wilson notes: "Critiquing others' work does not fit well within my cultural framework because it does not follow the indigenous axiology of relational accountability. Critiquing or judging would imply that I know more about someone else's work and the relationships that went into it than they do themselves" (p. 43).

Research strategy

Wilson observes that the use of an indigenous research paradigm requires the holistic use and transmission of information. Wilson clarifies that the researcher takes the role of storyteller rather than researcher/author. In storytelling, the storyteller has a relationship with the listener. Wilson notes, "instead of writing directly to readers, which is difficult without knowing their culture, and context, I choose to write to my children" (p. 9). The text is written in the first and second person, as a reflection of the storytelling tradition. The writing follows a cyclical pattern that introduces ideas or themes, then returns to them at intervals with different levels of understanding as is traditional in a worldview that recognizes the interconnectedness of all things living and nonliving.

Data-gathering instruments

A combination of methods, including participant observation, interviews with individual participants, and focus group discussions were used. Talking circles were used as a form of focus group discussions, as well as seminar-style conversations.

Participants

Indigenous scholars and the elders are co-researchers. Wilson describes the relationship that he had with the co-researchers and their relationship to the ideas they shared with him. "Cultural practices include the proper protocol for building of healthy relationships. One important indigenous research practice is the use of family, relations, or friends as intermediaries in order to garner contact with participants. This use of intermediaries has practical uses in establishing rapport with research participants and placing the researcher within a circle of relations. This in turn enforces the accountability of the researcher, as they are responsible not only to themselves but also to the circle of relations. In addition to being a culturally appropriate way of approaching potential participants, the use of an intermediary gives the participant an opportunity to ask candid questions about the nature of the research and the motives behind" (p. 129).

Ethics

On ethics, Wilson explains, "The ethics involved in an Indigenous research paradigm sometimes differs from the dominant academic way of doing things. I would like to use the real names of everyone I worked with on this research, so that you will know exactly who I am talking about. This goes against the rules of most university ethical research policies. However, how can I be held accountable to the relationships I have with the people if I don't name them? How can they be held accountable to their own teachers if their words and relationships are deprived of names? What I will do is write using the real names of everyone who has given me explicit permission to do so. I will use pseudonyms for anyone who I couldn't get in touch with to talk about it or who had any misgivings about the use of names" (p. 63).

(Continued)

(Continued)

Wilson further clarifies that "participants did not want anonymity because they understood that the information imparted, or story offered, would lose its power without knowledge of the teller. The entire notion of relational accountability would have been lost had I not honored the co-researchers by using their names" (p. 130).

Analysis

Wilson describes the analysis as collaboration between him and the co-researchers. It was also an ongoing process. Ideas were shared in indigenous research methods seminars and conferences where work on the project was presented. Indigenous protocols in each location where the research was conducted were observed. For instance, permission was requested to conduct the study and to write up the results.

❦ SUMMARY

The main emphasis is that postcolonial indigenous research methodologies challenge conventional research methodologies and contribute to alternative methods of doing research that draw from indigenous knowledge systems and the philosophies and worldviews of colonized and historical oppressed societies. Perspectives from Africa and from the indigenous people in Canada and Australia share a common understanding of an indigenous research paradigm informed by a relational ontology, epistemology, and axiology. The perspectives recognize a relational existence that promotes relations among people, the living and the nonliving, the environment/land, and the cosmos. Indigenous epistemology is viewed as knowledge that has a relationship with the people and has a place in the culture and the daily life experiences of the people. All perspectives agree to ethical principles that nurture harmony among people and to a relational accountability that emphasizes responsibility of the researchers and the participants to each other and the rest of the community, reciprocity, and rights of the researched to knowledge produced. Table 4.1 shows basic beliefs associated with a relational indigenous research paradigm.

Table 4.1   Basic Principles Associated With a Relational Indigenous Research Paradigm

How do we capture and interpret a reality that takes into account relations among people, the people's relation with the living and the nonliving, the cosmos, and a spiritual existence that promotes love and harmony? How can indigenous knowledge shed light on how this reality is captured and interpreted?	1. Reality is collectively constructed, taking into account the web of connection that the people have with the living and the nonliving. 2. Reality should be subjected to a critical analysis that interrogates colonizer/colonized, researcher/researched relationships. 3. Space for the construction of knowledge (i.e., interviews) is significant in coming to know the reality that is investigated. 4. Indigenous knowledge informs the reality that is known.
How do we capture knowledge that focuses on the formerly colonized and historically oppressed as the knower? How can indigenous knowledge shed light on how this knowledge can be captured and interpreted?	1. Elders are as important as libraries in providing knowledge about a phenomenon. Consultation of elders is vital. 2. Indigenous knowledge plays a vital role in informing theoretical frameworks, research questions, methods of data collection, and ethical protocols. 3. A cyclical approach as opposed to a linear approach to the research process is preferred.
How is ethical theory and practice in research defined? How can indigenous knowledge and the history of colonialism shed light on how this ethical theory and practice are defined?	1. Ethical theory and practice should address the role and responsibilities of the researcher in questioning the hegemonic role of colonialism and imperialism in the construction of knowledge. 2. The research process should be guided by accountable responsibility, respectful representation, reciprocal appropriation, and rights and regulations. 3. The ethical principle of consent should accommodate individual, community consent, group consent, and collective consent. 4. The principle of maintaining relations with the knower should be upheld by revealing research participants' names where they give approval.

In summary, postcolonial indigenous research methodologies include a discussion of ways to:

1. Decolonize and indigenize universalized research methodologies so that they are inclusive of indigenous knowledge, languages, worldviews, and philosophies and are respectful of the cultures of the colonized Other
2. Critique and resist colonizing hegemonies and promote liberating research approaches
3. Create new methodologies and methods based on the indigenous knowledge systems, languages, realities, ways of knowing, and value systems of the colonized Other
4. Situate the researcher and involve the researched in the research process so that indigenous voices can be privileged and research benefits the researched societies

KEY POINTS

- Postcolonial indigenous research methodologies challenge Euro-Western methodologies and contribute to the body of new methods informed by the worldviews and philosophies of the colonized Other.
- Indigenous knowledges provide the base from which new concepts, new theories, new forms of analysis, and new forms of methods are envisioned and practiced.
- Researchers discuss an indigenous research paradigm based on a relational ontology, epistemology, and axiology.

Activity 4.3

Read the study extract included here and answer the following questions:

1. From your reading so far and your own understanding of indigenous knowledge, make a list of the different forms of indigenous knowledge and how you would use them in designing a study.

2. Design a study that uses a postcolonial indigenous research methodology framework.

3. Define the term *indigenization* and use Adair et al.'s (1993) measure of indigenization to assess indigenization of research in the extract below. (Refer to page 100 of this text for this measure.)

Source: C. Grills and D. Longshore (1996), "Africentrism: Psychometric Analysis of a Self-Report Measure," *Journal of Black Psychology, 22,* 86–106. Used by permission from the Association of Black Psychologists.

Purpose

This article describes the development of a self-report measure of Africentrism, defined here as the degree to which a person adheres to the Nguzo Saba (Seven Principles) in African and African American culture. Beginning with a pool of the 25 Likert-type items, the authors tested the two alternative forms of Africentrism measure in a series of studies. The reliability (internal consistency) of the measure was found to be well above the minimum criterion for the purpose of group comparisons. Indicators of construct validity and known groups validity were also favorable. The authors recommend a 15-item version of the measure for future testing and conclude with hypotheses regarding the importance of Africentrism in assessing African-centered interventions.

Background

Efforts to assess the effectiveness of culture-based services will require tools by which the cultural characteristics of groups and individuals can be measured. If practitioners know the status of their clients on cultural characteristics considered relevant to effectiveness, culture-based services can be targeted more wisely. If individual level variability in cultural characteristics can be measured, researchers will be able to conduct more sensitive tests of culture based services by treating these characteristics as blocking variables or covariates in outcome analyses.

This article describes our progress in developing a self-report measure of Africentrism, defined as the degree to which a person adheres to the Nguzo Saba (Seven Principles) in African and African American culture. In a series of four studies involving African Americans and Whites, we evaluated the reliability and validity of two alternate forms of our Africentrism measure and concluded that a 15-item form is optimal for future testing.

Method

Our purpose, then, was to create a measure that would be broadly Africentric in its content and readily understandable by persons with a wide range of educational experience. In addition, we

(Continued)

(Continued)

wanted the Africentrism measure to be brief so it could be added to existing protocols for client assessment or research without creating an undue time burden. We also wanted the measure to be easy to administer. If completed by staff, it should require no special training. Ideally, however, clients should be able to complete it on their own. This section describes the initial development of items to be included in the measure and the criteria we used to assess its psychometric properties.

Because the Nguzo Saba represents a simple but comprehensive statement of Africentrism, they served as our guidelines for item development. Working from various statements of the Nguzo Saba (Karenga 1988a; Madhubuti, 1972; Perkins, 1992) and related constructs such as African-centered cultural precepts (Nobles and Goddard, 1993), we created a pool of 25 Likert-type items—one or more meant to represent each principle in the Nguzo Saba. Response options ranged from 1 (Strongly disagree), 2 (Disagree), 3 (Agree) to 4 (Strongly agree). To minimize the possibility of a response set, we worded some items positively so that agreement indicated views inconsistent with Africentrism.

Conclusion

Form A and Form B appear reliable for the purpose of measuring differences in Africentrism between groups of African Americans. Both forms were readily understood by respondents and can be administered by interviews, or self-administered within 3 to 4 minutes. Findings on validity also seem favorable to justify further work with this measure. Although Form C was not tested in the field, we believe it should be the focus of further psychometric testing. It is a minor revision of Form A, which was field-tested in three studies. Also, because the 15 items on Form C were drawn from Form A, not Form B, Form C retains specific relevance to African Americans.

SUGGESTED READINGS

Battiste, M. (2000). *Reclaiming indigenous voice and vision.* Vancouver: UBC Press.

Caballero, B. (2007). *Ethical issues for collaborative research in developing countries.* Available at http://www.ajcn.org

Chilisa, B., & Preece, J. (2005). *Research methods for adult educators in Africa.* Cape Town: Pearson South Africa.

Chilisa, B. (2009). Indigenous African centered ethics: Contesting and Complementing dominant models. In D. M Mertens & P. E. Ginsberg (Eds.), *The handbook of social science research ethics.* Thousand Oaks, CA: Sage.

Ellis, J. B., & Earley, M. A. (2006). Reciprocity and constructions of informed consent: Researching with indigenous populations. *International Journal of Qualitative Methods, 5*(4).

Hoppers, C. A. (Ed.). (2002). *Indigenous knowledge and the integration of knowledge systems.* Claremont: New Africa Books.

Goduka, I. N. (2000). African/indigenous philosophies: Legitimizing spiritually centered wisdoms within the academy. In P. Higgs, N. C. G. Vakalisa, T. V. Mda, & N. T. Assie-Lumumba (Eds.), *African voices in education* (pp. 63-83). Lansdowne, South Africa: Juta.

Gonzalez, M. C. (2000). The four seasons of ethnography: A creation-centered ontology for ethnography. *International Journal of Intercultural Relations, 24*, 623-650.

Kaphagawani, D., & Malherbe, J. (2000). Africa epistemology. In P. H. Coetzee & A. P. J. Roux (Eds.), *Philosophy from Africa: A text with readings* (pp. 205-216). Oxford, UK: Oxford University Press.

Louis R. P. (2006). Can you hear us now? Voices from the margin: Using indigenous methodologies in geographic research. *Geographic Research, 45*(2), 130-139.

Louw, D. J. (2001). Ubuntu: *An African assessment of the religious order.* Retrieved September 27, 2001, from: http://www.bu.edu/wcp/papers/Afrlouw.htm

Manuelito, K. (2004). An indigenous perspective on self-determination. In K. Mutua & B. B. Swadener (Eds.), *Decolonizing research in cross-cultural contexts: Critical personal narratives.* Albany: State University of New York Press.

Porsanger, J. (2004). An essay about indigenous methodology. *NORDLIT, 15,* 105-120.

Rigney, L. (1999). Internationalization of an indigenous anticolonial cultural critique of research methodologies. *Wicazo Sa Review, 14*(2).

Sefa Dei, G., Hall, B., & Rosenberg, D. (2002). *Indigenous knowledge in global contexts: Multiple readings of our world.* Toronto: University of Toronto Press Incorporated.

Wilson, S. (2008). *Research is ceremony: Indigenous research methods.* Manitoba, Canada: Fernwood Publishing.

CHAPTER 5

THEORIZING ON SOCIAL SCIENCE RESEARCH METHODS

Indigenous Perspectives

Language, myth, truth, ancestral memory, dance-music-art and science provide the sources of knowledge, the canons of proof and the stimulus structures of truth.

Molefi Kete Asante (1990, p. 19)

Our stories are our theories and method.

Melanie Carter (2003, p. 40)

For people of color have always theorized—but in forms quite different from the Western form of abstract logic. And I am inclined to say that our theorizing (and I intentionally use the verb rather than the noun) is often narrative forms, in the stories we create, in riddles and proverbs, in the play with language, since dynamic rather than fixed ideas seem more to our liking.

Barbara Christian (2000, p. 12)

OVERVIEW

Chapter 5 explores the role of language, oral literature, and storytelling as foundations and sources of the literature, philosophies, theories, and methods of data collection, analysis, and interpretation of research about, on, and with the colonized Other, accounting for two-thirds of the world population. The chapter llustrates how oral literatures and storytelling promote a postcolonial indigenous-based research process. The chapter further explores the place of indigenous languages in producing research reports.

LEARNING OBJECTIVES

By the end of this chapter, you should be able to:

1. Discuss the role of language and oral literature as basis for theorizing about postcolonial indigenous and methodologies
2. Discuss the term *ethnophilosophy* and its relevance in research methodology
3. Design a study that draws from ethnophilosophy to inform the methodology section of the study
4. Discuss the use of indigenous languages in writing research reports

Before You Start

Identify any literature written in a local language of the researched and the oral literature that you may want to review to inform your understanding of a research issue you want to study. Discuss some of the challenges you might encounter as you transport the information from the local language to the academic language required by your research committee or research sponsor.

▌ INTRODUCTION

How can we conduct research without using Western academic constructs and terminologies? How can the colonized Other talk about their experiences without the imposition of nonculturally cogent terms, concepts, and paradigms? How can we minimize the intrusion of terms in our research reports that may culturally and contextually lack contingency with the historically oppressed, marginalized colonized Other? Can research using Euro-Western academic languages accurately communicate the experiences of the two-thirds majority? What is the contribution of the languages stored in folklore, mythologies, and proverbs to the building of postcolonial indigenous conceptual and theoretical frameworks and the design of interventions to improve the quality of life of the people? Who is reading our research and in what and whose language? In Chapter 1, you learned that carrying out research in indigenous languages was an essential decolonization strategy. In Chapter 2, an argument was made that indigenous languages can play a significant role in contributing to the advancement of new knowledge, new concepts, new theories, new rules and methods, and techniques in research that are rooted in the colonized Other's ways of knowing and perceiving reality. In this chapter, I expand the discussion to illustrate the use of indigenous knowledge in building conceptual frameworks, challenging deficit theorizing, and informing research intervention strategies that valorize the culture and experiences of the colonized Other.

METHODS BASED ON ETHNOPHILOSOPHY

Zeverin Emagalit (2001) has used the term *ethnophilosophy* to refer to the collective worldviews of people that are encoded in language, folklore, myths, metaphors, taboos, and rituals. In defining ethnophilosophy in an African context, for example, Emagalit (2001) describes it as a system of thought that describes, analyzes, and tries to understand the collective worldviews of diverse African peoples as a unified body of knowledge. Elsewhere, Bagele Chilisa and Julia Preece (2005) describe ethnophilosophy as the experiences of the people encoded in their language, folklore, stories, songs, artifacts, culture, and values. These are the banks where knowledge is stored and can be retrieved to serve as literature against which other literature, predominantly written by Western-educated elites, can be reviewed. Community language, stories, songs, myths, and taboos can also serve as sources of information that can be triangulated with data from traditional methods such as interviews. Under the umbrella of ethnophilosophy, I discuss language, metaphorical sayings, proverbs, and oral literature as sources of knowledge that communicate other ways of data collection, analysis, and interpretation of the worldviews of postcolonial and indigenous societies.

Language, Metaphorical Sayings, and Proverbs

Language expresses the patterns and structures of culture and consequently influences human thinking, manners, and judgment. Culture is lived, and language, through all its manifestations, projects that life, giving it form and texture. In traditional oral societies, some forms of language are proverbs and metaphorical sayings, which uphold and legitimize the value systems of a society. For research problems to be understood within the value systems of the researched people, it is important to incorporate their language in the research process. Language analysis is commonly used by poststructural researchers, interpretive researchers, and those using a critical analysis perspective. It is, however, an important technique that needs to be emphasized in postcolonial and indigenous societies, where research problems have for a long time been defined from the perspective of Western-trained researchers who use Western languages to define the research problems. What follows is a discussion of the contribution of language stored in proverbs and metaphors in the construction of knowledge.

Proverbs and Metaphors as Conceptual Frameworks

A proverb is a short saying in common use that strikingly expresses some obvious truth or familiar experience (Guralnik & Solomon, 1980, p. 1144). Proverbs are used as tools to describe and express sociocultural events and practices and to hand down from one generation to another a community's cultural traditions and folklore; they also communicate expected codes of behavior. Kehinde Yusuf and Joyce Mathangwane (2003) describe proverbs as tools people use to persuade others in their culture to see the world and behave in a common way. "Proverbs, the world's smallest literary genre, are a most telling part of that serial narrative about humankind" (Schipper, 2003, p. 2) and articulate the very soul of society. Thus, they are important as a strategy for instructing, explicating, advising, praising, and nourishing members of a society on important social issues. Albert Gerard (1970) adds the following to the major functions of proverbs:

- Preserve the religious myths of the group
- Perpetuate the memory of a group's past in semi-legendary chronicles
- Promulgate the group's sense of collective identity and dignity
- Record the wisdom pragmatically accumulated by generations of ancestors in proverbs and gnomic tales
- Celebrate the prowess of kings and warriors whose high deeds have ensured glory of the group

J. L. Van Schaik (1998) classifies proverbs into seven functional categories: (1) community and family life, (2) leadership and teamwork, (3) youth, (4) behavioral guide, (5) hospitality and nourishment, (6) motivation, and (7) situation and human nature. Imagine that you wanted to conduct a study on leadership and teamwork in an institution. Van Schaik's classification on the functions of proverbs directs you to consult the researched's collective memories about leadership and teamwork stored in proverbs.

In addition to proverbs, metaphors also communicate values. A metaphor, according to Albert S. Hornby (1994), is "the use of a word or phrase to indicate something different (though related in some way) to the literal meaning" (p. 780). Ronald Wardhaugh (1989) reports that metaphors are used as vehicles of indirectness. They are used as substitution of direct words that would have been regarded as disrespectful, offensive, or taboo by a cultural group. Keith Allan and Kate Burridge (1994) argue that metaphors are used to avoid loss of face in cases where expressing one's experiences directly in written and spoken form can be considered a face-threatening act (Brown & Levison, 1987). Rudolf Schmitt (2005) adds that metaphorical sayings are used to uncover both objective and subjective patterns of thought and action and consequently to determine how individuals think and act. These metaphors are found in the oral literatures such as songs, folklore, and spoken language.

In proverbs and metaphors, we find philosophical and theoretical frameworks in which we can ground research that draws from the value systems of the communities to inform program interventions that address the needs of the people. Researchers in Africa (Omolewa et al., 1998; Youngman, 1998) have used language in the form of proverbs and sayings to explain indigenous people's understanding of researched topics. Frank Youngman (1998) demonstrates how the concept of lifelong learning is encoded in the language of the people by citing proverbs (p. 10):

Dilo makwati di kwatabolotswa mo go babangwe.	You get new ideas from others.
Noka e tladiwa ke dinokana.	A river becomes full from its tributaries.
Botlhale jwa phala bo tswa phalaneng.	The intelligence of an impala comes from its offspring.
Thuto gae golelwe.	There is always something to learn, no matter how old one is.
Kazena ua kuatua rune zena ua kengeza rune.	Do not say that because you were born long ago, you know everything (quoted by Otjiherero-speaking respondents).

Millicent Musyoka and Donna Mertens (2007) used the messages transmitted through proverbs to challenge deficit theorizing about people with disabilities and to build a conceptual framework for a curriculum for children with disabilities. Millicent Musyoka noted that her appreciation of individuals with disabilities in her community sprang from the following proverbs:

Kila chombo na wimbile.	Every ship has its own waves.
Kila mlango kwa ufunguo wakwe.	Every door has its own key.
Kila ndege huruka kwa ubawa wake.	Every bird flies with its own wings.

The proverbs, she explained, echo the saying that "everyone can learn, but everyone learns in different ways." The proverbs above energized and convinced policymakers, teachers, and curriculum and development officers to embrace change and improve the education and welfare of children with disabilities because the change and improvement is grounded in the value system of the community.

Using Proverbs to Explore Community-Constructed Ideologies

Proverbs, like stories, at times transmit ideologies of the powerful that perpetuate the dominance of some groups by privileging knowledge and practices that discriminate on the basis of gender, age, ethnicity, social class, ableness, and so on. These ideologies do not come out easily through traditional data collection methods, such as the interview method, because such methods use interview questions framed on the basis of the day-to-day language of research. Proverbs also communicate ideologies and worldviews that the researched may find too sensitive to discuss using explicit language. In a study on sexually risky behaviors, Bagele Chilisa, Tumani Malinga, and Poloko Mmonadibe (2009) asked adolescents to list proverbs that communicated messages on sexuality. Among the proverbs listed were four on multiple partners:

Monna poo ga a gelwe lesaka.	A man is like a bull, should not be confined to one kraal.
Monna phafana o a hapaanelwa.	A man is like a calabash, he must be shared.
Monna selepe o a adimanwa.	A man is an axe so he can be shared.
Monna nawa o a nama	A man, like a bean seed, spreads out.

Chilisa et al. (2009) noted that by far the dominant discourse expressed in these proverbs is that of unbridled male sexual drive in which the male person is represented as someone whose sex drive must find an outlet and whose scope of operation must know no limits. A man's infidelity is implicitly sanctioned because, like a bull, he should go outside his kraal to look for mates. Just as a bull can be rotated in several kraals to mate with other cows, a man can also meet the sexual needs of several women. In addition, in the same way that neighbors can share an axe used for chopping firewood or a calabash of water or drink, a man can be passed from one woman to the other. The proverbial metaphors, seeing man as an axe or calabash, also encourage women to *accept* sharing a man. The bean seed metaphor encourages males to spread their seeds (genes) as far and wide as possible. Such metaphors influence how people behave sexually and shape the societal attitude toward promiscuous behavior. To invoke proverbs in our research process is to engage in a dialogue about people's lives using their own literature as a frame of reference for discussion. Chapter 9 discusses the Mbizi group method (Nitza, Chilisa, & Makwinja-Morara, 2010), an indigenous feminist method that draws from community stories and proverbs to engage participants in a journey of empowerment, transformation, and healing.

Activity 5.1

Read the study extract included here and do the following:

1. Discuss the role of proverbs in the study.

2. Think of a topic that you want to investigate and list ways in which you may employ proverbs in your study.

3. Identify proverbs in the study that give legitimacy to the postcolonial indigenous worldview of relational ontologies and connectedness of the people to the living and the nonliving.

4. Discuss ways in which proverbs can marginalize the less powerful in a community and say how you would use such proverbs in your research.

Source: M. Kaplan (2002), "Employing Proverbs to Explore Intergenerational Relations Across Cultures," in M. Kaplan, N. Henkin, and A. Kusano (Eds.), *Linking Lifetimes: A Global View of Intergenerational Exchange* (pp. 39–64), Lanham, MD: University Press of America.

(Continued)

(Continued)

Background

The focus of the "What Is Age" poster that was displayed at the Indigenous Knowledges Conference is how proverbs can be used to enhance our understanding about intergenerational relations in various cultural frameworks. This poster originally was developed to supplement a Penn State University Cooperation Extension Web-based curriculum titled Proverbs to Promote Understanding Across Generations and Cultures. The target population for this outreach initiative was Extension educators and other professionals interested in working with children, youth, and adults to facilitate awareness of age- and culture-related stereotypes, and to stimulate critical thinking about intergenerational and cross-cultural relationships in people's lives. The curriculum package includes five activity modules (each drawing upon proverbs from different parts of the world), a series of overheads (22 pages), marketing card, and the 'What Is Age' poster (Kaplan, Ingram, and Mincemoyer, 2001).

The idea for the proverbs curriculum came from a 1999 study of proverbs about the aging process and patterns of intergenerational relations. This study, which is described below, consisted of a survey conducted with students and faculty at Hawai'i Pacific University. Respondents, all of whom were bilingual, were asked to list sayings that reflect cultural values and beliefs related to:

• The aging process,

• Views about the elderly people, and

• Patterns of communication between people of different generations

In addition to writing out the sayings and phrases they could recall in their native languages, respondents were asked to provide English translations and write comments about the cultural, philosophical, and historical significance of the proverbs they shared. Research team members (consisting of the author and three undergraduate research assistants) also searched for proverbs in languages other than English in books, articles, and websites. (For a more detailed report about the study presented below, see Kaplan, 2002.)

Survey results

Characteristics of the survey sample: Surveys were returned by 117 respondents, each of whom was fluent in a language other than English. In surveys that were completed and content analyzed, twenty-six different languages were represented. . . . The responses were re-categorized into four main language groups: Asian (N = 80, 67.8%) Pacific Island (N = 13, 11%), Western European (N = 20, 16.9%), and Eastern European (N = 5, 4.2%).

Views about the elderly and the aging process

The following basic themes were identified:

- There appear to be more positive than negative characterizations.

- For many of the languages that were considered, there is a juxtaposition of sayings that reflect strikingly positive views toward the elderly and sayings that reflect strikingly negative views.

- Characterizations of the elderly and the aging process are rich and varied and draw upon a wide range of metaphors, including those tied to the natural environment, animals and food.

- As a group, survey respondents provided more than twice as many sayings that convey positive views about elderly people than sayings that convey negative views: 83 of the 117 sayings provided about the elderly (70.9%) were positive, and 37 were negative (31.6%).

The following sayings reflect images of loneliness, vulnerability, and struggle:

- Swedish: "Unga lever sina liv i flock, vuxna i par, och gamla ensamma."["Youth goes in a flock, manhood in pairs, and old age alone."] (Mieder, 1986:558)

- Hawai'ian [survey]: "Elemakule kama 'ole moe I ke ala." ["An oldster who has never reared children sleeps by the roadside."]

- Hebrew: "Youth is a garland of roses, age is a crown of thorns." (Christy, 1888:20).

The following sayings expound on the "deterioration and decline" theme:

- German [survey]: "Wer rastet der rostet." ["The person who will rust."]

- French: "Un home est aussi vieux que ses arteres." ["A man is as old as his arteries."] (Davidoff, 1946: 8)

- Chinese (Mandarin) [survey]: "Sheng lau bing si." ["Born, old, sick, die."]

(Continued)

(Continued)

Several phrases were found that convey "like father, like son" theme:

- Spanish [survey]: "De tal palo, tal astilla." ["From such a stick, such a splinter."]

- Japanese [survey]: "Kaeru no ko wa kaeru." ["Children of frogs are frogs."]

- Korean: "Pu chon cha chon." ["Father hands down, son hands down."]

Other sayings make similar reference to the importance of ancestors:

- Hawai'ian [survey]: "Nona I ke kumu." ["Look to the source."] (Respondent's comments: "Seek knowledge from the ancestors.")

- Korean: "An twe myon cho sang ui t'at." ["Blame the ancestors for failure."] (Grant 1982).This saying highlights a concept of family in which "ancestors play an integral part."

- Zulu: "Ubuntu." [We are who we are today because of you who came before us."]. This sub-Saharan intergenerational concept was one of the driving themes of the Third Global Conference of the Federation of Aging held in Durban, South Africa in October 1997 (Newman, 1998).

The proverbs and phrases presented in this paper can be used to enliven formal and non-formal educational programs focused on intergenerational issues. This was the intent of "Proverbs to Promote Understanding Across Generations and Cultures" curriculum and the "What Is Age" poster displayed at Indigenous Knowledges: Transforming the Academy conference. The proverbs presented in these outreach education vehicles contain "lessons" related to age and aging, cultural differences and similarities, family dynamics, societal stereotypes, and intergenerational relationships. It is feasible that they may be productively drawn upon to embellish themes presented throughout an entire course on gerontology or intergenerational programs and policy study.

⬛ STORYTELLING METHODS

Stories are central to the lives of the colonized Other. They have been used to collect, deposit, analyze, store, and disseminate information and as instruments of socialization. This socialization is an important aspect in the research process because it foregrounds the responses that participants in a research study give. The socialization stories are thus important in understanding the participants' frame of reference. Stories are also a reflection of the values of a society and act as teaching instruments as well as commentaries on society, family, or social relations.

Researchers need to be aware, however, that not all stories are valuable to the building of communities. Some stories are written from the perspective of the powerful and are therefore oppressive. Such stories may exclude the voices of children, women, the poor, the disabled, homosexuals, and some ethnic or racial groups. Researchers should critique androcentric, anthropocentric, racist, heterosexual-centered, or ethnically biased and stigmatizing stories that build communities on foundations of exclusion, silencing, exploitation, and oppression. What is important for researchers to note, however, is that all stories are the circulating literature that is accessible to the people and informs their day-to-day experiences and practice. Any research-based interventions can either complement or compete with the knowledge transmitted through these stories.

The diversity of stories in postcolonial and indigenous societies is enormous. Among the forms of stories are folklore, folktales, legends, and mythical stories, stories in song and poetic forms, and stories and narratives that emanate from interviews and focus group discussions as researchers pursue their research interests. All these stories have a function. They fill the gaps and provide the missing literature, theories, conceptual frameworks, and research methods in a postcolonial indigenous research paradigm. What follows is a discussion about the functions of a story, showing how stories reflect the values of society, are socialization instruments, are data sources and analysis tools, and provide the missing chapters on the history, philosophies, theories, concepts, categories of analysis, and interpretation in research that invokes a postcolonial indigenous perspective.

Functions of a Story in Research

Folklores, folktales, stories in song and poetic forms, and the indigenous language through which they are communicated are the data collection and analysis tools that provide the missing chapters of the history, philosophies, theories, concepts, categories of analysis, and interpretation of data in research that invoke a postcolonial indigenous research perspective.

1. Stories are the tools of data collection, analysis, and interpretation that give another side of the story to deficit theorizing about the Other and allow the Other, formerly colonized and historically oppressed, to frame and tell their past and present life experiences from their perspectives.

2. Stories enable researchers to triangulate postcolonial indigenous values, belief systems, and community and family histories with other sources of knowledge.

3. They provide data from which to debate postcolonial indigenous perspectives on a variety of issues, for example, perspectives on gender relations.

4. Storytelling allows the researched to speak freely about all their relationships, including the role of spirituality in their life.

5. Stories can serve as vignettes that bring alive and make memorable the experiences of the people.

6. Stories and storytelling allow both listeners and tellers to gain understanding, to do self-analysis, and to take new decisions that enable people-owned research-driven interventions and development programs.

Daniel G. Solórzano and Tara J. Yosso (2001) describe functions of the counterstory narrative, which is a form of storytelling that can

- Build community among those at the margins of society by putting a human and familiar face to educational theory and practice
- Challenge the perceived wisdom of those at society's center by providing a context to understand and transform established belief systems
- Open new windows into the reality of those at the margins of society by showing the possibilities beyond the ones they live and demonstrating that they are not alone in their position
- Teach others that by combining elements from both the story and the current reality, one can construct another world that is richer than either the story or the reality alone (Delgado Bernal, 1998; Lawson, 1995).

Stories and Relational Accountability

Stories provide the literature that bears testimony to postcolonial and indigenous peoples' relational ontology with its emphasis on connectedness with the living and the nonliving. In Chapter 4, you learned that the Bantu people of southern Africa celebrate and honor their connectedness with the living and the nonliving through totems. For each totem, there is a story passed from one generation to another. For example, the Bangwato, an ethnic group in Botswana, do not eat a duiker because it is their totem. According to the legend, the duiker saved Ngwato in a war with his brother, Kwena. Ngwato is said to have taken shelter in a bush where the duiker was grazing. When Kwena and his followers saw the duiker, they concluded that Ngwato could not be anywhere near. The Bangwato to this day maintain a relational accountability to the duiker. They cannot eat or kill a duiker. There are many such practices. Southern African species preservation, for example, occurred through totemism. Many postcolonial societies and indigenous peoples share folktales, legends, and stories that connect them to nature and to the living and the nonliving.

Think of the many rituals that may still be practiced before a family meeting, a community gathering, or a family wedding or to mark the birth of a baby and so on. We learned for instance, that the Anishambe, one of the indigenous people of North America, use *aseema* (tobacco) as a cultural symbol for thanking people, asking for help, praying for information, and sharing stories. My grandmother used to require that we share every evening meal with the ancestors. As we gathered around the fireplace to eat our evening meal, we would first take a handful of our dinner and put it on the floor as a gift to the dead; then, we ate. In this way, we were always reminded of our connections with the ancestors. These practices and legends are the testimonies that give legitimacy to a postcolonial indigenous research paradigm with its emphasis on relational accountability. Sharing food, exchanging gifts, and communicating with the nonliving in prayer, in song, in dance, or in speech are indigenous ways of communicating a philosophy, a belief system, a thought, or a collective worldview of a group. These practices should provide the form and context against which research with the colonized Other is conducted; using them makes it possible to use multiple social theories in research with a postcolonial indigenous perspective.

Folklores and the Design of Research Interventions: Maori Mythos

Postcolonial indigenous research perspectives call for an inquiry process that creates a space within which the colonized Other can revalorize or return to their own life perspectives and culturally inculcated goals without the imposition of Western-cogent terms, concepts, and paradigms. Oral literatures such as mythologies and folklores give voice to the colonized Other's spiritual practices. These spiritual practices, if made central to the research process, can give legitimacy to interventions that resonate with the worldviews of indigenous peoples. The extract below shows how a mythology in Maori society valorized spirituality and formed the basis for an intervention to control smoking that resonated with the worldview of the Maori people.

Evidence in an Indigenous World

The tikanga Auahi Kore research set out to communicate within a fourth world paradigm that Māori traditionally have high regard for their bodies and particularly their breath and therefore smoking is not culturally appropriate.

The key risk (likely to be relevant to any fourth world research project) for The Quit Group undertaking this research as a national smoking cessation provider is the same risk that Smith succumbed to: using hapū-based mythos as a national generalization. This has been mediated by engagement with kaumātua (learned elders) involved in the tobacco control sector, but most importantly, by both using nationally communicated mythos and carefully acknowledging that hapū may well have different tikanga (customs/traditions) for this kaupapa (subject), and encouraging the communication of those local traditions in preference to research.

Establishing that smoking is a breach of the tikanga that treats breath and the body as tapu (restricted/inaccessible) lead us to the foundational mythos about the creation of Hine-ahu-one. The first created being.

Tane Mahuta (the deity of forests and humanity) was responsible for the creation of the first being, and in some hapū, this is a man called Tiki, and among many hapū, a woman. The reasons vary from hapū to hapū for his decision to create another being. The location of his creative act also varied, be it at a beach or at the genital area of Papatuanuku (the earth mother of Māori mythos). What seems to be commonly held by those who share this mythos is that Tane gave life to this creation through a hongi (pressing of noses and sharing of breath) and the recital of an ancient karakia (chant/prayer) (Orbell, 1995):

Tihei mauri ora, ki te whai ao, ki te Ao Mārama

Behold the breath of life, strive for the new world, the world of light (TPK, 1995)

For the purposes of tikanga Auahi Kore, it is the hongi and karakia that are particularly pertinent. They communicate that every breath is precious, is a creative act that Māori people share with Tane, and is the reason why Māori hongi when we greet each other. We literally share our life-breath with the other person. Consequently, we communicated in our research that it follows that smoking, a health damaging act, violates that gift of breath.

Māori mythos

The case study is one example of the use of mythos to address fourth world populations in a relevant manner on a public-health issue. The possibilities of application of fourth world paradigms will go as far as researchers wish to go. The example above is one form of mythos in Māori tikanga, kōrero pūrākau, or mythological stories that communicate a deep truth about the Māori world view.

There are other forms of mythos that may prove just as relevant. Whakatauaki (proverbs) and kīwaha (idioms) are either entry points into kōrero pūrākau or a reflection within themselves on the issues of the day. Waiata, waiata tāhwito, waiata-a-ringa and haka (types of songs and dances) similarly communicate through music the Māori world view and experience). Both give an insight to the supernatural world of Māori and particularly its holistic relationship with other aspects of life. Tā moko (tattooing of the body and face) and mahi toi (arts) are other forms of Māori evidence that communicate a variety of themes for those who take time to learn their meaning.

Source: G. Cram (2004a), *Evidence in an Indigenous World,* paper presented at the Australasian Society 2004 International Conference, October 13–15, Adelaide.

Folktales as Counternarratives: The Batswana Story of Origin

Let us imagine that a researcher wanted to study gender relations in a community and to trace the history of this asymmetrical relationship between men and women. Among the Tswana and Sotho-speaking of southern Africa, most people would locate the unequal relationship in the language, for example, in proverbs like: *Ga dinke di etelelwa ke e namagadi pele, di ka wela ka le mina.* (Women cannot be leaders). The story of origin would, however, defy this worldview. According to the Tswana story of origin, the people came from the hill of Lowe. When they came out, men and women were walking side by side, driving sheep, goats, and cattle. This story defies explanations that justify inequalities on the basis of traditions, revealing other traditional ways of viewing gender relations. It is an important contribution to knowledge production in the area of gender relations and could be used as an important entry point for a researcher who might be looking for intervention strategies to address inequalities.

Contemporary Stories

Stories continue to be created around the social problems that haunt communities. In Botswana, current stories about HIV/AIDS have one common characteristic: They show how communities have defined the problem and how often the definition is embedded in the values of the society. The stories encode in them the analysis of the problem and the prescribed solution.

A common story in Botswana is that HIV/AIDS is *Boswagadi,* which means an illness that inflicts those who indulge in love relationships with widows or widowers who have not performed the cleansing ritual. There is no cure for *Boswagadi.* The solution thus lies in avoiding widows and widowers. A researcher who incorporates these stories in the research process acknowledges the society's identification, analysis, and solution of the problem. In that way, the research does not disregard the community or impose knowledge from outside. The stories are community owned and therefore common knowledge. Reflecting on these stories during the research process creates an entry point that enables a dialogue in which information can be analyzed and false knowledge that impedes progress can be discussed. Such a framework is important for a participatory research approach in which the communities arrive at solutions to the problem and take immediate action.

Self-Praise/Identity Stories

Self-knowledge and self-identity were cherished attributes in most African cultures and were taught through self-praise stories. Almost every individual knew such a story. A self-praise story told the history and family tree of the individual, valued attributes of the family lineage, and any marked historical developments. What is important is that the definition of the self was related to the environment and its people, animals, birds, and vegetation. Today, most adults in villages still recite these self-praises, stories that define a person's complete existence and mark his or her self-identity without divorcing the person from core relations. Such stories would be good resources for psychological research on human and cognitive development as well as human behavior. The self-praise stories would help the researcher to understand better the participant and her or his values and self-image. Conventional research sums up the characteristics of participants under what is called demographic variables, which normally include age, education, and occupation. These demographic variables may add little value to a study, especially in rural communities where most adult village residents have little or no education and rely on subsistence farming for a living. The demographic variables in the conventional research process are individualistic and seek to understand the participant independent of the environment.

Self-praise may be an important complementary technique of gathering information on informants because it allows the researcher to understand the participants as they define themselves in relation to others around them and the environment. In their understanding of social reality, the self cannot be divorced from others, the spirits, and the environment. Such a worldview has to be built into the research process so that at each point, the researcher understands the participants' self-definition. It is an approach that gives the researched space to appreciate their identity and to heal from possible psychological harm that may have occurred because of deficit theorizing about their communities.

Songs

Stories are also told in song, in dance, and in poetic form. Songs, dance, and poems are an integral part of the oral literature that communicates historical information on events, public experience, and practice, especially experiences of the formerly colonized. Maenette Benham (2007) notes, for instance, that native Hawai'ians *mele* (songs) and *hula* (dance) tell stories about the history, people, and land. Benham uses the following song, written by Mrs. Ellen Wright in Prendergast in opposition to the annexation of Hawai'i by the United States, to illustrate the value of songs in reconstructing the history of the formerly colonized.

Na Pua: The Stories That Begin

Kaulana nāpua a' o Hawai`i	Famous are the children of Hawai`i
Kupa'a ma hope o ka 'āina	Ever loyal to the land
Hiki mai ka 'elele o ka loko 'ino	When the evil-hearted messenger comes
Palapala 'anunu me ka pākaha.	With his greedy document of extortion
Pane mai Hawai`i moku o Keawe.	Hawai'i, land of Keawe answers
Kokua nā Hono a'o Pi'ilani.	Pi'ilani's bays help
Kāko'o mai Kaua'i o Piilani.	Mano's Kauai lends support
Pa'apū me ke one Kakuhihewa.	And so do the sands of Kakuhihewa
'A'ole 'a'ekau'i ka pūlima	No one will fix a signature
Ma luna o ka pepa o ka 'enemi,	To the paper of the enemy
Ho'ohui 'āina ku'ai hewa,	With its sin of annexation
I ka pono sivila a'o ke kanaka.	And sale of native civil rights
'A'ole mākou a'e minamina	We do not value
I ka pu'ukālā a ke aupuni.	The government's sums of money

(Continued)

(Continued)

Ua lawa mākou I ka pōhaku,	We are satisfied with the stones
I ka'ai kamaha'o o ka 'āina.	Astonishing food of the land
Ma hope mākou o Lili'ulani	We back Lili'ulani
A loa'a'e ka pono a ka 'āina.	Who has won the rights of the land
(A kau hou 'ia e ke kalaunu)	(She will be crowned again)
Ha'ina 'ia mai ana ka puana	Tell the story
Ka po'e I aloha I ka 'āina.	Of the people who love their land

Source: S. H. Elbert and N. Mahoe (1976), *Na mele o hawai'i nei: 101 Hawaii songs*: Honolulu: University of Hawai'i Press, pp. 63–64.

Benham notes that the goal of such narratives is to invite participation of native people and their communities in the narrative process. This participation, it is noted, engages the researcher/scholar and native/indigenous people in building relationships that bring to the surface stories of experienced phenomenon and concrete evidence around pressing issues (e.g., historic hurt and pain). In this sense, narratives are the indigenous literature through which we can enter a dialogue with the researched on a given topic of interest. There are countless missing chapters on what the world needs to know about the postcolonial and indigenous people's histories and their resistance to colonizing ideologies of the former colonizers.

Songs are also a commentary on people's lives. Songs are for instance "capable of supplying subtle insights, local colour and details beyond what archives and other forms of oral traditions can provide" (Alagoa, 1968, p. 16). The social function of a song goes beyond the aesthetic as it also has a didactic role to play in teaching about social morality, societal values, and customs. Like proverbs, however, songs can serve as propaganda that perpetuates oppressive ideologies. In a study on sexually risky behaviors (Chilisa et al., 2009), Batswana adolescents cited the Setswana lyric, *Setlogolo Ntsha Ditlhogo,* as an example of an oppressive ideology that encouraged sexual exploitation of young girls by adults, especially relatives. *Ditlhogo* (heads) is a euphemistic expression that uncles traditionally used to request sexual favors from their nieces (although in the folksong, *ditlhogo* is restricted to a special relationship between a girl and her maternal uncle). Stories from the children revealed that the metaphor *ditlhogo* communicated sexual relations and expectations between uncles and their nieces and between cousins.

The song, *Setlogolo Ntsha Ditlhogo,* is structured in the form of a narrative about a journey the person undertook with her uncle. On the way, they rested, and the uncle asked the niece to give him *ditlhogo,* a special gift reserved for uncles. The niece asks her uncle what he means by *ditlhogo,* and he replies that anything can be *ditlhogo* and that a thigh, too, can be a *ditlhogo.* A thigh is a metaphor for sex. The uncle naughtily says that anything can be *ditlhogo,* but what he really wants is *serope* (thigh). The concept of *ditlhogo* gives maternal uncles privileged access to their nieces, who should afford them special treatment as a form of duty. This kind of song reinforces normative beliefs about adult/child relationships that make adolescents powerless to refuse to have sex with older people, especially close relatives; through songs such as this one, they are made to believe that the community approves of sexual relationships between young girls and their uncles or other adults.

Lyric Setlogolo Ntsha Ditlhogo

Lead voice:	ke tsamaile le malome	I travelled with my maternal uncle
Response:	A malala swii swii	
Lead voice:	Ko pele ra itapolosa	on the way we rested
Response:	A malala swiiswii.	
Lead voice:	A re setlogolo ntsha/mpha ditlhogo	He said "niece give me heads"
Response:	A malala swii, swii	
Lead voice:	Ka re ditlhogo tsa eng malome?	I said what head uncle?
Response:	A malala swiii swii	
Lead voice:	A re sengwe le sengwe ke ditlhogo	He said anything is heads.
Response:	Amalala swii swii	
Lead voice:	Serope le sone ke ditlhogo	Even a thigh is heads.
Response:	A malala swii swii	

Stories From Research Interviews

In qualitative research, the researcher can focus on the interview itself as a form of narrative or focus on stories that appear spontaneously in the course of the interview (Kvale, 1996). Teun A. Van Dijk (1993, pp. 132–133) suggests that the defining characteristics of narratives are:

- Stories about (past) human actions and cognitions, although descriptions of other events, objects, places, or circumstances may be part of stories, for example, as conditions or consequences to human actions
- Stories usually about events that are (made) interesting to the audience. The pragmatic interestingness is achieved by telling events/actions that are unexpected, extraordinary, deviant, or unpredictable, given the knowledge or beliefs of the audience
- Stories told to entertain, to influence the listener's aesthetic, ethical, or emotional reactions

From a critical discourse point of view, the narrative is "a socially symbolic act in the double sense that (a) it takes on meaning in a social context, and (b) it plays a role in the construction of that social context as a site of meaning within which social actors are implicated" (Mumby, 1993, p. 7).

Storytelling and Spirituality

When interviews are used as a strategy for collecting data and interviewees are invited to narrate their life experiences, they "naturally interject the spiritual aspects of their experiences into the research" (Walker, 2001, p. 20). Polly Walker (2001) gives an example of how, during a study on conflict transformation, Indigenous participants spoke openly of how the spirits and ancestors informed their day-to-day experiences and challenges in resolving conflicts. She cites excerpts from some of the aboriginal participants' stories, which describe the way the participants' ancestors assist in conflict transformation:

> If anything goes bad, I just talk to them. I believe in the spirits. I believe in the spirits getting us to reconcile . . . Another participants says, "When I am doing talks . . . how I psyche myself up is that I call on my mother and I can feel her on my shoulder." (p. 20)

Walker (2001) concludes that the research on conflict transformation would have been lacking without consideration of the spiritual experiences that the participants chose to share and that any silencing of such spiritual experiences can lead only to research results that are "inaccurate, incomplete, and invalid" (p. 20). It is, therefore, important to always interrogate the role of spirituality in postcolonial and indigenous communities' production, storage, analysis, and dissemination of knowledge. It is also important that researchers should interrogate their own perspectives toward spirituality, as it is most likely to affect the data obtained and its analysis and interpretation.

Stories as Information Dissemination Avenues

Imagine that you were to write your dissertation or research report in a story form. Shawn Wilson (2008) notes that stories enable writers to get away from the abstraction and rules that are dictated by the Western academic discourse and allow listeners to gain life lessons and draw conclusions from their personal perspectives. Wilson wrote his dissertation in a story form and shares with us his writing style.

My Writing Style

You will notice that the book is typeset in two different fonts: the main font denotes a more "academic" style; a different font is used for the personal narrative sections, which are initially addressed to my sons, Julius, Max and Falco. When I was originally writing my doctoral thesis, which led to this book, I felt that the dominant style of writing to an anonymous reader did not live up to the standards of relational accountability I was proposing. Indigenous epistemology is all about ideas developing through the formation of relationships. An idea cannot be taken out of this relational context and still maintain its shape. Terry Tafoya (1995) describes this in his Principle of Uncertainty. Just as Heisenberg theorizes in his Theory of Uncertainty in physics, that it is impossible to know both the velocity and the location of an electron at the same time (you would have to stop it to measure its location, or you would lose its location if it maintains its velocity), Tafoya postulates that it is not possible to know exactly both the context and definition of an idea at the same time. The closer you get to defining something, the more it loses its context. Conversely, the more something is put into context, the more it loses a specific definition.

So I was faced with the problem of trying to define or describe the ideas when doing so would take them out of their relational context. In an oral tradition, this problem is overcome by utilizing the direct relationship between storyteller and listener. Each recognizes the other's role in shaping both the content and process. Addressing parts of the book to Julius, Max and Falco became a device for me to try to provide both context and definition. Instead of writing directly to readers, which is difficult without knowing their culture and context, I chose to

(Continued)

(Continued)

write to my children. I further develop the relationships I have with the ideas through my relationship with my sons. I hope that this literary tool allows you to develop your own relationships both with me and with the stories in this book.

In my current thinking and writing process, it would probably make the most sense to address the entire book to my sons, but I have purposefully not gone back into my writing to switch it all to this style. As this foreword was one of the last things written in the preparation of this book, I am now at a point where I can address you directly. The writing process took me several years, and you may notice that my writing style changes, maybe matures, as the book progresses through the chapters. The chapters (other than this foreword) were pretty much written in the order they are presented: so in addition to putting forward ideas, they also represent a chronology of my maturation as a writer and Indigenous researcher.

The two "voices" may initially seem disjointed. Oftentimes, they either cover entirely different material, but they may repeat one another. It was my intention that they cover more or less the same ground, but with two different emphasizes—one academic, and one more personal. As my writing and thinking progressed, these voices became less and less distinct. Maybe I was finally beginning to internalize what it was that I was theorizing about. In final editing of the book, I tried to make a change so that the letters to Julius, Max and Falco begin to directly address you. By chapter four the difference between the voices becomes less clear. By chapter five, you might notice that I have more or less switched to one voice that incorporates both the personal and theoretical, but can't decide which font to use. Perhaps the book should switch to an entirely different font here, but I think that might be too confusing. Anyway, I hope that by then you will have internalized enough of the ideas to allow me to write the last parts (including this foreword) in a style that mixes the personal with the theoretical.

Source: S. Wilson (2008), *Research Is Ceremony: Indigenous Research Methods*, Winnipeg, Manitoba, Fernwood Publishing, pp. 8–9. Used by permission.

Apart from writing the dissertation in story form, research findings can also be summarized in forms compatible with communication systems in postcolonial and indigenous communities such as poems. In a study of Botswana youths' perspectives on gender, Michelle Commeyras and Mercy Montsi (2000) presented themes from data in poetic form. The words in the poems were taken from the essays that the youths wrote about what it would feel like if they woke up as the other sex. Following are stanzas from the poem that illustrate themes of discontentment from boys waking up as girls and girls' disapproval of the type of life that boys lead.

If I woke up tomorrow as a girl ...
I would feel disturbed, frightened, shocked,
and worried.
I would feel embarrassed, humiliated and
Disappointed
I would feel lonely, depressed and mentally
disturbed.
I might as well commit suicide.

If I woke up tomorrow as a boy
I would not ...
bully others
impregnate a girl and run away

(Commeyras & Montsi, 2000, p. 343)

Activity 5.2

The story below illustrates how pervasive the dominant academic systems have been in guiding indigenous research and teaching of indigenous knowledge. Read it and answer the following questions:

1. What lessons and personal perspectives do you draw from the story?

2. Think of ways in which you may transform an interview script or focus group interview script into a storyline like the one below.

3. How would you honor indigenous methods and ethics in writing a storyline from interview scripts? Would you write the names of the interviewees or use pseudo names?

Source: H. Harris (2002), "Coyote Goes to School: The Paradox of Indigenous Higher Education," *Canadian Journal of Native Education,* *26*(2), 187–196. Used by permission.

(Continued)

(Continued)

Coyote was once again fed up with running around all day in the hot sun for a few scrawny gophers and rabbits. Dirt up his nose, dirt in his eyes, and what for? Barely a mouthful. Coyote had tried getting food at the supermarket one time like the Human People do but got the shit kicked out of him for that. So, once again, he went to his brother, Raven, to ask him for advice.

Coyote said, "Raven, there's got to be an easier way to get fed. I tried the supermarket—got beaten up. Tried to get money from welfare but came up against the Devil's Spawn in a K-Mart dress. Nothing's worked so far. You got any other ideas?"

"Well," Raven said thoughtfully, "the White Humans seem pretty well fed and they say that the key to success is a good education. Maybe you could go to school."

"Humm," Coyote mused, "maybe I'll try it. Couldn't hurt."

Well, Coyote went off to the city to the university because that's where Raven said adults go to school.

In a few days Coyote was back. "Well my brother," Raven inquired, "did you get your education?"

"Not exactly," Coyote replied, "education is as hard to get as a welfare cheque. To get an education like the teachers at the university takes at least 10 years—that's a Coyote's entire lifetime—and in the end, you don't get paid much anyway.

"When I got to the university, they asked me what program I was in. I didn't know so they sent me to this guy who told me about the programs. I kinda liked the idea of biology—if I learned more about gophers maybe I could invent a great rabbit trap. But in the end I settled on Native Studies. Now that's something I can understand—I've known these guys for thousands of years, even been one when it suited me."

"So I went to my introduction to Native Studies course and, can you believe it, the teacher was a white guy? Now how much sense does that make? I saw native people around town—any one of 'em has got to know more about native people than some white guy."

"When I asked this guy what Indian told him the stuff he was saying, he said none—he read it in a book. Then I asked who the Indian was who wrote the book. And he said, it wasn't an Indian, it was a white guy. Then I asked him what Indian the guy who wrote the book learned from and the teacher got mad and told me to sit down."

The next day I went to my Indians of North America class. I was really looking forward to meeting all those Indians. And you know what? There was another white guy standing up there and not an Indian in sight. I asked the teacher, "Are we going to visit all the Indians?" He said, No. So I asked him, "How are we going to learn about Indians then?" And he said, just like the other guy, from a book written by a white guy. So I asked him if I could talk to this guy who wrote the book and the teacher said, "No, he's dead."

"By then, I was getting pretty confused about this education stuff but I went to my next class—Indian Religions. And guess what? When I went in, there wasn't another white gut standing up at the front of the room—there was a white woman!"

"I sat down and I asked her, 'Are we going to the sweatlodge?' 'No.' 'Sundance?' 'No.' 'Yuwipi?' 'No.' 'Then how are we going to learn—no wait, I know—from a book written by a dead white guy! I'm starting to get the hang of this education business."

"So then I go to my Research Methods class thinking I've got it figured out. In this class, the teacher (you've got it—another white guy) said that our research must be ethical, that we must follow the guidelines set out by the University for Research on human subjects. The rules are there, my teacher said, to protect the Indians from unscrupulous researchers. Who made these rules I asked—you guessed it—a bunch of white guys. They decided we need protecting and that they were the ones to decide how best to protect us from them. So I told my teacher that I wanted to interview my father. The teacher said, you've got to ask the ethics review committee for permission. What?! I've got to ask a bunch of white guys for permission to talk to my own dad? That can't be right. I was confused all over again."

"So I sat down and thought about all this for a long time. Finally I figured it out. If white guys teach all the courses about Indians and they teach in the way white people think, then to find Indians teaching the way Indians think, all I had to do was give up Native Studies and join the White Studies program!" (pp. 194–196).

IN WHAT LANGUAGE IS THE STORY TOLD?

In Chapters 1 and 2, you learned that writing and carrying out research in indigenous languages is a critical decolonization strategy. What follows is a discussion of methodological challenges and practices in researching and producing research reports in ways that give legitimacy to indigenous languages.

Language Rights and Research

Today, an imposed hierarchy of languages continues to inform in whose language the discipline of research is conducted and debated and its findings disseminated. In Africa, for instance, the language of the former colonizers—English for former British colonies, French for former French colonies, and Portuguese for former Portuguese colonies—remains the official language of instruction in all academic institutions and in public discourse. In addition, one or more languages of majority ethnic groups are selected as national languages and may be taught up to secondary school level. It then remains the responsibility of the remaining minority ethnic groups to see how they develop their languages. In the United States, English is the dominant language, and government supports the protection of Native American languages. In contrast, "U.S English has not extended that kind of gesture to the Chicano people," thus violating their linguistic rights and perpetuating the annihilation of not only their language, but also their culture (Demas & Saavedra, 2004, p. 215). The diversity of languages spoken but not necessarily written poses possible threats to the linguistic rights of the formerly colonized and indigenous peoples and to the validity and credibility of research studies.

What happens when the myriads of stories in postcolonial indigenous communities are told and written in Western languages? Who benefits when research reports are written and disseminated in Western languages? In whose language should research be conducted and data stored and analyzed? What outlets are available for reports and journal articles written in local languages?

Elsa M. Gonzalez and Yvonna S. Lincoln (2006) discuss language and its role in research and advance the argument that researchers must produce research reports that are multilingual and multivocal. The authors recommend that researchers not familiar with the languages of the researched should work with translators and interpreters throughout the research process, and those authors should present data in more than one language, including the language in which the data were collected. In addition, researchers should review literature that is written in the local language of the researched. Aroztegui Massera (2006) reflects on how she presented bilingual texts in her doctoral dissertation as follows:

The personal accounts this dissertation is based upon were collected in Spanish. The general criteria I used for translation is that, whenever possible, I translated the original word or sentence into English inside a parenthesis. However, the act of translation always implies the loss of information. Therefore, every time a testimony is recalled, I place the original Spanish transcript and the translation into English, together within the document. The purpose for this is to allow the reader who knows Spanish to read the original version. The difficulty in translating is mostly a cultural problem. Some words that are essential to understanding the meaning of the narratives have a specific meaning within the context of the group interviewed: Uruguayan female former political prisoners. Such words, although they might have a Standard English translation, would lose an important part of their meaning because these meanings are created by the context within which they are used. For very frequently used words, I use the original word in Spanish, in italics, and clarify the meaning only once, in this appendix. (cited in Lincoln & Gonzalez, 2008, pp. 787–788; excerpt used by permission.)

The second example illustrates the use of bilingual texts in data collection and analysis where the researcher is not fluent in the native language and seeks assistance from a local/native partner. Richard Nader (2005, cited in Lincoln & Gonzalez, 2008) reflects on methods regarding language in data collection and analysis as follows.

South Koreans were interviewed either in the Korean language or in English. The language of the interview was determined according to each participant's preference. Korean language interpretation was provided by a Korean graduate student matriculating for her masters in science journalism on a paid basis. (p. 38)

All Korean language interviews were transcribed into Korean, checked for accuracy by the interviewer and subsequently translated into English. English translation questions were clarified through discussion between the research assistant and the researcher. The researcher and the assistant discussed the English version of each Korean language interview before and following analysis. A post-interview assessment was conducted for Korean language interviews where the researcher was not in attendance to ascertain the quality of the interview and potential interviewer effects or bias in the data collected. (pp. 39–40)

The researcher and assistant met frequently and practiced interviews together, being aware of non-verbal communication, interviewing using successful Korean communication methods (e.g., limited hand gestures, no antagonistic language), and by developing documents in Korean language according to styles appropriate to South Korean culture. (p. 41; excerpts used by permission.)

In the third excerpt, Xiaobo Yang (2005) collected data in her native language, Chinese, but wrote the dissertation in the academic language of the institution, English in her case. On reflection of this practice she observes,

> Using a second language to write a naturalistic inquiry research report based on the motherland language is a great challenge for the researcher. When you translate every sentence, you feel so guilty, because you lose much information, which can only be expressed and understood with one's own language and cultural tacit knowledge. So be careful and prepare well, if you want to choose the way the researcher did. (p. 251)

By and large, to decolonize research methodologies, researchers are advised to use bilingual texts in all the stages in the research process.

SUMMARY

Indigenous languages and oral literature provide some of the missing chapters on the histories and experiences of indigenous peoples, peoples in the third world, historically oppressed groups, and in general the colonized Other. The oral literature has the potential to form the basis for theoretical and conceptual frameworks in designing research studies, to serve as evidence to debate the deficit literature about the formerly colonized, and to offer intervention strategies that resonate with peoples' value systems and ways of knowing.

KEY POINTS

- Language, oral literature, and storytelling are important sources of literature on the history of the formerly colonized and can provide new insights into other ways of theorizing about methodologies in social science research.
- Language, oral literature, and storytelling provide an entry point from which researchers can engage in a dialogue with the researched about social issues of concern.
- There is need to always review oral literature and literature written in the language of the researched and to produce research reports that are multivocal and multilingual.

Activity 5.3

Make a list of the oral literature, legends, folktales, proverbs, idioms, contemporary stories, and songs in your community that you think can inform theory and practice in social science research.

SUGGESTED READINGS

Benham, M. K. P. (2007). On culturally relevant story making from and indigenous perspective. In D. J. Clandinin (Ed.), *Handbook of narrative inquiry: Mapping a methodology.* Thousand Oaks, CA: Sage.

Cram, G. (2004, October 13-15). *Evidence in an indigenous world.* Paper presented at the Australasian Society 2004 International Conference, Adelaide.

Gonzalez, G., & Lincoln, Y. (2006). Decolonizing qualitative research: Nontraditional forms in the academy. In N. K. Denzin & M. D. Giadina (Eds.), *Qualitative inquiry and the conservative challenge*, (pp. 193-214). Walnut Creek, CA: Left Coast Press.

Lincoln Y. S., & Gonzalez, G. (2008). The search for liberatory decolonizing methodologies in qualitative research: Further strategies for liberatory and democratic inquiry. *Qualitative Inquiry, 14*(5), 784-805.

Nitza, A., Chilisa, B., & Makwinja-Morara, V. (2010). Mbizi: Empowerment and HIV/AIDS prevention for adolescents girls in Botswana. *The Journal of Specialists in Group Work, 35*(2), 105-114.

CHAPTER 6

CULTURALLY RESPONSIVE INDIGENOUS RESEARCH METHODOLOGIES

[To decolonize the research methodologies is] to argue that people must enter the world of scientific and scholarly analysis from the path of their historically and culturally developed perspectives. These perspectives are not counter to the universal truth, but simply access the universal through the window of one's particular worldview.

Naim Akbar (1991, p. 248)

We stand at the threshold of a history marked by multivocality, contested meanings, paradigmatic controversies, and new textual forms. At some distance down this conjectural path, when its history is written, we will find that this has been the era of emancipation: emancipation from what Hannah Arendt calls the "coerciveness of Truth," emancipation from hearing only the voices of Western Europe, emancipation from generations of silence, and emancipation from seeing the world in one color.

Egon Guba & Yvonna Lincoln (2005, p. 212)

OVERVIEW

I have discussed a postcolonial indigenous research paradigm as a worldview that articulates the shared aspects of ontology, epistemology, axiology, and research methodologies of the colonized Other discussed by scholars who conduct research in former colonized societies in Africa, Asia, and Latin America and among indigenous peoples in Australia, Canada and the United States. In this chapter, you will learn about the relationship between methodology, methods, and philosophical assumptions on the nature of reality, knowledge, and values; implementation of an indigenous research and examples of evolving and culturally responsive indigenous methodologies; and the way that rigor and credibility are addressed in these methodologies.

LEARNING OBJECTIVES

By the end of this chapter, you should be able to:

1. Design a study that uses a postcolonial indigenous methodology
2. Compare and contrast the postcolonial indigenous methodologies discussed in the chapter
3. Discuss validity and reliability in postcolonial indigenous methodologies

Before You Start

Discuss the quotations at the beginning of the chapter and their relevance to what you have learned so far.

REGIONAL, NATIONAL, AND LOCAL SPECIFIC METHODOLOGIES

A growing number of methodologies are written from the experiences of postcolonial Indigenous researchers in national and regional geographic locations, as they encounter methodological imperialism and deficit-driven and damage-centered research and literature, which chronicle only the pain and hopelessness of the colonized and which entrench existing structures of domination. These methodologies draw from the philosophical and theoretical assumptions of a postcolonial indigenous paradigm to emphasize the unique contribution of sociohistorical, cultural, and political factors to social science research. The main emphasis is that people should be understood within their social context, which is inevitably influenced by their cultural, political, and historical contexts. For example, some argue that most data-gathering instruments are biased and not applicable to non-Western contexts because "they are often based on individualistic westernized assumptions and theories that mostly neglect context dynamics in which meanings emerge, and within which they continue to exist" (Roos, 2008, p. 661). Contexts and cultures among the colonized Other may differ from region to region and, within each region, by location, nationality, or ethnic group. To illustrate culturally responsive methodologies is to acknowledge the local histories, traditions, and indigenous knowledge systems that inform them. A recognition of the diversity in culture and contexts should be seen not as promoting fragmentation of knowledge but rather as giving voice to all, irrespective of race, location, and ethnic group. Some of these methodologies are well developed, specifying the principles underlying the research methodology: ways of identifying a research issue; reviewing of literature; selecting data collection, data analysis, and interpretation and dissemination procedures; and establishing an ethical framework. Others are still evolving. The challenge is locating and internationalizing indigenous culturally responsive methodologies and integrating Western culture-informed perspectives with indigenous culturally based methodologies in ways that permit dialogue between researchers, policymakers, communities, and nations. In this chapter, I emphasize those postcolonial indigenous culturally specific methodologies that are not common in the research methodology literature and show how philosophical assumptions about the nature of reality, knowledge, and values converge with theory and practice to inform culturally specific methodologies. The methodologies discussed here are not the only ones in the evolving literature of methodologies informed by a postcolonial indigenous research paradigm. The following are discussed:

- Kaupapa Maori research methodologies
- Methodologies based on the medicine wheel
- Afrocentric methodologies

Let us begin with a discussion of the relationship between a paradigm, methodology, and methods.

PARADIGM, METHODOLOGY, AND METHODS ▮

A methodology summarizes the research process, that is, how the research will proceed. Building a methodology starts with a choice of the research paradigm that informs the study. The process is, therefore, guided by philosophical assumptions about the nature of reality, knowledge, and values and the theoretical framework that informs comprehension, interpretation, choice of literature, and research practice on a given topic of study. Diagram 6.1 illustrates parts that make up a paradigm.

Methodology becomes the place where assumptions about the nature of reality, knowledge, values, and theory and practice on a given topic converge. Diagram 6.2 illustrates the relationship. Methods are the tools used for gathering data and are an important component of the methodology.

Building the methodology of a study begins with a standpoint on the following questions:

Paradigm. What paradigm informs your methodology? Is it the postpositivist paradigm, interpretive paradigm, transformative paradigm, or a postcolonial indigenous paradigm?

Theoretical framework. What theories inform the choice of your research topic, the research questions you ask, the literature reviewed, data collection methods, analysis, and interpretation? Is it an indigenous knowledge-based

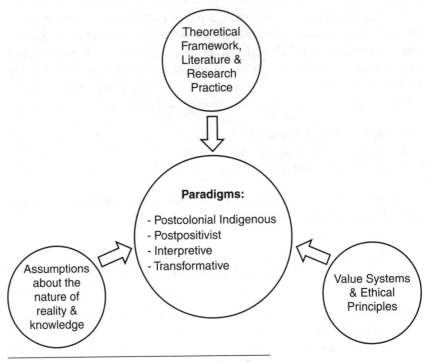

Diagram 6.1   Parts That Make Up a Paradigm

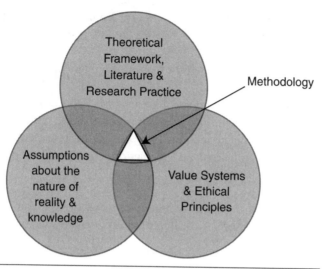

Diagram 6.2   Methodology as Convergence of Three Parts

theory, postcolonial theory, critical race-based theory, feminist theory, critical theory, or a combination of some of the above.

Research approach. Is it a quantitative participatory approach study, for instance, a survey? Is it a qualitative participatory approach study, for instance, an ethnographic study? Is it a combination of qualitative and quantitative participatory approach study?

Data collection. What assumptions about the nature of reality, knowledge, and values inform your data collection methods? Are you, for instance, adopting a decolonization of methods approach that inserts an indigenous data collection method into a study guided by a Euro Western-based paradigm? Or is it a decolonization approach within a postcolonial indigenous research paradigm? What assumptions guide the selection of participants in the study (sampling), the setting of the study, and the techniques of data collection? What role do the following play in your choice of data collection and sampling procedures: ethnophilosophy, philosophic sagacity, cultural artifacts, and decolonization of interviews? Are you using any of the following: proverbs and metaphors as conceptual frameworks, storytelling methods, songs and poems, talk circles, or indigenous knowledge-based interview guides? See Chapters 5 and 7 for a discussion of these strategies.

Data analysis. What theory informs the data analysis and interpretation approach? Is it any one of the following: an indigenous knowledge-based theory, postcolonial theory, critical theory, feminist theory, critical race theory, or a combination of these theories and others?

Ethics. What is the theory of ethics that informs the study? Take, for example, the role of the researcher as a transformative healer with responsibilities to others. These responsibilities involve the application of theories and the literature review that inform the research process, along with the four general principles of relational accountability, respectful representation, reciprocal appropriation, and rights and regulations proposed in a postcolonial indigenous research paradigm.

Validity. By what and whose standards are the design, data collection, analysis, and interpretation of research findings deemed valid and reliable?

▌ VALIDITY AND RELIABILITY: AN OVERVIEW

Whatever the paradigmatic assumptions that guide the research process, the resulting studies should be convincing enough that research participants can see themselves in the descriptions. In addition, all stakeholders, practitioners, and policymakers should feel confident to act on the findings and implications of the studies. A criterion for judging the validity of a study is thus an important methodological component. Methodologies described in this chapter assume a qualitative approach. This is not to say indigenous methodologies use only qualitative methods. As noted in Chapter 4, indigenous research approaches may begin with a qualitative approach that can inform the development of theories and concepts, which can be tested for efficacy using quantitative methods. Qualitative methods are best for theory building and can involve diverse social constructs and theories that are novel and unique. The quantitative methods complement the qualitative approach in indigenous research by testing, refining indigenous research theory, and integrating it into the global knowledge economy. I will thus focus on validity from a postcolonial indigenous perspective.

Rigor in Qualitative Research

One major concern in qualitative research, as in quantitative research, has to do with the confidence that researchers and consumers of research studies can place in the procedures used in the data gathering, the data collected, its analysis and interpretation, and the related findings and conclusions. The researcher has to be aware of possible threats to the credibility of the research study. For instance, quantitative researchers frequently describe qualitative research as subjective and therefore inherently unreliable and invalid. They also maintain that participants may lie, distort the truth, or withhold information. When that happens, the researcher is misled by incomplete, inaccurate, or biased data. This has led to rigid procedures and language that inform validity and reliability of qualitative research studies. Yvonna Lincoln and Egon Guba (1985; Creswell, 2009) have proposed that the validity and reliability of qualitative research studies should be judged under criteria different from those used in quantitative research. The following terms in qualitative research were suggested to describe validity and reliability: *credibility* for internal validity, *transferability* for external validity, *dependability* for reliability, and *confirmability* for objectivity. Procedures and strategies for establishing rigor and ensuring the credibility, transferability, dependability, and confirmability of qualitative research studies were also established. Today, there is a concern that an overemphasis on the criteria and language in judging validity in qualitative research can lead to oversimplified, mechanical procedures that reduce data to controllable elements, fragments, and predetermined structures (Brabeck & Brabeck, 2009; Cram, 2009; Koro-Ljungberg, 2010; Lincoln, 2009). I will nevertheless begin the discussion with a review of this oversimplified version of validity to enable a contrast with validity and reliability with postcolonial indigenous critique framework.

Credibility

Credibility is the equivalent of internal validity in quantitative research. Qualitative research is characterized by multiple realities and therefore multiple truths. Research evidence is therefore credible if it represents as adequately as possible the multiple realities revealed by the participants. The participants should also be able to recognize the descriptions and interpretations of their human experience as accurate and true. Following are some of the common strategies for enhancing the credibility of qualitative research studies.

Prolonged and substantial engagement. The credibility of a study may be threatened by errors that occur when research participants respond with what they think is the desired social response (Krefting, 1991) or when they resist intrusion into their communities by deliberately giving false information. I have noted that in most postcolonial indigenous societies, building rapport requires a process that connects the researcher to the researched through sharing of values or practices that recognize that both researcher and researched are connected to each other, to the cosmos, and to the environment. I noted, for instance, that practices such as tobacco smudging among the Anishambe, one of the indigenous peoples of North America, is a way of building relationships with people and gaining their trust. Prolonged time in the field and engagement with participants is important in enhancing the credibility of a study. The assumption is that as more time is spent in the field, rapport with participants will increase, and they will volunteer different and more sensitive information than they do at the beginning of a research study. The researcher should also observe long enough to identify salient issues. Researchers know they have spent enough time in the field when information, themes, patterns, trends, and examples are repeated. When this happens, the researcher may leave the field.

Peer debriefing. The researcher should engage in discussions with peers on the procedures for the study, findings, conclusions, analysis, and hypothesis. The peer should pose searching questions to help the researcher confront her or his own values and to guide the research process. In a postcolonial indigenous paradigm, peer debriefing should also occur with research participants, who ideally should be co-researchers, and with the sages and elders of the community who are knowledgeable on the subject of discussion.

Negative case analysis. During the data analysis, it should not be expected that all cases will fit the appropriate categories. It is important to document negative cases. Lincoln and Guba (1985) state that when a "reasonable" number of cases fit, negative case analysis provides confidence in the hypothesis that is being proposed. Working hypotheses can be revised based on the discovery of cases that do not fit.

Progressive subjectivity. Researchers should monitor their own developing constructions and document the process of change from the beginning of the study until it ends. The researcher can share this statement of beliefs with the peer debriefers, who may be research participants, elders of the community, or sages; peers can challenge the researcher who has not kept an open mind but found only what was expected from the beginning.

Member checks. This is the most important criterion in establishing credibility. The researcher must verify with research participants the themes and patterns that are developing as a result of data collected and analyzed. Member checks can be formal and informal. For example, at the end of an interview, the researcher can summarize what has been said and ask if the notes accurately reflect the person's position. Drafts of the research reports can be shared with members for comments.

Triangulation

Triangulation is another strategy for enhancing the credibility of a study. It is based on the assumption that the use of multiple methods, data sources, or investigators can eliminate biases in a study. There are various ways of triangulating data. Among them are methodological triangulation, investigator triangulation, triangulation of data sources, and theoretical triangulation (Krefting, 1991).

Methodological triangulation. This refers to the comparison of data collected by various means, for example, data from structured interviews, talk circles, observations, diaries, documents, oral literature, storytelling, songs, language, proverbs and metaphors, and artifacts.

Triangulation of data sources. This is based on the importance of varying the times during which events are observed, space where they are observed, and participants in the study.

Triangulation of investigators. Triangulation of investigators occurs when more than one researcher participates in the study. The assumption is that the team members bring a diversity of approaches that help to investigate the phenomena from multiple perspectives. Commonalities in their interpretations make a strong case for the credibility of the findings. Collaboration of two or more researchers, one Western and others indigenous or local, can enhance the credibility of a study.

Theoretical triangulation. This refers to the comparison of ideas from different theoretical perspectives, including indigenous knowledge theories that inform conceptual frameworks, the design of interview guides, data analysis, and interpretation.

Referential Adequacy

In qualitative research, the researcher is the measurement tool, and the trustworthiness of the human instrument has to be established. Mathew B. Miles and Michael Huberman (1984) have suggested that the trustworthiness of the human instrument is enhanced if the following four conditions are fulfilled:

1. The researcher is familiar with the setting and phenomenon under study.
2. The researcher has a strong interest in conceptual or theoretical knowledge and has the ability to conceptualize the large amounts of qualitative data.
3. The researcher has the ability to take a multidisciplinary approach.
4. The researcher has good investigation skills.

Reflexivity

The truth-value of qualitative study is also affected by the closeness of the relationship between the research participants and the researcher, which develops during the prolonged interaction considered necessary to establish credibility (Krefting 1991). This closeness creates difficulties in separating the researchers' experiences from those of the participants. Reflexivity is a strategy to help ensure that the overinvolvement of the researcher is not a threat to the credibility of the study. Reflexivity in this context refers to the assessment of the influence of the researcher's background and ways of perceiving reality, perceptions, experiences, ideological biases, and interests during the research. The researcher is the main data collection instrument. The researcher also analyzes, interprets, and reports the findings. It is important, therefore, that the researcher's thoughts, feelings, frustrations, fears, concerns, problems, and ideas are recorded throughout the study.

Qualitative researchers keep a record of these observations in journals. A journal serves as a diary that records all events that affect the way the study is conducted, analysis is made, interpretation is reached, and conclusions are made. You may wonder about the exact nature of information recorded and how it is used in writing the research report. Following is a checklist on some of the information that you may find useful to record after an interview session. The checklist is by no means exhaustive.

Post Interview Impressions

1. What was the emotional tone—laughter, sadness, anger, and so on? If expressed, what was the context, for example, what was the interviewee/s talking about? Any sudden change in emotional tone? If so, when?

2. Difficult or easy interview to conduct? In what sense?

3. What was your relationship with the interviewee/s? How did you get on with them? How do you think they saw you? Did they ask questions about you? If so what?

4. Were there any difficult or embarrassing moments during the study (for you and/or the interviewees). If so, what?

5. Did anything surprise you in the data collected, for example, unanticipated turns or raising of unfamiliar issues?

6. Did you face any ethical dilemmas?

Responses from these questions can be used to report on methodological reflections and challenges in a study.

Transferability

Transferability is the equivalent of external validity in quantitative research. Quantitative researchers randomly select representative samples from populations so they can generalize findings to the target populations. Qualitative researchers focus on situational unique cases, and generalization of findings is not always necessary. A biographical study, for example, might represent one life perspective not transferable to any other life situation. In contrast, in an ethnographic study, the researcher might wish to generalize or transfer findings to similar situations. Transferability of research findings in qualitative research can be enhanced through sampling and dense description of the setting of the study. In qualitative research, small samples are selected purposively. The researcher selects participants who are knowledgeable on the topic under study to build a sample that is specific to the needs of the study. There are, nevertheless, a variety of purposive sampling strategies that can be used.

Snowball sampling. In this approach, the researcher selects a few participants who have the information that is important for the study. These selected participants help identify others who they believe have knowledge or information on the phenomenon under study. Take, for example, sages or elders in the community who are vested with indigenous knowledge.

Intensity sampling. Sites or individuals are selected in which the phenomenon of interest is strongly represented.

Homogenous sampling. In this approach, selected participants are very similar in experience, perspective, or outlook. This approach is used when the intention of the researcher is to describe the experiences of subgroups of people who share similar characteristics.

Random purposive sampling. This involves randomly selecting from a group of participants who were identified because of their knowledge in the researcher's area of interest. The approach is used when too many participants are selected purposively for all to be included in the sample.

Dense description. Sampling alone does not provide enough information for those who read the research study to decide if findings are applicable to other settings. The researcher must provide dense background information about the research participants, research context, and setting so that those reading the study can determine if there are similar settings to which findings of the study can be applicable or transferable.

Dependability

Dependability is the equivalent of reliability in quantitative research. In qualitative research, the notion of reliability, where emphasis is on replication or reoccurrence of behavior under observation, is problematic because human behavior is never static. Moreover, qualitative research seeks to study the uniqueness of these human occurrences. Replication is not feasible or defensible in qualitative research. Rather, the important question is whether the results are consistent with the data collected. Variability is thus expected, and consistency is defined in terms of dependability. Dependability may be enhanced by using a number of strategies such as dense description of methods used in conducting the study and triangulation. These are described under credibility of the study. Other methods include stepwise replication technique and code-recode procedure.

Stepwise replication. In this procedure, two researchers or teams analyze the data separately and compare results.

Code-recode. The researcher codes data, waits a week or two, and recodes the data to see if the results will be the same.

Confirmability

Confirmability is the equivalent of objectivity in quantitative research. It refers to the extent to which findings in a study can be traced to data derived from the informants and the research settings, and not to the researcher's biases. Some of the strategies for enhancing confirmability, namely, reflexivity and triangulation, are discussed under credibility. Another important strategy is auditing. The strategy involves an external auditor following through the steps in the progression of a research study to try and understand how and why decisions were made. Auditability also implies that another researcher could arrive at comparable conclusions, given the same data and research context. Table 6.1 summarizes the strategies with which to establish trustworthiness in qualitative research and the criteria for each strategy.

VALIDITY: A POSTCOLONIAL INDIGENOUS FRAMEWORK

As noted in Chapter 1 and Chapter 4, an ethics theory built on relationships and responsibilities to the researched informs every aspect of the postcolonial indigenous research process, from choice of topic and data collection instruments to data analysis and dissemination of findings. In other words, "every research activity is an exercise in ethics" (Clegg & Slife 2009, p. 24). Validity with a postcolonial critique framework starts with a call for recognition of conceptual frameworks, theoretical frameworks, and data collection and analysis methods derived from the researched's frames or reference and indigenous knowledge. In this context, validity is the researcher's responsibility to go beyond banked book research methodologies to imagine other possibilities, to accommodate the researched's ways of knowing, and to wish for the researched what we would wish for ourselves. Concepts of fairness, ontological authenticity, educative authenticity, catalytic authenticity, and tactical authenticity, as well as positionality, voice, critical subjectivity, or self-reflexivity (Guba & Lincoln, 2005), resonate with postcolonial indigenous perspectives of validity.

Fairness. This can be described as a quality of balance that enables all participants' and stakeholders' views, perspectives, claims, concerns, and voices to be visible in the research texts. Omission of the views of any one of those involved becomes a form of marginalization or a way of silencing them.

Table 6.1   Summary of Strategies With Which to Establish Trustworthiness

Strategy	Criteria
Credibility	Prolonged and varied field experience
	Triangulation
	Member checking
	Peer examination
	Referential adequacy
	Reflexivity (Field journal)
Transferability	Sampling
	Dense description
Dependability	Dependability audit
	Dense description of research methods
	Stepwise replication
	Triangulation
	Peer examination
	Code-recode procedure
Confirmability	Confirmability audit
	Triangulation
	Reflexivity

Source: Adapted from L. Krefting (1991), "Rigor in Qualitative Research: The Assessment of Trustworthiness," *American Journal of Occupational Therapy, 45*(3), 214–222. Used by permission of The American Occupational Therapy Association.

Catalytic and tactical authenticities. In this strategy, a given inquiry is able to prompt action on the part of the research participants; the researcher/evaluator is involved in training participants in specific forms of social and political action, if the participants desire such training. The ethical theory for postcolonial indigenous research paradigm begins with assumptions about the research participants as co-researchers; thus, it assumes some level of involvement, which may require training of the researcher by the research participants or vice versa.

Ontological and educative authenticity. This criterion determines a raised level of awareness, in the first instance, by individual research participants and, in the second, by individuals about those who surround them or with whom they come into contact for some social or organizational purpose. In a postcolonial indigenous research paradigm, research is defined as ceremony (Wilson, 2008), and each activity in the ceremony is marked by acknowledging relationships that people have with each other and the environment, as well as the moral and spiritual-based obligation that they have for each other, the community, and the environment at large.

Positionality or standpoint judgments. Standpoint judgments are informed by standpoint theory. The main argument in standpoint theory is that knowledge is always referenced to some standpoint argument (Thompson & Gitlin, 1995). What counts as knowledge is tied to the interests and perceived purposes of knowledge of different interest groups.

Specific communities and research sites as arbiters of quality. Methods such as the participatory rural appraisal require researchers to learn from the communities and initiate a participatory approach in which research participants and other members of the community make judgments on the quality and accuracy of the analysis and interpretation of the data that is gathered. In addition, communities have established ethics guidelines that guide the research process and define quality standards. Developing countries and indigenous communities have also come up with their own ethics review boards and ethical guidelines. The Maori, for instance, have *Guidelines for Research and Evaluation with Maori* (Ministry of Social Development, 2004); in Australia, the aborigines have the *Mi'kinaw Research Principles and Protocols* (Aboriginal Research Centre, 2005).

Voice. This criterion indicates the extent to which a text has polyvocality. In more participatory forms of research, voice includes a researcher's voice in the text, letting research participants speak for themselves, either in text form or through plays, forums, town meetings, or other oral and performance-oriented media communications forms designed by research participants themselves (Guba & Lincoln, 2005). In Chapter 5, for example, I discussed how some forms of oral literature, such as folklores and stories, speak about the histories of the indigenous people. What are the multiple ways in which indigenous methodologies give voice to the colonized and the historically marginalized? What are the multiple ways through which interview transcripts can be reproduced to preserve the voices of research participants? Some research participants, as we observed in Chapter 4, want their names in the research reports.

Critical subjectivity or self-reflexivity. Shulamit Reinharz (1992) discusses three selves that researchers bring into the research process: the research-based self; brought selves, which historically, socially, and personally create our standpoints; and situationally created selves. She argues that each of these selves comes into play in the research inquiry and has a distinctive voice. The postcolonial indigenous research paradigm requires the researcher to critically reflect on self as knower, redeemer, colonizer, and transformative healer.

▌ ACCOUNTABILITY, RESPECTFUL REPRESENTATION, RECIPROCITY, AND RIGHTS AND RESPONSIBILITIES

In Chapter 4, it was noted that an ethics theory in a relational postcolonial indigenous paradigm contributes to the debate on ethical research by adding the four Rs of relational accountability, respectful representation, reciprocal appropriation, and rights and responsibilities. A postcolonial indigenous perspective requires an analysis of social contexts that involve specific attention to conditions of social injustices. The researcher has to pay attention to issues of concern to the colonized researched and those who are disadvantaged, to the history of the researched, to the history of the methods used, and to the literature on the colonized researched. The researcher has to move the research from deficit- and damage-centered research to investigation that builds communities and restores hope and belief in their capabilities to resolve challenges that they encounter. Postcolonial indigenous ethical theory borrows from appreciative inquiry perspectives (Reed, 2006), desire-centered research perspectives (Tuck, 2009), and positive psychology to focus on the strengths of communities, reveal the positive aspects of resilience and the acts of resistance, and the survivance needed for social change. Postcolonial indigenous ethical theory defines research as respectful when it benefits the participants. This requires that research participants play a pivotal role in making decisions on the research to be conducted, the research questions to be addressed, the analysis of the data, and the dissemination of findings. Refer back to Chapter 4.

Within communities of the colonized, there are wide variations in age, socioeconomic background, sexual orientation, ethnicity, health, ableness, language spoken, and so on. The postcolonial indigenous perspective includes efforts to interrogate and include in the research process all dimensions of diversity in order to give appropriate representation in accordance with the spirit of relational ontology. A postcolonial indigenous ethical theory recognizes power sharing within diversity as an integral part of fairness and social justice and as a means to challenge power structures in order to transform lives. Research must interrogate power dimensions that arise between the researcher and the researched; power that comes with the choice of methods or techniques used in a study; power that comes with academic discourse; power that comes with the unfortunate Western ideology that sees the world in binary opposites of colonizer/colonized, first world/third/fourth world; and power that comes from archival literature, which in most cases is informed by deficit- and damage-centered research.

You are encouraged to use the four Rs to evaluate the ethical theory from a postcolonial indigenous perspective in the studies discussed. As you read this chapter, you will learn about context specific indigenous-based ethics, standards, and criteria for defining and evaluating the validity or credibility of data collection, analysis, and interpretation of research findings. A methodology is good only if stakeholders, research participants, and policymakers are convinced of the rigor in the research process as well as the authenticity of the research findings. What follows is a discussion of the regional, national, and local specific postcolonial indigenous research methodologies. The methodologies bring with them non-present possibilities and complexities of validity.

KAUPAPA MAORI RESEARCH METHODOLOGY

What is Kaupapa Maori research? Kaupapa Maori research encompasses the different sets of ideas and issues that are claimed as being important in doing culturally safe, sensitive, and relevant research in the Maori community (Bishop, 2008a, b; Smith, 1999, 2008). *Kaupapa* literally means a Maori way or philosophy, a term used to describe traditional Maori ways of doing, being, and thinking encapsulated in a Maori worldview or cosmology (Henry & Pene, 2001).

Kaupapa Maori research has been defined as "research that is culturally safe, that involves the mentorship of *kaumātua* that is culturally relevant and appropriate, while satisfying the rigor of research undertaken by a Maori researcher, not a researcher who happens to be Maori" (Irwin, 1994). Russell Bishop (2008a, b) frames the discourse on Kaupapa Maori research in the context of the Treaty of Waitangi and discusses Kaupapa Maori research as a research that address the ideologies of Western culturally superiority. Marewa Glover (1997) describes Kaupapa Maori as "a desire to recover and reinstate *mautaranga* Maori, the indigenous system that was in place before colonization" (p. 3). Kaupapa Maori as a theory is also discussed as a localized critical theory (Smith, 1999); it "is a local theoretical positioning that is the modality through which the emancipatory goal of critical theory, in a specific historical, political, and social context, is practiced" (Smith 2000, p. 229). It is further described as a social project that "weaves in and out of Maori cultural beliefs and values, Western forms of education, Maori aspirations and values, Western forms of education, Maori aspirations and socioeconomic needs, and Western economies and global structures" (Smith, 2000, p. 233).

According to Smith (2000), Kaupapa Maori research can be summarized as research that (1) is related to being Maori, (2) is connected to Maori philosophy, (3) takes for granted the validity and legitimacy of Maori language and culture, and (4) is concerned with the struggle for autonomy of the Maori. Six principles that guide Kaupapa Maori research are outlined as follows:

1. *(tino) rangatiratanga* (relative autonomy principle)
2. *Taonga tuku iho* (cultural aspirations principle)
3. *Ako Maori* (culturally preferred pedagogy)
4. *Kia piki ake i nga raruraru o te kainga* (mediation of socioeconomic and home difficulties principles)
5. *Whanau* (extended family structure principle)
6. *Kaupapa* (collective vision, philosophical principle)

What follows is a discussion of *Te Matahauariki: The Creative Relationship Framework* (Parr, 2002), which is used by the Te Matahauriki Institute "to research and understand Maori culture both in a traditional sense, and also as an evolving, dynamic expression of identity" (p. 2). It is a methodology employed by Te Matahauriki as it attempted to identify and analyze those fundamental Maori concepts, philosophies, beliefs, values, customs, ethics, and practices that inform Maori law and jurisprudence (Parr, 2002, p. 4). The Te Matahauriki program objective is

a contribution to an intellectual climate to realize a vision of socially inclusive laws and political and legal institutions in Aotearoa/New Zealand derived from two polyphyletic traditions, which will have sufficient flexibility and robustness to meet the future needs of citizens of Aotearoa/New Zealand as individuals and as collectivities. (Parr, 2002, p. 4)

What follows is a brief discussion of the processes, selection of participants, their role, and the principles that guide the methodology.

The Process and Methods of the Creative Relationship Framework

Identifying the literature. Research was undertaken on a variety of sources for implicit and explicit and operational definitions and operational examples of Maori jurisprudence (Benton, 1999).

Consultation with Te Pu Wanangu (skilled or wise person). Seminars were held with key individuals, experts in *tikanga* (the correct way of doing things), and scholars both Maori and Pakeha (white New Zealanders).

Selection of participants. Benton (cited in Parr, 2002) describes the *Te Pu Wananga* as follows:

> They have been gifted with a long life (the majority being in their 70s and 80s). Their memory and knowledge of Maori culture and their reflections on where to go from here span more than four generations, starting with knowledge of their own mentors—their own parents, grandparents and other elders—and now in their position as *tohunga kaumātua*, parents and grandparents or great-grandparents themselves, their younger kinsfolk look up to them for advice and wisdom. (p. 5)

Conducting the seminars. A series of semistructured, in-depth, participant-driven discussions are conducted in a series of seminars. Participation and seminar discussions are guided by the four principles of the creative relationships framework: (1) intention and reflexivity, (2) rapport—formation of research relationships, (3) *utu* reciprocity, and (4) the reiterative process.

Intention and reflexivity. This refers to the ability of those participating in the seminar discussion to do self-research that enables them to understand their own context. In addition, participants also have to be able to transverse their own culture and that of others. Parr (2002) notes,

> Closely related to the ability to reflect upon oneself and the enriched understanding ensuing from such reflections is the ability to traverse both cultures. Until you are comfortable with your own culture and secure in your understanding of it, arriving at a worthwhile understanding of another culture will be problematic. For a creative relationship, to also be cross-cultural, what is necessary are the skills to operate effectively within both cultures and across cultures in an

inter-disciplinary capacity. In order to experience this, a researcher must have a solid understanding of themselves, their own culture, beliefs, values and epistemologies. Only then can a proper understanding of another culture be attempted. (p. 12)

Knowing oneself in terms of the social, cultural, and political context in which the research is conducted has become an important topic of discussion, with various procedures suggested for self-research (Cram, 2009; Mertens, 2009, 2010a; Symonette 2004). One of the procedures on self-research is built around the Johari window, not indigenous to non-Westerners (Mertens, 2009). Remember that it may be counterproductive to reject applicable Western ideas simply because they originate from the West. The Johari window is discussed as an example of a research procedure borrowed from the West that can enhance the process of self-research that is critical in relational ethics theory in indigenous research.

The Johari window developed by Joseph Luft and Harr Ingham in the 1950s is used as a model to understand and teach self-awareness for personal development and to improve communications, interpersonal relationships, group dynamics, team development, and intergroup relationships. Anne Bell (2001) modified the Johari window to enhance self-awareness, and Donna Mertens (2009) modified the context and probing questions to fit research and evaluation contexts. A graphic representation of the Johari window used by Bell (2001, cited in Mertens, 2009, p. 78) is illustrated in Box 6.1.

Box 6.1: Johari Window

	Things I know about myself	Thing I don't know about myself
Things others know about me	Open area	Blind area
Things others don't know	Hidden area	Unknown area

Mertens explains each quadrant and the self-awareness questions as follows:

The open area. One's comfort zone, it allows for personal growth, self-disclosure, and receiving feedback from others. She suggests the following questions to expand one's open area.

- How open am I about my own processes of learning about social justice and my own socialization?
- What kinds of things about myself do I share easily with others?
- How do I use myself and my experience in my research?
- What is open for discussion in my interactions with others?

The hidden area. It represents self-knowledge about which a person is conscious but which they choose not to disclose to others. People in relationships can decide on what they choose not to disclose by asking the following questions, suggested by Bell (cited in Mertens, 2009):

- What do I avoid disclosing about myself? Why?
- What are my motivations for not disclosing certain things?
- What do I hide that I might disclose?
- What do I hide that I think could interfere with good research or evaluation? Is my rationale clear and conscious?

Blind area. Having the potential to impede good working relationships, this area contains cultural beliefs and prejudices about others that have been normalized as a result of socialization. Bell (cited in Mertens, 2009) suggests the following questions:

- What am I likely to not perceive due to my own socialization positioning?
- What have I learned that was previously in my blind area?
- How open am I to feedback, and how do I respond when others give me feedback?
- What important insights/learning have I gained from inviting feedback in the past?

The unknown area. This is the area that the person and those with whom they are working are aware of; it represents unexplored area. Bell (cited in Mertens, 2009) suggests questions to ask in this area as follows:

- What was previously unknown to me and (to others) which I now know about myself?
- How did I become aware of this?
- What other puzzles intrigue me and call me to further exploration?

These self-awareness questions can be used to guide the principle of self-questioning in the creative relationships framework.

Source: Mertens, D. M. (2009). *Transformative research and evaluation.* New York: The Guilford Press. Used by permission.

Rapport: Formation of research relationships. Rapport expresses a state of harmony between people through relationship and connection (Parr, 2002). It requires mutual respect and trust, generosity, affection, and enjoyment of the other's company, and it is enhanced by face-to-face interaction, involvement in the community, and other personal interactions. The method also requires that "the researchers prove their genuineness, worthiness, integrity appropriateness, and any number of characteristics that may be desired by research subjects" (Parr, 2002, p. 15).

Utu *reciprocity.* Looks at the sorts of things that are reciprocated. Parr (2002) notes that through reciprocity, a feeling of connectedness is created. Connectedness removes the need for empowerment, feelings of separateness or distance, and the need to be in charge.

The reiterative process. Reciprocity is manifested through the reiterative process. The reiterative process is "one of many journeys between participants—journeys that shape and enhance the venture that lies between them" (Parr, 2002, p. 20). The process entails recycling descriptions and emerging analysis and conclusions. Transcripts created from the seminars are taken back to the participants for comment and analysis; and every participant is free to indicate any material that they may not wish to be disclosed publicly. The reiterative process principles are as follows:

1. The names of all those present at the seminar are recorded and indicated at the beginning of the transcript.
2. Transcribing begins immediately after the seminar.
3. The speaker's own words should be faithfully transcribed, omitting repetitions but refraining from correcting grammar or polishing styles.
4. In the transcription, the nature of gaps should always be indicated within square brackets, for example: [inaudible], [too many people talking at once], [interruption], [pause].
5. The transcript is thoroughly reviewed by the research team as soon as possible.
6. Words are added only when necessary to provide links or clarify meaning.
7. Thereafter, the transcript is given back to participants.
8. The participants have ample time to comment on the transcript.
9. The participants must validate the transcript as an accurate account of what they said and want to say.
10. In all matters of doubt or dispute, the speaker's decision must be accepted as final.
11. Senior members of the team are required to carefully consider all suggestions from participants.

12. Thematic analysis is then carried out on the transcripts.
13. Themes identified are taken back to participants for comment.
14. Options for future participation are discussed.

Ethical Issues in the Creative Relationship Framework

The creative relationship framework discusses the following ethical issues:

Subjective responsibility of the researcher. The researcher must be genuine and committed to the participants and the ongoing relationship formed with them. The researcher has to be constantly self-questioning to reflect on how factors such as age, gender, social class, ethnicity, or race may limit holistic understanding of issues in the study.

Objective responsibility. The researcher should remain committed to sound quality research and ensure that "all genuine interests are served by honest, robust research generated through meticulous attention to detail, personal integrity, and a real commitment to co-participants" (Parr, 2002, p. 25).

Participants' responsibility. Participants define their role during the course of the research.

Participants and consent. Participants have a right to an informed consent. They are informed of the purpose of the study, the anticipated consequences of the research, the identity of funders and sponsors, the anticipated uses of material gathered, the possible benefits of the investigation, and the degree of anonymity and confidentiality that would be afforded participants. The issue of consent in the creative relationship framework is ongoing and is defined by "the context and circumstances of the relationship as much as by the participant themselves" (Parr, 2002, p. 27).

Mutual respect and reciprocity. A *koha* is laid down as an acknowledgment that both sides have power during the process. The laying down of the *koha* remains "a powerful recognition of the right of others to self determination" (Parr, 2002, p. 28). The creative relationship framework clearly shows validity concepts that are anchored in roles and responsibilities of the researcher to the researched as well as responsibilities of the researched to one another. Offering *koha* is recognition of power sharing and responsibilities that connect all those involved in the research process.

Activity 6.1

Discuss the data collection, methods, sampling procedures, and data analysis and ethics in the creative relationship framework methodology and illustrate how this methodology is a space where assumptions about the nature of reality, knowledge, and values informed by a postcolonial indigenous research paradigm converge with theory and practice on the given topic.

▮ CYCLICAL POSTCOLONIAL INDIGENOUS RESEARCH METHODOLOGIES: THE MEDICINE WHEEL

Postcolonial indigenous scholars emphasize the circular and cyclical nature of methodologies embedded in postcolonial indigenous cultures. This circular and cyclical characteristic emerges from a worldview that recognizes the interconnectedness and interdependence of all things and from the integration of spiritual beliefs, values, and experience as valid ways of coming to know a reality. "Seeking truth and coming to know necessitates studying the cycles, relationships and connections between things" (Sefa Dei et al., 2002, p. 9). In this context, communications with the natural world and ancestors, as well as knowing that comes through dreams, visions, and intuitions, form an integral part of the research process (Walker, 2001). Polly Walker (2001), a Cherokee woman, discusses a cyclical indigenous methodology that draws from the Medicine Wheel.

> The Indigenous paradigm that underlies my research emphasizes the interconnectedness of all things. It is both ancient and modern and expressed through the American Indian Medicine Wheel. The Medicine Wheel Paradigm encompasses a holistic integration of humans and the natural world, including all beings, processes and creations. In this paradigm, the Four Directions, or Four Grandfathers, represent a complex system of knowledge. The following introductory explanation illuminates the research I conducted within this paradigm.

> As a Cherokee woman using methodologies based on the Medicine Wheel, I integrated all aspects of human experience represented on the Wheel. In the Medicine Wheel methodology, the East represents

the Spiritual aspects of experience. In the East, researchers acknowledge their interconnectedness with the research participants and the wider community. Research from the Eastern position integrates a wide range of senses in coming to know. The South represents the Natural World. In the South, researchers honor and utilize emotional experience, speaking from the heart with authenticity. The West represents the bodily aspects of knowing. In the West, researchers are encouraged to go within themselves, discovering what is important in relation to the connections between self, others, nature and traditional teachings (Bopp et al., 1989). The North represents the mental processes of balancing intellect with wisdom. In the North, researchers work within the community to find solutions that are balanced and restore harmony to the community as a whole (Huber, 1993: 358–360; Bopp et al., 1989). (pp. 18–21; excerpt used by permission.)

Maria Gonzalez (2000), illustrates the cyclical approach in ethnography by employing the four seasons of spring, summer, autumn, and winter. Gonzalez notes that the four-seasons strategy is "my attempt to reformulate the task of ethnography, as it might be viewed through the methodology of a circular ontology, as experienced and often expressed by Native American Indian culture" (p. 626). The researcher's activities in the field are illustrated by employing metaphors that communicate indigenous communities' activities during the four seasons. The methodology of circular ontology describes the role of the ethnographer in the field; the methods, activities, and procedures to be followed; and the possible threats to knowledge production using the four seasonal activities as metaphors to guide the process. The methods and procedures correspond to the conventional process in ethnography, namely, gaining entry, collecting data, compiling data for analysis, and writing the report. The use of the Medicine Wheel and the four seasons as guiding frameworks in the ontology of connectedness illustrate relationships, the cyclical nature of all experiences, and the way this can inform a research process grounded on indigenous knowledge.

The East. In the Medicine Wheel methodology, the East represents the spiritual aspects of experience. The aboriginal perspective sees the earth as alive, thinking, creating, cautioning, offering a new humane alternative, and responding to kindness, respect, prayers; this view requires researchers to respect the rituals performed in coming to know a reality. Stories, songs, prayers, and rituals are meaningful sources of understanding the researched, individually and collectively (Battiste, 2000). The East is also the direction of spring and a place of beginning. In Gonzalez's (2000) creation-centered ontology of ethnography, the spring is the time when an ethnographer can prepare for what is ahead. Preparation cannot begin until permission to do the research is given. It is a time in which the human instrument is being prepared for fieldwork. Walker (2001) notes that in the East, researchers acknowledge their interconnectedness with research participants and the wider community, integrating a wide range of senses in coming to know.

The South. The South represents the natural world and is the direction of summer (Battiste, 2000; Gonzalez, 2000; Walker, 2001). It requires knowledge, understanding, appreciation, and utilization of indigenous peoples' languages, metaphors, symbols, characters, stories, teachers, and teachings. In the South, researchers honor and use emotional experience, speaking from the heart with authenticity. This methodology requires the ethnographer's deep involvement with the culture:

> The skilled ethnographer in the field learns to believe in the circle of time, and in the inevitability of changes. If there is too much focus on one's specific experience, the product of ethnography will be narrow and non-holistic. It will not capture the essence of the culture. Rather, each and every experience within the culture is an example of the whole culture. (Gonzalez, 2000, p. 642)

The West. West is the direction of autumn and represents the bodily aspects of knowing. In the West, researchers are encouraged to go within themselves, discovering what is important in relation to the connections between self, others, nature, and traditional teachings (Bopp, Bopp, Brown, & Lane, 1989).

The North. North is the direction of winter and represents the mental processes of balancing intellect with wisdom. In the North, researchers work within the community to find solutions that are balanced and restore harmony to the community as a whole (Bopp et al., 1989; Huber, 1993, pp. 358–360). Researchers take up their responsibilities as transformative healers and make a conscious effort to work with the communities to bring about change.

❚ THE AFROCENTRIC PARADIGM

Afrocentricity is a worldview whose origin is attributed to Molefi Kete Asante's works, *Afrocentricity* (1988b), *The Afrocentric Idea* (1988a), and *Kemet, Afrocentricity, and Knowledge* (1990). This perspective places the

African ways of perceiving reality, ways of knowing, and value systems on equal footing with other scholarly examinations of human experience. It is an African-centered worldview, which establishes a conceptual framework for how the world is seen and understood. It is culturally specific and draws on African philosophical and theoretical assumptions and serves Africans, just as classical Greek civilization serves as a reference point for Europe (Diop, 1978). Drawing from the Afrocentric paradigm, Asante (1990) came up with three basic beliefs that guide the research process. Ruth Reviere (2001) has summarized these as follows:

- Researchers must hold themselves responsible for uncovering hidden, subtle, racist theories that may be embedded in current methodologies.
- Researchers must work to legitimize the centrality of African ideals, values as valid frames of reference for acquiring and examining data.
- Researchers maintain inquiry rooted in strict interpretation of place.

According to Reviere (2001), the insistence on a clear definition of space is the central distinguishing characteristic. An Afrocentric inquiry must be executed from a clearly defined Afrocentric place and must include a clear description of this location (Reviere 2001). Queeneth Mkabela (2005) added that an African-centered methodology focuses on Africa as the cultural center for the study of African experiences and interprets data from an African perspective. She went on to say that Afrocentrists argue for pluralism in philosophical views, without hierarchy. All cultural centers are to be respected, and thus, the diversity that is characteristic of Africa is accommodated as the researcher shifts from one cultural space to another. Eboni Baugh and Lisa Guion (2006) argue that although Afrocentric methodology is suggested for use with Africans and people of African descent, it can also serve as a guide for research with other marginalized groups and indigenous peoples because it addresses issues pertinent to most formerly colonized societies. The Afrocentric method and methodologies require researchers to develop relationships with the researched, to reaffirm those relationships, and to use methods that may not be conventional for use with Western populations; the approach is collaborative, allowing the community to participate and provide input during all stages of the research process (Baugh & Guion, 2006).

Culture and the Afrocentric Methodologies

The Nile Valley civilization is considered to be the geographic and historical foundation of cultural commonalities derived and shared among the continent's approximately 6,000 tribes and countless descendants (Ramsey,

2006). Asante (1987, 1990) is credited with identifying *Ma'at* and *Nommo*, extracted from the Nile Valley civilization, as the two principles intrinsic to African cultures. *Ma'at* is the quest for justice, truth, and harmony and, in the context of research, refers to interrogating the manner in which the research process is in harmony with the culture of the people and pursues issues of truth and justice. *Nommo* describes the creation of knowledge as a vehicle for improvement in human life and human relations (Reviere, 2001, p. 711). Seven cardinal virtues—truth, justice, rightness, propriety, harmony, order and balance, and reciprocity—are derived from *Ma'at* and *Nommo*. These, together with conceptions of reality based on *ubuntu*, should provide a code of conduct and a standard of aspiration for ethical and moral behavior. What follows is a discussion of important *ubuntu* components that should inform relational ways of perceiving and knowing reality.

Religiosity

Spirituality is an important component of *Ubuntu*. Desmond Tutu, explaining Ubuntu, notes that *Ubuntu* is an organic relationship between people such that when we see another we should recognize ourselves and God in whose image all people are made. Elsewhere, I note (Chilisa, 2005) that our understanding of humanness or reality—in Botswana, for example—is influenced by our connectedness to the earth (*lefatshe*) and all its inhabitants, including animals, birds, plants, and the spirits (*Badimo*). I note that this connectedness is embraced and celebrated through taboos and totems. Batswana see the human and physical world as one and self and world as one; separating them from their traditional conceptions of God can deplete their source of knowledge as a people (Tournas, 1996, p. 43). The existence of being and behavior is not easily separated from the supernatural and nature. People do not live a simple existence made up of hierarchies; rather, they are embedded in a web of relations and interconnectedness that extends to nonliving things. Understanding this type of reality requires a back and forth movement that connects to this web of relations. In Chapter 4, totems of the Bakalanga of Botswana were illustrated and their relevance to the research process discussed.

Ubuntu and Respect for Self and Other Through Consensus Building

In the *ubuntu* context, to exist is to respect others and oneself. Ubuntu embraces the importance of agreement and consensus (Louw, 2001).

In African traditional culture, when issues are discussed at the *Kgotla* (community gathering space), there may be a hierarchy of importance among speakers, but every person gets an equal chance to speak up until some kind of agreement, consensus, or group cohesion is reached. The role of the people in consensus building is etched in the language that guides the discussion. Agreement and consensus should, however, not be confused

> with outmoded and suspect cravings for an oppressive universal sameness . . . True *Ubuntu* takes plurality seriously. While it constitutes personhood through other persons, it appreciates the fact that other persons are so called precisely because we can ultimately never quite stand in their shoes or completely see through their eyes. When Ubuntist reads solidarity and consensus, s/he therefore also reads alterity, autonomy and cooperation. (Louw, 2001, p. 6)

Ubuntu and the Other: Respect for Particularity, Individuality, and Historicity

Ubuntu respects particularity, individuality, and historicity (Louw, 2001). In the *ubuntu* ethical framework, "we expose ourselves to others to encounter the difference of their humanness so as to inform and enrich our own" (Sindane, 1994, pp. 8–9). *Ubuntu* incorporates dialogue, preserving the Other in their Otherness, in their uniqueness, without letting the Other slip into distance. It embraces a perception of the Other that is never fixed or rigidly closed but adjustable or open ended. According to Louw (1994), when the *Ubuntu* read consensus, they also read open-endedness, contingency, and flux.

Self-Determination and Rebirth

Ubuntu has survived colonialism and cultural imperialism, but it still suffers marginalization by dominant Western discourses tied to market profits in a capitalist world economy. *Ubuntu*-informed research in this context is a long process of going back and forth to question subversive research practices that continue the violence and oppression of postcolonial indigenous communities. The *We* in the I/We relationship is emphasized to facilitate a rebirth of a people relegated to the lowest position in the Euro-Western scale of human hierarchy and to the fourth world in the global market economy. In ethics, the We allows us to invoke the concept of African renaissance and Africanization in research.

The African renaissance is a unique opportunity for Africans to define ourselves and our agenda according to our realities and taking into account the realities of those around us. It's about Africans being agents of history and masters of our destiny. Africa is in a transformative mode. The renaissance is about African reflection and African redefinition. (Makgoba, Shope, & Mazwai, 1999, p. xii)

Ubuntu is an inherent part of our rebirth; thus, we define our agenda taking into account the realities of those around us. Africanization refers to a process of placing the African worldview at the center of analysis (Teffo, 2000, p. 107). Validating this view, Kwesi Prah (1999) noted,

We cannot in all seriousness study ourselves through the eyes of other people's assumptions. I am not saying we must not know what others know or think of us. I am saying we must think for ourselves like others do for themselves. (p. 37)

The assertions raise questions such as who should do research among formerly colonized, historically colonized societies and in indigenous communities or culturally complex societies. Jelena Porsanger (2004), for example, noted that some extreme opinions hold that only Indigenous researchers may conduct research "on, with, and about indigenous people." Porsanger rejects this extreme view, observing that Indigenous scholars and indeed those scholars from formerly colonized societies cannot be privileged on the basis of their background because there are a great variety of insider views, some of which may not be sensitive and responsive to the needs and intents of indigenous communities. The "I am we" *ubuntu* principle makes provision for

the rationale, modulation and interconnectedness of the categories of race, class, gender, ethnicity and their respective isms . . . and all those things which Europeans and westerners see as either/or opposites, binaries, or dichotomous thinking. (Tetreault, 1993, cited in Goduka, 2000, p. 71)

From this perspective the *ubuntu* worldview addresses researchers from all worlds to see themselves first as related and connected by the same goals of commitment to build harmony among communities they study; to reciprocate by giving back to communities for what they take; and to strive for truth, justice, fairness, and inclusiveness in the construction of knowledge. A research approach informed by an *ubuntu* worldview requires researchers to contextualize conventional research methods and ethical principles, taking into consideration the history of colonialism and its effects on the formerly colonized; the culture of the African people based on Ma'at and Nommo and the seven cardinal principles of truth, justice, rightness, propriety, harmony, order and balance, and reciprocity that emanate from Ma'at, and contemporary African theorizing on Africanization and Ubuntu. What follows is an ethical framework that focuses on researcher's and researched's relationships and responsibilities of researchers. The framework is informed by the ubuntu principle of "I am we, I am because we are," Ubuntu principles of religiosity; respect for self and Other through consensus building; and respect for particularity, individuality, and historicity.

RESPONSIBILITIES OF RESEARCHER AS TRANSFORMATIVE HEALER

Ubuntu informs our construction of harmony, justice, and reciprocity as much as it is informed by *Ma'at* and *Nommo*. In discussing the responsibilities of a researcher, one has therefore to go back and forth to invoke the seven virtues of Ma'at and to explain the application of Ubuntu-based ethical relationships between them. The application of the seven virtues of *Ma'at* constructs the social scientist researcher as a transformative healer (Ramsey, 2006). The role of a transformative healer involves self-reflection and self-questioning about the researcher's responsibilities as well as relationships with others, the living and nonliving. The meaning of a transformative healer, however, has to be understood in the African context from which it emerges. In the African context, before a healer could be allowed to perform classical healing rites, he or she has to undergo intensive study of self, to understand how self is unique yet related to the whole, and to identify his or her life purpose. The healer has to be a living example of how to resolve crises, challenges, and difficulties (Ramsey, 2006). Elsewhere, I (Chilisa, 2009) have outlined the following as roles and responsibilities that a transformative healer needs in order to reflect on and make choices about what is ethical.

1. Researcher as a colonizer, researched as the colonized
2. Researcher as knower/teacher and researched as an object/subject/ known/pupil
3. Researcher as a redeemer, researched as the problem
4. Ethical responsibilities of researchers in the application of theoretical frameworks and literature review to inform the research process

I look at how each of these challenges manifests in the research process and discuss the questions that researchers who assume the responsibilities of a transformative healer need to ask themselves in order to carry out research informed by an I/We relationship.

Researcher as Colonizer, Researched as Colonized

The colonizer/colonized, researcher/researched relationships can be a starting point to begin to review events and practices in the research process so that the ethical responsibility of a healer engaged in a transformative journey is not compromised. As producers of knowledge, researchers make assumptions about the power relations between themselves and the researched, and they are consciously or unconsciously guided by these assumptions. These assumptions inform the researchers' interactions with the researched, the kind of knowledge that can be produced, and the way it can be produced. The colonizer/colonized relationship interrogates power relations with regard to researchers as privileged elites researching within and operating with Western models of thought. The concern is with Eurocentrism as a science that privileges Western ways of knowing and perceiving reality.

In this framework, postcolonial Indigenous researchers can assume many identities. They can operate at the level of colonizer co-opted by the dominant Western discourse on methodology, which uses Euro-Western standards as universal truths against which the Other, formerly colonized societies that are marginalized by globalization, are researched and written about. At another level, researchers can operate as healers, challenging and resisting the blind Euro-Western application of methodologies across all cultures. At this level, they are members of the formerly colonized and marginalized, writing about and rewriting what has been written about the Other, Others, and themselves. These multiple positions require knowledge production approaches that are multiple, interconnected, and sensitive, engaging researchers with ethical issues that position them as healers who need to heal themselves before they can assist others to heal. Researchers need to ask the following questions:

1. Whose side am I on?
2. Do I challenge and resist dominant discourses that marginalized those who suffer oppression?
3. Who am I writing about? Self or Other/s or both?
4. What needs to be rewritten?

Researcher as Knower/Teacher, Researched as Object/Subject/Known/Pupil

At another level, the power relations operate within spaces of researched as subject/object and researcher as knower. Researchers act as knowledge imperialists and colonizers when they claim authenticity of description, interpretation, and dissemination of results under the guise of scholarship and authority in the area of study. The researched become objects and "passive onlookers." In this objectification and "thingfication of people" (Loomba, 2005), researchers do not ask the researched if they agree in the way their lives are described and interpreted. bell hooks (1990) notes that, in such instances, researchers become the authoritative authors who are not sensitive to the voices of the researched but are more interested in their standing as authorities in the subject they write, a field in which the researched cannot participate. A transformative/healer reflects and raises the following questions:

1. Do the researched own a description of themselves?
2. Have the voices of the researched been captured in a way that the researched recognize themselves, know themselves, and would like others to know them?

Reviere (2001, p. 711) has proposed five canons as the criteria against which research should be judged to ensure its accuracy in reflecting the lived experiences of all people including Black people. These five canons—*ukweli* (truth), *kujitolea* (commitment), *utulivu* (calmness and peacefulness), *uhaki* (justice), and *ujamaa* (community)—are derived from the seven cardinal African virtues of truth, justice, rightness, propriety, harmony, order and balance and reciprocity, which form the basis of an Afrocentric research methodology. The five canons speak to procedures and strategies for establishing rigor in research and establishing credibility, trustworthiness, dependability, validity, and reliability as commonly known in quantitative research. *Ukweli* seeks truth grounded in people's experience. The canon of *ukweli* shifts the emphasis from objectivity to truth, fairness, and honesty and how these can be achieved. *Ukweli* requires researchers to establish whether the conclusions reached are representative of only their own position or whether they represent a consensus of the researched and other opinions. *Kujitolea* requires the researcher to emphasize how knowledge is structured and used over "the need for dispassion and objectivity" (Reviere, 2001, p. 716). *Utulivu* requires that researchers actively avoid creating, exaggerating, or sustaining divisions between or within communities, but rather strive to create harmonious relationships between and within groups. *Ujamaa* requires that theory and practice be informed by the aspirations and interests of the community, while *uhaki* requires the encouragement and maintenance of harmonious relationships between communities and groups. In addition to prolonged and substantial engagement, peer debriefing, member checks, triangulation, and reflexivity (Creswell 2009; Krefting 1991), Reviere (2001) has proposed an African-centered procedure informed by the five canons of *ukweli, uhaki, utulivu, ujamaa,* and *kujitolea.* The procedure is as follows: truth, validity, and reliability of findings from an Afrocentric perspective:

- Involve a group of self-identified Afrocentric research scholars who meet once or twice per month to discuss relevant issues uncovered by the inquiry and provide feedback on whether the inquiry and the researcher's interpretation of the data embody the principle of Afrocentrism as understood in the Afrocentric research community.
- Use the Internet and e-mail system to solicit views and critiques of African scholars worldwide.
- Initiate direct correspondence with well-established scholars, including those of Afrocentric orientation, to dialogue on the ideas and findings generated by the inquiry.
- Analyze the data from an Afrocentric perspective using the Afrocentric canons and, in addition, use one's own experience and knowledge of the subject matter, as well as consulting with the wider community for interpretation of data.

Researcher as Redeemer, Researched as the Problem

Researchers are also implicated in the imperialist agenda when they participate in the Othering of the researched through deficit discourses and theories or literature that construct the researched as the problem. Elsewhere, I (Chilisa, 2005) discuss the position of a researcher co-opted into the dominant Western deficit discourse about the historically colonized, resisting this discourse and failing because of the overwhelming literature that has normalized and constructed as facts and common sense the deficit discourse about the Other. Common among these deficit discourses is the normalized thinking that blames the devastating epidemic of HIV and AIDS on a "permissive female sexuality," a thinking perpetuated by a colonial discourse on sexuality that equated African women with animals (Chilisa, 2006; Collins, 2000). This deficit thinking and constructions about the African should propel researchers to review, critique, and think afresh the steps in carrying out research. Scholars researching non-Western societies need to ask themselves the following questions:

1. What psychological harm, humiliation, embarrassment, and other losses, if any, have these theories and body of knowledge caused the researched?
2. What is the body of indigenous knowledge of the colonized that researchers can use to counter theories and to rebut the body of knowledge that may cause humiliation and embarrassment to the researched?

These questions make it increasingly important for researchers to familiarize themselves with colonial epistemologies and their social construction of the colonized, formerly colonized, and historically oppressed groups to understand the theoretical landscape and literature within which the international community of researchers are encouraged and coerced to operate. Healers/transformative researchers should debate these theories and literature to expose the possible psychological harm and loss of whatever kind that has occurred over the years because of these theories. Postcolonial theories provide an important framework through which Western-educated researchers can explore the possible biases in the literature we read, identify the knowledge gaps that have been created because of the unidirectional borrowing of Euro-Western literature, and bring to a halt the continuing marginalization of other knowledge systems, which occurs because of the dominant Euro-Western research paradigms and their discourses on what can be researched and how it can be researched. A transformative healer needs to reflect and raise the following questions:

1. What assumptions, prejudices, stereotypes informed the review of literature?
2. How do the literature and theories reviewed portray the researched?
3. Is there any deficit thinking or theorizing in the literature reviewed?
4. What evidence is there to bring to question the literature reviewed?
5. What are the gaps in the literature?

Ethics for researchers researching in historically oppressed, formerly colonized societies should involve going back and forth to retrieve marginalized and dominant literatures to review, analyze, and challenge colonizing and deficit theorizing and interpretations and to create counternarratives that see the past differently and envision a transformative agenda for the researched. Ethics also involves defining literature and theorizing in the context of formerly colonized societies. Literature is our language: proverbs, cultural artifacts, legends, stories, practices, songs, poems, dances, tattoos, lived experiences such as our fight against HIV/AIDS, personal stories, and community stories told in weddings, funerals, celebration, wars, ritual songs and dance, and silence. In Chapter 5, it was shown how Frank Youngman (1998) and Michael Omolewa et al. (1998) used proverbs to provide an indigenous concept of lifelong learning and literacy. Bagele Chilisa and Julia Preece (2005) also show how the Batswana legend on the origin of human-kind can be used as a reference point in countering Western theorizing on gender relations and Western perceptions on African tradition and gender. In an ongoing study to examine sociocultural, family, and social influences on Batswana adolescent sexual behaviors, the investigators collected meta-phorical language and sayings such as proverbs, popular legends, community stories, songs, rituals, myths, and taboos that communicate messages on sex, sexuality, and gender relations. The collection is to provide baseline literature that enables the researchers to include African indigenous voices in framing issues on gender relations, sexuality, and adolescent behavior.

As more and more indigenous scholars and scholars from formerly colonized societies begin to make choices on what they research and to delve into areas that colonial epistemologies dismissed as sorcery, research-ers who assume their responsibilities as healers will be confronted by real limitations of Western hegemonic ethical standards, such as the principle of informed consent of the researched. A transformative healer will seek to go beyond Euro-Western research issues of power that mainly focus on the "I the researcher" and the "you the researched" to more involving I/We rela-tionships that see reality differently.

Ethics Built on a Deep Respect for Religious Beliefs and the Practices of Others

How do we study or come to understand a reality that does not separate the physical from the nonphysical? Data collection, both quantitative and qualitative, always begins with biographical information of the researched. Often, however, information is sought based on an I/You relationship, where emphasis is on the individual. Ethical protocols built on an I/We relationship would embrace biographical information that includes the researched's lin-eage and totemism, as they relate to the topic of inquiry. Totemism embraces religion and spirituality.

An I/We relationship informed by an *ubuntu* worldview requires research to be conducted with care, love for one another, empathy, and compassion that is derived from an understanding of a human nature that embraces all as created by God. Dalene Swanson (2009) reveals how the concept of "I am because we are, I am we, and we are because I am" served as a point of reference in applying the concept of reflexivity in researching school mathematics among a poor community in postapartheid Africa. The *ubuntu* worldview she argued, allowed her to disrupt and decolonize dominant deficit thinking by promoting compassion, care, togetherness, empathy, and respectful ways of doing research that allowed researchers to see themselves in the researched. An *ubuntu* worldview, from this perspective, is an African contribution to any researcher's reflexivity and critical journey into the lives of others. Julie Laible (2000) calls this way of knowing a loving epistemology. She explains it as away of knowing where the production of knowledge should include a journey of the researcher and the researched into each other's lives.

ETHICS THAT UNDERSCORES THE IMPORTANCE OF AGREEMENT AND CONSENSUS, DIALOGUE, AND PARTICULARITY

Under African eyes, an I/We relationship emphasizes respect for the self, the other, and others; it implies a unification of the self with the environment. The deontological and consequential ethical framework based on the Western mode of individualism places emphasis on a one-on-one contractual agreement where relationships between the researchers and the researched are entered through signed consent forms. An I/We relationship invites us to further ask the following questions: Whose consent is asked? Is it consent from the I, the Other, or others? Consent to do what? Is it consent to write and describe the Other and then to extrapolate or generalize the written story to the rest of the community, even though its members were not involved? The consent under Euro-Western eyes carries with it a desperate hidden desire to make the I speak for those whose consent has not been sought. In the I/We relationship, if it is made known to the researched that the consent includes allowing the researcher to use the researched to speak for others, the story would be different for it would be told from multiple perspectives.

In the I/We relationship, consent agreements would invoke consensus arrived at through circles of discussion where membership is informed by the intricate web of connections that are the basis of relationships based on I/We principles. In Botswana, for example, even after an institutional review board gives consent that research can be carried out, the researcher has to consult with the chief of the village, who in turn calls the people to a village council to deliberate on an issue and reach a consensus. If the researcher is allowed to do the research, then she or he may visit households to interview the identified key informants and still have to ask for individual and group consent. In an African setting, a husband may seek the views of his wife and children before he consents to speak. In most cases, people will decline to speak on behalf of family members, preferring everyone in the family who is affected to participate in the dialogue. From the I/We relationship emanate four types of consent: individual consent, community consent, group consent, and collective consent. Mkabela (2005) refers to the process as collective ethics and concludes that when collective ethics is translated into the research process, it would include:

- An appreciation of the importance of individuals in the research group
- An understanding that research is part of a very complex (community) whole
- Respect for heritage authority
- The inclusion of elders and cultural committees in the research process
- An understanding of the interconnectedness of all things (including the spiritual) and required long-term perspective in dealing with research issues.
- An understanding that researchers must act in an appropriate way and respectful way to maintain the harmony and balance of the group (community).

The Afrocentric methodology reveals data collection methods and ethic protocols based on the principles of respect for the I and the Other, researcher responsibilities, connectedness, togetherness, social justice, and harmony as embodied in the I/We relationship principle. The *Mmogo* method (Roos, 2008) is an example of connectedness and togetherness-informed methods. It derives its name from the Setswana word, *Mmogo*. Setswana is one of the indigenous languages of southern Africa. The word *Mmogo* means "relatedness, co-ownership, togetherness, co-construction and interpersonal threads" (Roos, 2008, p. 660). The method uses visual images as key to meaning making. An extract on the Mmogo method procedures follows.

Activity 6.2

Read the extract on the method and answer the questions that follow:

1. In what ways does the Mmogo method depart from Western social science research preoccupations, with the individual as the social unit of focus?

2. How are the networks and relations of people with each other and the environment brought into focus through this method?

3. Discuss fairness, catalytic and tactical authenticities, voice, and reciprocity in the context of the Mmogo method.

Source: V. Roos (2008), "The Mmogo–Method: Discovering Symbolic Community Interactions," *Journal of Psychology in Africa, 18*(4) 659–668.

Research design

The Mmogo method is best applied in explorative and descriptive research designs. An inductive approach assists the researcher to gather data on the different relational levels of social structures and meaningful actions in which participants engage by means of a visual narrative. A visual narrative is regarded as the stories about people's past and present experiences, values, and the socially created meanings that are inextricably connected to their social, cultural, and contextual settings (Moen, 2006). A visual narrative assists the participant as well as the researcher to "tell sociological stories that embody the flow of human experience" (Harper, 2004, p. 724).

Participants and setting

The Mmogo method is particularly suitable for research in which visual images are key to meaning making through the process of objectification (Reavey & Johnson, 2008). Engaging vulnerable people in a way that does not rely primarily on verbal accounts can allow them to tell stories that they would not have otherwise have been able to do. The Mmogo method may be applied in a community setting with smaller groups consisting of eight to ten participants to allow for optimal group interaction between participants.

Data-gathering materials

Data-gathering materials are selected from familiar cultural items within a community. These items should symbolize the cultural embeddedness of behavior within a particular context and should be used to create objects with symbolic and socially constructed meanings. In an African context, this may include clay, grass stalks, wood pieces, needles, cloths, beads, or colourful buttons. In some cultures, such as the Zulu culture, the use of specific colours is particularly meaningful (Fiedeldey-Van Dijk, 1994).

(Continued)

(Continued)

The material that is chosen should reflect the integrity of the particular context in which the data are obtained. The cultural items should be as non-directive as possible and preferably familiar to the community in which the research is conducted. In addition, these items should be able to reflect the social processes based on the shared understandings that communities use to communicate (Keesing & Starthern, 1998). The inclusion of particular materials is decided on after observing the natural living environment of the people who are going to participate in the research. Wagner (2007) is cautious about using cultural items since the variations, arrangements, and modifications that could be used in visual presentations could reflect both naïve and manipulative human agency. It is therefore recommended that the materials be limited to basic, culturally familiar items; and that all participants be provided with the same materials.

Data collection procedure

In line with the principles of community psychology and social constructionism, the researcher does not enter the community as an expert, but as someone who, together with the members of the community, co-constructs reality. The process of entering communities for research purposes is characterized by open and transparent communication, respect, caring and an ethical attitude. Ethical community-based research refers to an understanding and respect for different cultures and their values (Roos, Visser, Pistorius & Nefale, 2007). Harrell and Bond (2006) refer to this as a grounding of oneself in a stance of *informed compassion*. Data are only gathered after the specific culture has been explored, together with the manifestations of cultural expressions, which could assist in limiting assumptions and overgeneralizations; and after informed consent has been obtained from community leaders, gatekeepers and individuals (Harrell & Bond, 2006; Roos et al., 2007).

Participants are divided into groups and are then provided with the familiar cultural items, which are used to make their visual presentations. An open-ended research question (phrased as a statement) based on the proposed research, is then asked, for example: *Please make anything with the materials that you were provided that will tell us about your . . .* This statement is open to the interpretation of the participants. The participants are then provided with an opportunity to create their visual presentations, and may also engage in group discussions on any topic of their choice. Copious field notes are taken about the discussion and visual presentations, which are then analyzed for content, narrative, or discourse.

Once the visual presentations have been completed, the researcher asks individual participants to give an account of their presentations. After each participant has shared the meaning of their visual presentations, all the participants are invited to comment on the others' presentations, contributing to the co-construction of rich descriptions. Copious field notes are made about the visual presentations and the discussions, which are then analyzed for content, narrative, or discourse. The locus of meaning shifts away from the empirically objective, but gains significance in the way that the participants engage with and interpret the subject (Wagner, 2007). The visual presentations are photographed and the discussion is transcribed verbatim.

Data analysis

Building the collective narrative involves a multilevel process of collecting, analyzing, and reconstructing the data. The Mmogo method aims to go beyond the isolated individual when trying to understand human functioning and studies social life through exploration and inspection. The process of exploration enables the researcher to explore the cultural nuances of community life, while the process of analysis refers to establishing the validity of the data (Klunklin & Greenwood, 2006). Inspection should be "flexible, imaginative, creative, and free to take new direction" (Blumer, 1969, p. 44), since the social contexts in which people participate and the historical conditions are constantly changing. The analysis involves both the analysis of the visual images as well as the interview data, with and without the participants (Reavey & Johnson, 2008). In the first stage of the analysis, the explicit and conscious meanings of the visual presentations are narrated by the participants. The visual images are analyzed by the participants themselves when they are asked about each object that was made. Banks (2001) refers to this level as the "external narrative" (p. 11). Each participant tells what was presented in their visual presentation, which Banks (2001) refers to as the "internal narrative." Creating this narrative "comes from the intermental life experiences and intramental images that are not accessible to direct observation" (Moen, 2006, p. 7)

(Continued)

(Continued)

On the second level, the group's narrative is added to the research process by inviting the participants' narrative about what the visual presentation prompts them to respond to, including the social context within which the presentations have been made. Then the apparent patterns, themes, or relationships are provisionally discussed with the participants. The participants are asked to link their visual presentations with the initial open statement. Through carefully questioning the underlying meanings of the visual presentations, the researcher encourages participants to provide insight into the symbolic meanings that underpin the presentations, as well as insight into communal practices and behavior. Data from the focus group discussions are transcribed and analysed according to the principles of thematic content analysis. The third level includes the researchers' examination of the types of images that were made while reading the accompanying textual description of the data (Reavey & Johnson, 2008).

Rigour

The inclusion of the context as a collective relationship provides contextual triangulation of the findings.

Ethical aspects

The Mmogo method supports the view that the community should be actively involved in the research process. Therefore, ethical aspects have to make provision for an acknowledgement of the community (by consulting with the appropriate authority structures such as the chiefs of a community), and permission to conduct the research must be obtained from the powers of structures. From the very beginning, the community is involved in the planning and conducting of the research. Community members should be included in the research team and outcomes of the research. Acquiring knowledge of how the community functions, including customs, norms, leadership styles, and other cultural expressions of social organizations, is important both in the research and in the interpretation of the findings (Harrel & Bond, 2006; Keesing & Strathern, 1998; Roos et al., 2007).

SUMMARY

The chapter has demonstrated the major implications of pragmatic assumptions and culture for indigenous methodologies. Three methodologies were discussed as exemplary of culturally responsive methodologies. The methodologies discussed illustrated how relational dimensions between researchers and research participants are cultivated and how culture-specific practices inform relational-based research processes that produce valid research with defined criteria for judging the process and outcomes of a qualitative research inquiry. The methodologies offer opportunities for a dialogue between Western scholars and indigenous scholars to engage in partnerships to decolonize Euro-Western methodologies and to make indigenous knowledge part of national and international discussions.

KEY POINTS

- Pragmatic assumptions in culture-specific contexts and theory and practice on a given topic converge to inform a methodology in a study.
- Interconnectedness and relational ontology and epistemologies form an important framework within which to discuss the culturally responsive indigenous research methodologies discussed in this chapter
- A growing number of methodologies draw from the philosophical and theoretical assumptions of a postcolonial indigenous paradigm to emphasize the unique contribution of sociohistorical, cultural, and political factors to social science research.
- Rigor is a standard requirement of any research inquiry, and indigenous methodologies have theory and culture- and context-driven criteria for judging the validity of an inquiry.

Activity 6.3

1. From your reading so far and your own understanding of components of a methodology, make a list of the different forms of data collection methods, sampling procedures, ethical protocols, and ways of addressing validity that emerge from a discussion of postcolonial indigenous research methodologies.

2. Design a study that uses a culturally responsive postcolonial indigenous research methodology framework.

SUGGESTED READINGS

Asante, M. K. (1987). *The Afrocentric idea*. Philadelphia: Temple University Press.

Asante, M. K . (1990) *Kemet, Afrocentricity, and knowledge*. Trenton, NJ: Africa World Press.

Chilisa, B. (2009). Indigenous African-centered ethics: Contesting and complimenting dominant models. In D. M. Mertens & P. E. Ginsberg (Eds.), *The handbook of social research ethics* (pp. 407–442). Thousand Oaks, CA: Sage.

Cram, G. (2004, October 13–15). *Evidence in an indigenous world*. Paper presented at the Australasian Society International Conference, Adelaide.

Cram, F. (2009). Maintaining indigenous voices. In D. M. Mertens & P. E. Ginsberg (Eds.), *The handbook of social research ethics* (pp. 308–322). Thousand Oaks, CA: Sage.

Gonzalez, M. C. (2000). The four seasons of ethnography: A creation-centered ontology for ethnography. *International Journal of Intercultural Relations, 24,* 623–650.

Koro-Ljungberg M. (2010). Validity, responsibility, and aporia. *Qualitative Inquiry, 6*(8), 603–610.

Lincoln, Y. (2009). Ethical practices in qualitative research. In D. M. Mertens & P. E. Ginsberg (Eds.), *The handbook of social research ethics* (pp. 150–169). Thousand Oaks, CA: Sage.

Mkabela, Q. (2005). Using the Afrocentric method in researching indigenous African culture. *The Qualitative Report, 10*(1) 178–189.

Parr, R. (2002). *Te Matahauariki methodology: The creative relationship framework* (*Te Matahauariki* Institute Occasional Paper Series). Hamilton: University of Waikato.

Roos V. (2008). The Mmogo method: Discovering symbolic community interactions. *Journal of Psychology in Africa, 18*(4), 659–668.

Walker, P. (2001). Journeys around the medicine wheel: A story of indigenous research in a Western University. *The Australian Journal of Indigenous Education, 29*(2), 18–21.

CHAPTER 7

DECOLONIZING THE INTERVIEW METHOD

Traditional social sciences have stubbornly refused to interrogate how we as researchers create our texts.... That we are human inventors of some questions and repressors of others, shapers of the very contexts we study, coparticipants in our interviews, interpreters of others' stories and narrators of our own, is sometimes rendered irrelevant to the texts we publish.

Michelle Fine (1994, p. 14)

OVERVIEW

Researchers want to engage the researched in a conversation on what has been written about them and what dreams they have about improving their quality of life. This chapter critiques the dominant interview method from a postcolonial indigenous perspective and offers alternative interview strategies that reflect postcolonial indigenous worldviews. The critique relates to the asymmetrical relations between the interviewer and the interviewee and among interviewees and to the dominance of Western academic disciplines' theories, terms, and concepts in shaping interview questions and analyzing interview transcripts. The chapter further discusses indigenous interview strategies, based on philosophic sagacity, that invoke indigenous worldviews of the colonized Other to inform the type of questions that can be asked and data analysis approaches that can be used. The alternative interview strategies require the researched to critique the literature written about them, to introduce the indigenous knowledge that informs their experiences, and to enter into a dialogue with the researcher on the researcher's questions of interest.

LEARNING OBJECTIVES

By the end of the chapter you should be able to:

1. Critique conventional interview approaches
2. Discuss the postcolonial indigenous interview strategies
3. Envision other ways of conducting interviews, informed by postcolonial indigenous worldviews and perspectives

Before You Start

Read the quotation above and discuss the challenges it raises with particular reference to research on postcolonial indigenous societies.

❦ THE CONVENTIONAL INTERVIEW METHOD: AN OVERVIEW

The conventional interview method, like other data collection methods, leans toward individualistic, Westernized assumptions and theories that ignore postcolonial indigenous value systems. Postcolonial indigenous worldviews lean toward communities' togetherness, cooperation, and connectedness. A focus on individuality is a Western preoccupation (Cannella, 1997). The individual interview is, for instance, built on the assumption of an "individual knower, focussing on the concept of the individual researcher (aware of his own limitations and capabilities as a human instrument), talking, with rare exceptions, to an individual informant" (Viruru & Cannella, 2006, p. 184). There is an expectation, for instance, that a researcher should avoid "getting involved in a real conversation in which he or she answers questions asked by the respondent or provides personal opinions on the matters discussed" (Fontana & Frey, 2005, p. 660). Let us take a close look at the conventional interview method.

The Interview Structure and Questions

The interview has been defined as a purposeful conversation, usually between two people (Bogdan & Biklen, 1982), or a conversation with a purpose (Lincoln & Guba, 1985). Interviews can be divided into individual and group interviews and further categorized according to the manner in which interview questions are structured. When we classify interviews according to the way interview questions are structured, we come up with three types: the unstructured or nonstandardized interview, the semistructured interview, and the structured or standardized interview.

The unstructured or nonstandardized interview. The unstructured interview starts with a general question in the area of study. This is usually accompanied by a list of topics to be covered in the interview. This type of interview allows for flexibility and makes it possible for researchers to follow interests and thoughts of informants. Interviewers freely ask questions in any order, depending on the answers. An example of an unstructured interview is the focused life story interview discussed later in this chapter.

The semistructured interview. These are focused interviews that have questions contained in an interview guide. They focus on the issue to be covered. The sequencing of questions is not the same for every participant as it depends on the process of the interview and answers from each individual participant. The interview guide ensures that the researcher collects similar types of data from all informants. See interview questions based on the theory of planned behavior, also discussed in this chapter.

The structured or standardized interview. In this type of interview, the interview schedule contains a number of pre-planned questions. Each research participant is asked the same questions in the same order. The advantage of standardized interviews is that they are time saving and reduce interviewer effect; analysis of the data is easier. The disadvantage is that they direct the informants' responses and therefore are not appropriate for qualitative research (Holloway & Wheeler, 1996).

Interview Questions

There are disagreements on the type of questions that can be asked. James Spradley (1979) distinguishes between descriptive, structural, and contrast questions, while Michael Patton (2002) distinguishes between experience and behavior questions, opinion and value questions, feeling questions, knowledge questions, sensory questions, and background and demographic questions.

Descriptive questions: Ask research participants to talk about the social scene with which they are familiar.

Structural questions: Help research participants demonstrate how they organize their life experiences.

Contrast questions: Require participants to distinguish between objects and events.

Experience and behavior questions: Ask participants to describe what they do.

Opinion and value questions: Seek understanding on how research participants think about the things they do and experience.

Feeling questions: Ask how research participants feel as opposed to how they think about their experiences.

Knowledge questions: Require factual information.

Sensory questions: Ask about things experienced through the senses.

Background and demographic information: Require information on the characteristics of the interviewee.

▌ POSTCOLONIAL INDIGENOUS INTERVIEW METHODS

From the discussion of the interview method, it is clear that there are fairly well established rules and codes, which draw from a Western archive of knowledge systems and values, to inform how interviews can be conducted. A postcolonial indigenous research paradigm offers other possible interview methods, which privilege relational ways of knowing that valorize respect for relations people have with one another and with the environment. Gabo Ntseane (2009), in her study on rural women's transition to urban business success, reflects on how an interview with a key informant ended up in a dialogue among three people. According to Ntseane, the key informant, who was the owner of the business, wanted one of her employees to join in the discussion because she had more authoritative knowledge on some aspects of the business. Ntseane notes that during the interview, the employer and the employee helped each other to elaborate on different aspects of the business. At times, they asked each other questions, and at times, they directed the questions to the researcher. She notes that the procedure she was compelled to adopt by the researched was different from the typical interview procedure. The procedure adopted valorized collective construction of knowledge and love and respect for the connections and relationships that participants had with one another.

Another concern about the individual interview method has been the visibility of the researched in the finished research report. Conventional educational research methods require that data from the researched be treated with confidentiality, which in most cases is ensured by not revealing the researched people's names. But what if the researched person wants to be visible in the scripts? Why should the names of the informants remain anonymous when the informants want them revealed? The researched women in Ntseane's (2009) study wanted readers to associate the stories in the study with their names and businesses. They argued that because they did not have the writing skills to document their stories, telling them to Ntseane was the only way to tell their communities and the generations to come about their knowledge and contributions to women's business in Botswana. Unfortunately, Ntseane could not reveal the names because it was against the stipulated research ethics of her university.

These experiences in the field reveal an African orientation toward individual and community production of knowledge and an appeal for visibility where the position of the researched as a producer of knowledge is clearly marked. In Chapter 4, you learned that a postcolonial indigenous paradigm favors using the names of everyone who participates in the research, if they permit it. This ensures that the researcher is accountable to the participants, and the participants are in turn accountable to their communities. For a postcolonial indigenous perspective, information or stories told by participants lose their power if the storyteller is not known. What follows is a discussion of two individual interview methods based on relational ways of knowing.

A Relational Interview Method: The Diviner/Client Construction of a Story

One of the most ancient interview strategies is the interviewing, analysis, and interpretation etched in the *dingaka* (diviners) practices of the people of southern Africa. Dingaka interview their client about an issue by using a set of as many as 60 bones symbolizing divine power, evil power, foreign spirits (good or bad), elderly men and women, young and old, homesteads, family life or death, and ethnic groups that include *Makgoa* (white people) to stimulate a discussion surrounding the client's life and problem (Dube, 2001). The pieces represent experiences, networks, and relationships among people and with the environment and together make up a theory of social life. In constructing a story, the diviner consults the patterns of the divine set as the client throws them to the ground. The diviner asks the client to confirm the interpretation of the set as a true story about his her life troubles. In the process, neither the set nor the diviner has exclusive knowledge. The client is invited to talk freely about his or her life and to reject the constructed story if it does not tally with her or his life experiences. The process demonstrates a postcolonial indigenous relational way of knowing in the following ways:

1. In the context of the diviner and the client, there is no absolute knowledge; the diviner and the client construct the story together, guided by an indigenous theory of social life symbolized by the divine set.

2. The divine set symbolizes a complex, expansive, and infinite context within which the interview and construction of the story take place. The complex context in many ways symbolizes the many connections and web of relations that the client has with other people, the land, and the environment. What is important to note is that context is brought to the consciousness of both the diviner and the client through symbolic representations of the environment of the client's life.

3. The story in whatever form is read and agreed upon. No interpretation occurs in the absence of the three: diviner, client, and symbolic representations (Chilisa, 2005).

A Relational Interview Method: The Focused Life-Story Interview

Shane Edwards, Verne McManus, and Tim McCreanor (2005) described a method they call the focused life-story interview and how this method enabled each individual to construct his or her story in relation to the connections he or she had with other people. Robert Atkinson (1998) defines the conventional life-story approach as follows:

> A life story is the story a person chooses to tell about the life he or she has lived, told as completely and honestly as possible, what is remembered of it, and what the teller wants others to know of it, usually as a result of a guided interview by another . . . A life story is a fairly narrating of one's entire experience of life as a whole, highlighting the most important aspects. (p. 8)

In keeping with the principles of a postcolonial indigenous research paradigm, the focused life-story interview method invokes relational ways of knowing to enable the use of an interview guide that brings to the discussion ways in which people are connected with one another and the environment, as well as topics absent from the standard vocabulary of academic disciplines. In Activity 7.1, an article by Edwards et al. (2005) illustrates how the individual is part of the collective and how procedures of the focused life-story interview valorize the web of connections that people have with those around them and with the land and the environment.

Activity 7.1

Read the study extract included here and respond to these questions.

1. Discuss the concepts of fairness, voice, and ontological and educative authenticity discussed in Chapter 6 in the context of the extract.

2. Discuss ways in which the focused life-story interview differs from a conventional life-story method of data collection.

Source: S. Edwards, V. McManus, & T. McCreanor (2005), "Collaborative Research Within Maori on Sensitive Issues: The Application of Tikanga and Kaupapa in Research on Maori Sudden Infant Death Syndrome," *Social Policy Journal of New Zealand, 25,* 88–104. Used by permission.

The individual as part of the collective—The notion of whanau

Many research participants are often part of larger collective or whanau groupings. These whanau groupings are not based on blood connections but can be conceptualized as whanau based on history, experience, the context or the Kaupapa or connected through association constituting a whanau relationship as determined by the participants (Durie 2004, Walker 1990). For us this meant that we were not only working with individual participants but with whanau members as well, and thinking about our families and the impacts of research in these circles.

Researchers need to be happy with the project and the people with whom they will be working in order for the research to be successful and beneficial to the stakeholder groups. It is not only about participants' possible uncertainty about "research vampires" but acknowledgement also that the researcher has personal tapu and mana that could be affected; as such, a researcher needs to be aware and acknowledge this, both as an individual and as a

(Continued)

(Continued)

member of other collective groups as there is the potential to be "touched" by the research itself or the participants themselves.

. . . For many Maori researchers karakia plays a central part of research pedagogy. In traditional times all activity took place with karakia present throughout. The effect of successive colonial acts to limit connectedness to Maori spirituality meant that karakia did not and continues not to play a central role in the everyday lives of Maori as previously experienced. This is still the same in the majority of situations today. Nevertheless karakia is still a powerful force in preparing a researcher for activity (Shirres, 1997). This is especially so when coming into contact with other people and heightened when the purpose is of sensitive nature. Some researchers are known to do their own karakia before they engage in research activity. They also repeat this process in situations that call for it and at the completion of the activity. Following interviews and field research many researchers will often find places to wash their hands with water to lift the tapu associated with human encounter.

Our chosen data collection method, known as focused life story interviews, sits comfortably within qualitative social science investigation. This method is based on the life story model discussed by Olson and Shopes (1991) and Anae (1998). Focused life story interviews are very appropriate for sensitive topics as they encourage a reflective, narrative style where the interviewee sets the pace and the interviewer listens, clarifies, probes, and possibly brings up topics which need to be covered in the interview that have not arisen spontaneously in the course of the conversation. This particular style allows for a relaxed, almost conversational approach to data interview. The hope was that the participants would feel safe and supported enough to talk through the very difficult circumstances surrounding the loss of their babies. The MSP care worker was the key to our highly positive experiences and most certainly enhanced the participant's appreciation of the sessions. This interview method is also consistent with the principles that underpin a Kaupapa Maori research framework within which the mana of the participants and the information that has been shared is upheld, and our respect and appreciation for the contribution are conveyed.

To start the interviews, the participants were asked to construct an outline of their life, paying special attention to those aspects (themes) that relate to whakapapa, relationships, family structure, economic/employment issues, education, identity, sense of belonging, access to amenities and other aspects of community that impact on the health and well-being of whanau. Multiple themes evolved and arose spontaneously throughout the course of interviews and these have added to the richness and diversity of the data. At times, when it appeared that an interview had gone "off-track," with gentle guidance the participants were able to continue with their story. They were encouraged to expand on ideas, elaborating and providing detail wherever this was possible and appropriate.

Philosophic Sagacity and the Interview Method

Another way to approach indigenous interviews is sagacity, a reflective system of thought based on the wisdom and the traditions of people (Emagalit, 2001, p. 4). From this perspective, the theory of knowledge and questions about knowledge can be found in the wisdom and beliefs of wise elders of the communities, who have not been schooled in the formal education system (Kaphagawani & Malherbe, 2000). This is an important epistemological assumption, given that most postcolonial indigenous thought systems have not been documented. Methods based on philosophic sagacity enable researchers to consult a large body of knowledge from the sages that is not available in the written literature. Queeneth Mkabela (2005) describes these sages as elders and members of cultural committees and suggests that they should be included in the research process. Cora Weber-Pillwax (2001) adds that the sages, who could be the elders, members of cultural committees, or any identified key informant, should play an important role in critiquing the written literature on the subject of research. This is how Weber-Pillwax describes the approach.

One of the steps that I have sometimes taken in preparation for interviews is to select specific excerpts from relevant literature that I feel would speak to the person with whom I will be working. I would make these excepts available to the people involved in my work by reading aloud or having them read on their own, and then giving a brief interpretation of what I thought the author was saying would then contextualise the focus of our work together and put my ideas forward as to how this selection fitted or raised questions. The contribution to the discussion would flow easily from this introduction . . . The process is one where indigenous people, many of whom are not able to read the English texts, can participate in the direct analysis of written knowledge and worldviews from other cultural groups and also be active partners in the co-creation of contemporary indigenous knowledge. I believe that this seemingly simple approach has potential for ensuring the vitality of the intellectual contributions that indigenous elders are making in the area of indigenous scholarship. (p. 171)

The interview method based on philosophic sagacity enables researchers to explore ways in which sages can be interviewed to analyze and give interpretations or commentaries on the oral literature stored in their languages and cultural artifacts, as well as the literature written about them. In addition to individual interviews, discussion-based interviews with more than one person contributing are a common practice. What follows is a discussion of indigenous focus group interviews.

▌ INDIGENOUS FOCUS-GROUP INTERVIEWS

The Western-based focus group was developed in the 1930s because of dissatisfaction with the individual interview. It is a discussion-based interview in which multiple research participants simultaneously produce data on a specified issue. The researcher takes a less directive and dominant role. In focus group interviews, the researcher can use unstructured or semistructured questions, as is done in individual interviews. Audiovisuals such as pictures, cartoons, and photographs can be used to stimulate a discussion. Most focus groups consist of between 6 and 12 people. The basic principle is not to allow the group to be so big that participation by all is impossible or so small that it is not possible to cover a number of issues.

The focus group interview is compatible with real communication systems in natural settings. For instance, most of the time when people want to address problems, they meet in groups of more than two people to hold a dialogue. In addition, the group interaction in focus group interviews allows more realistic perceptions of issues. Members within the group can, for example, challenge participants with extreme views, and thus, more realistic information is obtained on issues. Information is also checked for accuracy as members question, complement, and corroborate what others say. In addition, the researcher can cover a wide range of issues. The main disadvantage of Western-based focus group interviews is that a few assertive individuals may dominate the discussion. What follows is a discussion of indigenous interview methods that promote equality among participants.

Many non-Western communities use various kinds of group discussion when issues must be addressed. One can think of community interviews, where selected members of a community are invited for a discussion by a chief, headperson of a ward, village leader, or a wise person such as a sage. When researchers follow informants to their homes, most of the family members invite themselves to the discussion. In African contexts, for instance, it may be appropriate to distinguish focus group interviews where the facilitator determines the group membership and other focus group interviews where the identified key informant is joined by others, either because of invitation by the key informant or because of community or family values. The home is a space marked by family togetherness. When researchers visit homes to interview key informants, they should be aware that the overriding value is family togetherness, sharing, and doing things together. Postcolonial indigenous research methods call for the recognition and valorization of the variety of focus group interviews, such as community focus group interviews, family focus group interviews, and others.

Talking Circles

We have noted that one of the disadvantages of the Western-based focus group interview technique is that members do not necessarily have equal opportunity to be heard. Talking circles are based on the ideal of participants' respect for each other and are an example of a focus group method derived from postcolonial indigenous worldviews. In African contexts and among indigenous peoples, there are many occasions when people form a circle. It could be around the fireplace, during celebrations when they form circles to sing, or in games when children form circles to play. In each of these occasions, a person is given a chance to speak uninterrupted. The talking circle symbolizes and encourages sharing of ideas, respect of each other's ideas, togetherness, and a continuous and unending compassion and love for one another. The circle also symbolizes equality of members in the circle.

From Canada, Peggy Wilson and Stan Wilson (2000) explain that group members sit "in a circle that represents the holism of Mother Earth and the equality of all members" (p. 11). A common practice in talking circles is that a sacred object—a feather, a shield, a stone, a basket, or a spoon—is passed around from speaker to speaker. These sacred objects symbolize collective construction of knowledge and the relations among group members. Refer to Chapters 8 and 9 for the use of these objects in talking circles. The holder of the object speaks uninterrupted, and the group listens silently and nonjudgmentally until the speaker has finished. A talking circle may consist of as few as two people (Lavallée, 2009) and as many as 12 people. In most instances, a complete talking circle comprises four rounds (Wilson & Wilson, 2000). The number of talking circles may vary because of time restraints, rules, and norms of each group. For instance, Lavallée (2009) conducted a total of nine circles to complete a talking circle. See Chapter 9 for more on sharing circles and the Anishnaabe symbol-based reflection method.

Interviews and Data Analysis

One of the challenges that researchers have is organizing the volumes of data from interviews in a way that it will be easy for use. Organizing data starts with open coding. Open coding refers to the process of breaking down data into themes, patterns, and concepts to create a meaningful story from the volume of data. The patterns, concepts, and themes become codes that are then identified across data generated through different data-gathering techniques, such as the individual and the focus group interview. Concepts, themes, and patterns are developed as researchers read through the data and ask critical questions, which may come from the abstract vocabulary of a discipline or a theory within a discipline. Euro-Western academic discipline-related language continues to dominate analysis procedures, interpretation, and reporting procedures. During the reporting, for instance, the researcher pulls together the voices of the interviewees to create generalizations, patterns, or sameness communicated in Euro-Western academic discipline language. The voices of the researched cease to exist except when cited to illustrate a theme or a pattern.

Lawrence Neuman (2003, p. 458) has summarized seven Euro-Western academic discipline-related strategies for qualitative data analysis:

1. *The narrative.* Tell a detailed story about a particular slice of social life.
2. *Ideal types.* Compare qualitative data with a pure model of social life. Postcolonial indigenous scholars challenge the "pure model of social life" to which the data are compared. Often, the West is used as the norm against which all others should be compared, with the end result that postcolonial indigenous social life is stereotyped and then ruled inferior and demonized.
3. *Success approximation.* The researcher repeatedly moves back and forth between data and theory until the gap between them shrinks or disappears.
4. *The illustrative model.* The illustrative method requires a researcher to apply theory to a concrete historical situation or social setting or to organize data on the basis of a prior theory. The questions indigenous scholars

ask are: Whose theory is it? Who wrote it, and how does it portray the researched? "There is a disturbing failure to recognize that these people (the poor and grassroots people in non-Western developing countries) do theorize in their communities as part of their community life, and that they are not only articulate but also able to interpret their experiences" (Elabor-Idemudia, 2002, p. 227).

5. *Path dependency and contingency.* Begin with an outcome and trace a sequence of events back to origin to see a path that constrained the set of events.

6. *Domain analysis.* Locate the included terms within cover terms that make the cultural domain.

7. *Analytical comparison.* Identify many characteristics and a key outcome, and then check agreement and difference among the characteristics to learn which ones are associated with the outcome.

It is evident from the strategies listed above that the Western-based interview method works within a standard vocabulary, terms, concepts, and categories of analysis of given disciplines, with their associated theories; above all, it is a mode of Western social science research, with its emphasis on the individual as the social unit of focus. Recently, colleagues and I embarked on a study to design a theory-driven intervention to change sexually risky adolescent behaviors. We agreed that the theory of planned behavior (TPB) should inform the intervention. TPB is a theory of the predictors of individual behavior that has been frequently applied to understanding health behaviors. The TPB asserts a specific relationship among beliefs, attitudes, intentions, and behavior. More specifically, the TPB posits that intentions to perform a specific behavior are determined by three factors: (1) attitudes toward the behavior, which are seen as reflecting behavioral beliefs about the consequences of performing the behavior; (2) subjective norms toward the behavior, which reflect individuals' beliefs about whether specific referent persons (e.g., peers, romantic partners, parents, the church, etc.) would approve or disapprove of the behavior, and (3) perceived behavioral control over the behavior, which involves individuals' beliefs that they have the necessary resources, skills, and opportunities to perform the behavior. We used the theory to guide our qualitative interview to elicit adolescents' views on risky sexual behaviors by asking the following questions:

- What is good about multiple partners, abstinence, and male circumcision? (behavioral beliefs question)
- What is bad about multiple partners, abstinence, and male circumcision? (behavioral beliefs question)

- Who approves of multiple partners, abstinence, and male circumcision? (normative beliefs question)
- Who disapproves of multiple partners, abstinence, and male circumcision? (normative beliefs question)
- What is easy about having multiple partners, abstinence, boys performing male circumcision? (control beliefs question)
- What is difficult about having multiple partners, abstinence, and boys performing male circumcision? (control beliefs question)

Clearly the questions are limited and constrained by the theory in its attempt to delineate individual participant intentions, which according to the theory depend on an individual's attitudes toward the behavior, subjective norms toward the behavior, and perceived behavioral control. Such construction of interview guides is limited in the extent to which it accounts for the broader social context surrounding behavior.

Interviews and Analysis Based on the Medicine Wheel

From the discussion above, it is clear that every discipline, be it sociology, education, or psychology, has its own language, vocabulary, concepts, terms, and theories that guide research interview questions. The argument is that researchers can base interview questions on theories, concepts, and terms that come from postcolonial indigenous worldviews. In Chapter 5, for instance, it was shown how researchers can derive theories and concepts from proverbs, myths, folklore, and so on. In this chapter, I extend the discussion on the methodology based on the Medicine Wheel by illustrating interview questions informed by the four quadrants of the Medicine Wheel. Terry L. Cross, Kathleen Earle, Solie, H. Echo-Hawk Solie, and Kathryn Manness (2000), in their study of Native American communities, designed interview and focus group questions based on the four quadrants of the Medicine Wheel. They defined the four quadrants as context, body, mind, and spirit (Cross et al., 2000, as cited Mertens, 2009).

- The *context* includes culture, community, family, peers, work, school, and social history.
- The *mind* includes our cognitive processes such as thoughts, memories, knowledge, and emotional processes such as feelings, defenses and self-esteem.
- The *body* includes all physical aspects, such as genetic inheritance, gender and condition, as well as sleep, nutrition and substance use.

- The *spirit* area includes both positive and negative learned teachings and practices, as well as positive and negative metaphysical or innate forces (Cross et al., as cited in Mertens, 2009, pp. 20–21).

Sample questions for each quadrant include (Cross et al., 2000, as cited in Mertens, 2009).

- *Context quadrant:* "How does your program draw upon extended family and kinship to help parents help their children? (for service providers)" (p. 103).
- *Body quadrant:* "Have you or your child (children) participated in any cultural activities to improve physical health? Examples include: special tribal celebration with food served to mark the occasion, herbal or plant remedies for certain illnesses, smudging or other ways of cleansing for special occasions, or tribally based recreational opportunities such as dancing or playing games" (p. 103).
- *Mind quadrant:* "How has the program helped you develop strategies that use Indian ways for addressing the needs of your child? (for parents)" (p. 104).
- *Spirit quadrant:* "Have you or your family participated in any rituals or ceremonies to help restore balance to your lives, either through the purging of negative forces or the development of positive forces? Do you use any Indian traditional remedies to restore balance in the spiritual area (example: sweat lodge)?" (p. 104).

The questions clearly draw from Native American worldviews, use their indigenous knowledge, and valorize their spiritual practices and people's relations with each other. The data were further fitted into the four quadrants of context, body, mind, and spirit for analysis and interpretation (Mertens, 2009). The interview questions and the data analysis and interpretation further illustrate how postcolonial indigenous worldviews can be used as frameworks with their own language, vocabulary, concepts, terms, and theories, used either alone or to complement Euro-Western academic discipline frameworks.

SYMBOLS IN POSTCOLONIAL INDIGENOUS INTERVIEW METHODS

Discussions in this book show that postcolonial indigenous interview methods use symbols such as sacred objects, drawings, crafts, sculptures, tattoos, dance, song, written literature, and so on for various reasons. In the talking circle method, for example, objects symbolize the connection of participants to each other and the collective construction of knowledge. This is similar to the relational interview method based on the diviner/client construction of a story, where objects bring to the participant's consciousness the many connections and web of relations that the participant has with other people, the land, and the environment. In the Mmogo method discussed in Chapter 6, participants made visual representations of their experiences using materials derived from their culture. The interview then focused on these visual images. In contrast to the Mmogo method, in the Anishnaabe symbol-based reflection method (Chapter 8), participants select a symbol—in the form of a sacred object, a sculpture, song, or dance—that communicates their life experiences and explain how it led them in a journey of their search for identity and transformation. Cross et al. (2000) bring another dimension to interviews by showing how symbolism in the Medicine Wheel worldview enabled the researchers to conduct interviews and data analysis informed by the four quadrants of the Medicine Wheel: context, body, mind, and spirit. Weber-Pillwax (2001) adds to these methods an approach where the researcher brings to the interview some written literature for the participants to critique. This method could include sages as elders and members of cultural committees commenting and giving interpretations on literature stored in cultural artifacts.

It is thus clear from these examples that cultural artifacts store worldviews and can be used as stimulants in individual and focus group interviews. These cultural artifacts, which include pottery, sculptures, home painting, and basket weaving by ordinary women and men, may bring to life worldviews, topics, and other categories of thought otherwise missing in the literature. Discussed here are two examples of artifacts that a researcher can bring to the interview to engage sages in a dialogue on a given topic of a research.

The Kente Legend

According to Asante legend, weaving began after two hunters observed the spider Anante creating an intricate web. They copied the technique and brought their cloth to their chief, Oti Akenten. Kente (see Figure 7.1) has been worn since the late 17th century, when imported silk cloth was unraveled to obtain silk threads for inclusion in local hand-woven textiles. The legend on the Kente communicates African perspectives on production and ownership of knowledge. It is clear from this legend that the Africans recognized collective production and ownership of knowledge by

Figure 7.1   Kente wrapper

Source: Ghana, Asante. 20th Century, Rayon. Collection of the Newark Museum.
Gift of Mr. and Mrs. William U. Wright, 1985 85.366.

all, including animals and all creatures in the environment. For instance, the contribution of the spider to the weaving of Kente is acknowledged. The communication between the spider and the hunters could also illustrate the African-valued connectedness with the environment, including living and nonliving things. The legend would seem to suggest that a discussion of context in a study would be incomplete without describing the nonliving and living in the community and how people relate to the living the nonliving and the environment in general. The legend opens spaces for new discussions on context in research that researchers can bring to the interviews with sages.

Bamana women of Mali are the creators of the unique cloth design called *bogolanfini* (mud cloth), shown in Figure 7.2. This cloth has a pattern of circular motifs. The central panel symbolizes motherhood, known as the "the mother of the cloth." Each configuration has a name that is descriptive of the beliefs and values of the Bamana. Letters of the alphabet, both Chinese and Arabic, have remained the recognized ways of communicating in writing. The Bamana cloth design captures others forms of representing and storing information. These forms of writing and storing information have to be recognized, collected, and brought to interviews with sages so that they can be analyzed and interpreted for use as baseline literature on research topics of interest. The literature on motherhood stored in the cloth, for example, supports the argument for the mother-centered, woman-centered African feminisms discussed in Chapter 9.

Figure 7.2 *Bogolanfini* (mud cloth)

Source: Artist Guacho Diarra. Mali, Bamana. Cotton and paint. Collection of the Newark Museum. Purchase 1986 The Members' Fund 86.47.

⬛ CONDUCTING A POSTCOLONIAL INDIGENOUS INTERVIEW

From the discussion in this chapter, we can draw the following principles about a postcolonial indigenous interview.

1. The interview process is guided by a relational way of knowing and therefore brings into the process objects that communicate equality among participants; recognize and celebrate participants' connection to each other and to the environment; and teach respect, love, and harmony among all those participating in the interview process.

2. The researched, who are the knowers, draw from their web of connection with land, the environment, the living, and the nonliving to engage in a dialogue on the issue of discussion.

3. The research participants have the following roles among others: critiquing the literature written about them; bringing to the discussion indigenous knowledge such as worldviews, the myths, folktales, language, and proverbs that inform their frames of reference; and entering into a dialogue with the researcher on the researcher's questions of interest.

These principles should inform guidelines for preparing and conducting an interview. What follows are suggestions on how to conduct the interview.

Starting the interview. Indigenous research is viewed as ceremony. Interviews should thus start by recognizing and celebrating participants' relationships with the cosmos and those around them. In Chapter 4, it was noted, for instance, that among the Anishambe, one of the indigenous people of North America, the offering of *aseema* (tobacco) facilitated the interview. Aseema among the Anishambe is a cultural symbol that is used to ask for help, to share information, and to thank people. Researchers must identify the cultural symbols that will allow them to gain entry to the setting and conduct interviews. See also the example on the focused life-story interview discussed in this chapter.

About the participants and the researcher. While starting a Western-based interview requires the researcher to document common sociodemographic information such as age, sex, occupation, and so on, a postcolonial indigenous interview method also requires documentation of the participants' and the researcher's relations with others, with the cosmos, and with the topic of the research. The researcher shows respect to the participants by saying who they are, describing their relationship with the participants, and explaining researchers' interest in the research topic. Participants in turn tell their lineage stories, which connect them to one another, to the community in general, and to the cosmos. For instance, in the example of the focused life story, participants were asked at the beginning of the interview to construct an outline of their life by paying attention to themes that related to *whakappa,* relationships, and family structure.

Rituals and symbolism during the interview. Participants use cultural symbols of their choice to communicate collective construction of knowledge, sharing of ideas, or equality among all involved. Cultural symbols to facilitate discussions are common in talking circles. To conduct focus group interviews using talking circles, researchers must dialogue with participants on the cultural symbols to be used and the ground rules associated with the symbolism, which should guide the discussion.

Giving voice to the participants. One of the most important considerations in indigenous research interviews is that participants should decide if their names can be used in the research manuscript and when and how they can be used. Take, for example, the role of sages in analyzing and interpreting cultural artifacts or critiquing literature written about their people. It may be important to credit the analysis and the interpretation to individual sages so that academic scholars can acknowledge them by referencing their work. The sages' critique of the written literature also requires recognition that can be achieved by giving details of who they are. There is thus need to devote ample time to a discussion with participants on the use of their names in the research manuscript.

The following practical guidelines, which are also common with Western-informed interviews, can be used to inform the interview process.

1. As a researcher, deal efficiently with the practicalities of interviews; for example, ensure that the tape recorder, batteries, and microphone are in good working order and properly set if you are going to use them.
2. Take care as to where the respondent and interviewer sit so that they are not too close to cause cultural discomfort and not too far apart to create a sense of power boundary. Also, take care of the effects of direct sunlight, noise, and others forms of interruptions.
3. It is important at the start of the interview to allow the respondent to relax by conducting introductions in a manner that encourages dialogue. For example, ask if there is something they would wish to know about the interview procedure before you start.
4. Help the participants to position themselves within the discourse of the study by asking them questions that allow them freedom to express their perspectives.
5. Always aim at asking simple (not loaded) questions, one at a time.
6. Be an attentive listener (Avoid conducting interviews when you are tired).
7. Be sensitive not to pursue issues that appear to be complicated or sensitive too early in the interview.
8. Take note of answers that need follow-up later in the interview.
9. Give the participant time to reply. Do not attempt to cover a silence with another question (unless you want to clarify the initial question).
10. Keep reassuring participants about the importance of their replies. Indicate that what they are saying is interesting to you, for example, by making comments such as "that is quite interesting" or "that is a very interesting way of describing it."
11. Watch for non-verbal clues of boredom or embarrassment and then respond appropriately, perhaps by changing the line of interviewing.
12. Try to end interviews on a positive note, for example, by giving the participants an opportunity to ask questions and give their opinion about their experience of the process.
13. Summarize the main points raised and ask participants if your summary is a correct interpretation of their view.

SUMMARY

This chapter advanced the argument that interview structures, type of questions asked, and analysis of the data produced from the interviews are predominantly informed by Western academic disciplines. Interview methods based on philosophic sagacity, employing cultural artifacts as interview stimulants, and informed by postcolonial indigenous worldviews were discussed as alternative strategies that give voice to marginalized communities.

KEY POINTS

- The conventional interview method works within a standard vocabulary, terms, concepts, and categories of analysis informed by Western academic disciplines with their associated theories and a Western social science research culture with its emphasis on the individual as the social unit of focus.

- In postcolonial indigenous societies, researchers conduct interviews as privileged elites and knowers who are researching and operating with Western models of thought and conducting interviews within frameworks of Othering ideologies supported by deficit theories and literature that constructs the researched as the problem.

- Researchers should use indigenous knowledge to guide interview question structures, types of questions asked, and data analysis procedures.

- Researchers should recognize indigenous people who have expertise and knowledge.

- Researchers should highlight reviewed literature about the researched and dialogue with the researched to enable them to participate in a critique of the literature produced about them.

Activity 7.2

1. Compare and contrast the narrative analysis strategy of data analysis with the diviner and client approach.

2. How does the diviner and client's analysis and interpretation strategy compare with the illustrative and successive approximation methods?

(Continued)

(Continued)

3. Simulate a focused life-story interview.

4. Videotape the interview and later use it to evaluate the interview skills, the structure of the interview, and the questions asked.

5. To evaluate the videos, first create a checklist informed by a post-colonial indigenous paradigm for use in the evaluation.

SUGGESTED READINGS

De Vault, M. L. (1999). *Liberating method: Feminism and social research.* Philadelphia: Temple University Press.

Edwards, S., McManus, V., & McCreanor, T. (2005). Collaborative research within Maori on sensitive issues: The application of *Tikanga* and *Kaupapa* in research on Maori sudden infant death syndrome. *Social Policy Journal of New Zealand, 25,* 88–104.

Scheurich, J. (1997). *Research method in the post-modern.* London: Falmer Press.

Viruru, R., & Cannella, G. (2006). A postcolonial critique of the ethnographic interview: Research analyzes research. In N. Denzin & M. Giardina (Eds.), *Qualitative inquiry and the conservative challenge* (pp. 175–192). Walnut Creek, CA: Left Coast.

CHAPTER 8

PARTICIPATORY RESEARCH METHODS

Research with the Indigenous community is a commitment that extends well beyond the final report, dissertation, peer-reviewed article submission, or conference presentation. It is a lifelong relationship and commitment. If contacted by the community, even many years after the completion of a research project, the research team must be prepared to assist the community with their requests.

Lynn Lavallée (2009, p. 24)

OVERVIEW

Discussed in this chapter are participatory research approaches that enable the colonized Other in the third and fourth worlds, as well as those discriminated against and marginalized on account of their gender, ethnicity, age, religion, social class, or ableness, to collectively share and analyze their knowledge, life experiences, and conditions and to use indigenous knowledge as a frame of reference to plan and to act. Two types of participatory action research are presented, one with an emphasis on participants as co-researchers and another with an emphasis on personal and social transformation. Participatory rural appraisal (PRA) is provided as an example of a participatory action research approach. Finally, appreciative inquiry is introduced as one of the methods for promoting healing and transformation in participatory research.

By the end of this chapter, you should be able to:

1. Analyze the role of participatory action research for the oppressed and disempowered groups
2. Distinguish between participatory action research with participants as co-researchers and a transformative participatory action research approach
3. Discuss transformative participatory action research as a decolonizing research approach
4. Explain indigenous methods in participatory action research.

Before You Start

Search your library databases for articles that use participatory action research with the historically oppressed, the disempowered, marginalized groups, indigenous peoples, and the formerly colonized in developing countries. List the variety of names used to describe research with a participatory approach and the disciplines where participatory action research has been used.

ACTION RESEARCH: AN OVERVIEW

The emphasis in this book so far has been that the exploited, the poor, and the marginalized should participate as knowers in the entire research process, which includes defining the research issue, collecting the data, analyzing and interpreting the data, writing the report, and disseminating the findings. There remains, however, a missing link between research output and implementation of findings that can bring about social change. Perhaps your reflections on the following questions can define your stance toward participatory action research.

1. As a social science researcher, do you think that you and the researched should collaborate in discovering scientific facts as well as implementing the findings from the research inquiry?
2. What is your reaction to the view that once communities have participated in the research process, they should wait for professionals—for example, social workers, nurses, and teachers—to implement findings from research studies?
3. How many research findings from doctoral dissertations and master's theses do you think get implemented?

4. Do you think it would be possible for you to conduct a dissertation study in which a community participates in the research process and, together with the community, you implement the research findings?
5. What is your reaction to the quotation at the beginning of the chapter?

There is a continuing debate on the relationship between research and social action. One view is that social science research should aim solely to discover scientific facts. Linking social science research findings to action, it is argued, should be left to other professionals, who may be looking for scientific facts to aid the improvement of human welfare. Another view is that it is important for the advancement of science and for the improvement of human welfare to devise strategies in which research and action are linked (Whyte, 1991). You have learned in previous chapters that decolonization of research methods calls for the researched to participate in the research process and for researchers to be committed to an action-oriented research process, in which researchers are activists dedicated to social transformation. This also calls for researchers who theorize and conduct research using healing and social-justice methods informed by the worldviews of those whose histories, experiences, and voices have been distorted and marginalized. An overview of action-oriented research will enable you to understand the general principles and steps of action research and to appreciate the decolonization and indigenization process of conventional action research.

The Action Research Cycle

The idea of action research is attributed to Kurt Lewin, a social psychologist from Germany. Action research is a process of doing, reflecting on the action, drawing conclusions, and then reflecting again on the process. It became popular in the 1980s as a mode of inquiry for practitioners: for example, adult educators, teachers, social workers, nurses, and agricultural extension workers. The argument advanced by these practitioners was that some forms of inquiry require a continuous cycle of practice and reflection based on real life experience. It was also argued that such practice-based research inevitably required involvement by the practitioners instead of relying on outside experts to observe, analyze, and solve social problems. Action research also emerged as a tool for engaging the exploited, the poor, and disempowered groups in a process of collective inquiry with the aim of empowering them to have greater control in decision making about various aspects of their lives. There is a basic sequence that all action-oriented studies follow. Stephen Kemmis and Robert McTaggart (2000, p. 563) describe the sequence as a spiral of self-reflexive cycles involving the following:

Planning a change. This involves identifying and inviting community members to participate in the research, forming partnerships with all stakeholders, bringing about full participation of community members in defining research questions, and also planning the research design and data collection methods.

Acting and observing the process and consequences of change. This involves full participation of community members in putting the plan into action, for instance, mapping out the activities for data collection or making decisions on strategies to get a plan in motion; community members observe, monitor, analyze, and evaluate outcomes.

Reflecting on these processes and consequences. This includes self-reflection by the researcher and participants, and addressing the following: what they have learned, if it will change the way they think and do things, whether they are willing to change, how they evaluate the significance of findings, and whether the intervention proposed is appropriate based on the findings.

Replanning. This involves the researcher and the community in the collaborative design of an intervention.

Acting and observing again. The intervention is implemented, observed, monitored, and evaluated.

The self-reflexive cycles are informed by six principles (Winter, 1996) that are common to all action research initiatives. The principles are as follows:

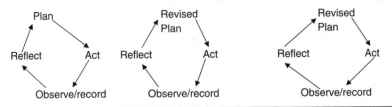

Figure 8.1   The Basic Action Research Cycle

Source: Viswanathan M., Ammerman A., Eng, E., Gartlehner, G., Lohr, K. N., Griffith, D., Rhodes, S., Samuel-Hodge, C., Maty, S., Lux, L., Webb, L., Sutton S. F., Swinson, T., Jackman, A., & Whitener, L. (July 2004), *Community-Based Participatory Research: Assessing the Evidence. Evidence Report/Technology Assessment No. 99.* (Prepared by RTI-University of North Carolina Evidence-based Practice Center under Contract No. 290-02-0016). AHRQ Publication 04-E022-2. Rockville, MD: Agency for Healthcare Research and Quality.

Reflexive critique. This involves a self-questioning, self-critical thinking where biases about the researched, tendencies to exclude local and indigenous knowledge, tendencies toward deficit theorizing about the researched, and the conception of researcher as knower are questioned.

Dialectic critique. Here there is an emphasis on the role of context in understanding the problem. Context includes the researched and researcher's beliefs about conceptions of reality, the way this reality can be known, and the context-informed ethical principles that should guide the process of knowing.

Collaboration. Collaboration entails a basic acceptance that researchers and researched communities should work together, and that everyone has something worthwhile to contribute.

Risking disturbance. Researchers and participating communities must have willingness, intentions, and commitment to change as a result of the research process.

Creating plural structures. Here, researchers and participating communities acknowledge and honor multiple voices and interpretations throughout the research process.

Internalizing theory and practice. Researchers are called on to recognize the link between theory and practice and to use the link to develop new insights and practice.

Decolonization of Action Research

Research to increase voice and participation of the colonized Other requires indigenization and decolonization of the basic action research model. This indigenization has led to two types of action research: one that I will call the participant as co-researcher approach and the other, the participatory transformative research approach.

Participant as Co-Researcher

In the participant as co-researcher approach, the level of participation of the researched is limited to helping with the research questions, research design, analysis, authoring of research manuscripts and dissemination of findings. The following questions can be used to evaluate the extent of participation and the presence of the voice of the researched in the participant as co-researcher approach.

- How are the research questions produced?
- Whose research questions are they?
- Do the research questions energize the researched to engage in a dialogue about their material world?
- What methods and theories are used to accurately generate and record marginalized voices, as well as indigenous and local knowledge predominantly excluded through Euro-Western conventional methodologies?
- With what and with whose theories are research questions and analysis of data conceptualized?

Meera Viswanathan et al. (2004, pp. 15–16) summarizes critical elements in community-based participatory research, a form of participatory action research that engages communities as co-researchers in the research process. Table 8.1 shows areas in the research process where community members can participate and describes their roles, the benefits of their participation to the research and the community, and research challenges. The emphasis in the approach depicted in the table is on the role of community members as co-researchers participating in (a) identifying and defining the research question, (b) making decisions about the research design and data-gathering instruments, (c) data analysis and interpretation, and (d) coauthoring the report.

Table 8.1   Critical Elements in Community-Based Participatory Research (CBPR)

CBPR Implementation and Potential Impact				
Research Element	CBPR Application	Community Benefits	Research Benefits	Research Challenges
Assembling a research team of collaborators with the potential for forming a research partnership	Identifying collaborators who are decision makers that can move the research project forward	Resources can be used more efficiently	Increases the probability of completing the research project as intended	Time to identify the right collaborators and convincing them that they play an important role in the research project

A structure for collaboration to guide decision-making	Consensus on ethics and operating principles for the research partnership to follow, including protection of study participants	The beginning of building trust and the likelihood that procedures governing protection of study participants will be understood and acceptable	An opportunity to understand each collaborator's agenda, which may enhance recruitment and retention of study participants	An ongoing process throughout the life of research partnerships that requires skills in group facilitation, building consensus, and conflict accommodation
Defining the research question	Full participation of community in identifying issues of greatest importance; focus on community strengths as well as problems	Problems addressed are highly relevant to the study participants and other community members	Increased investment and commitment to the research process by participants	Time consuming; community may identify issues that differ from those identified by standard assessment procedures or for which funding is available
Grant proposal and funding	Community leaders/members involved as a part of the proposal writing process	Proposal is more likely to address issues of concern in a manner acceptable to community residents	Funding likelihood increases if community participation results in tangible indicators of support for recruitment and retention efforts, such as writing letters of support, serving on steering committee or as fiscal agents or co-investigators	Seeking input from the community may slow the process and complicate the proposal development effort when time constraints are often present

(Continued)

Table 8.1   (Continued)

CBPR Implementation and Potential Impact				
Research Element	CBPR Application	Community Benefits	Research Benefits	Research Challenges
Research design	Researchers communicate the need for specific study design approaches and work with community to design more acceptable approaches, such as a delayed intervention for the control group	Participants feel as if they are contributing to the advancement of knowledge vs. as if they are passive research "subjects," and that a genuine benefit will be gained by their community	Community is less resentful of research process and more likely to participate	Design may be more expensive and/ or take longer to implement Possible threats to scientific rigor
Participant recruitment and retention	Community representatives guide researchers to the most effective ways to reach the intended study participants and keep them involved in the study	Those who may benefit most from the research are identified and recruited in dignified manner rather than made to feel like research subjects	Facilitated participant recruitment and retention, which are among the major challenges in health research	Recruitment and retention approaches may be more complex, expensive, or time consuming

Formative data collection	Community members provide input to intervention design, barriers to recruitment and retention, etc., via focus groups, structured interviews, narratives, or other qualitative method	Interventions and research approach are likely to be more acceptable to participants and thus of greater benefit to them and the broader population	Service-based and community-based interventions are likely to be more effective than if they are designed without prior formative data collection	Findings may indicate needed changes to proposed study design, intervention, and timeline, which may delay progress
Measures, instrument design and data collection	Community representatives involved with selecting the most appropriate intervention approach, given cultural and social factors and strengths of the community	Participants feel the intervention is designed for their needs and offers benefits while avoiding insult; provides resources for communities involved	Intervention design is more likely to be appropriate for the study population, thus increasing the likelihood of a positive study	Time consuming; hiring local staff; may be less efficient than using study staff hired for the project
Data analysis and interpretation	Community members involved regarding their interpretation of the findings within the local social and cultural context	Community members who hear the results of the study are more likely to feel that the conclusions are accurate and sensitive	Researchers are less likely to be criticized for limited insight or cultural insensitivity	Interpretations of data by non-scientists may differ from those of scientists, calling for thoughtful negotiation

(Continued)

Table 8.1   (Continued)

CBPR Implementation and Potential Impact				
Research Element	CBPR Application	Community Benefits	Research Benefits	Research Challenges
Manuscript preparation and research translation	Community members are included as coauthors of the manuscripts, presentations, newspaper articles, etc., following previously agreed-upon guidelines	Pride in accomplishment, experience with scientific writing, and potential for career advancement; findings are more likely to reach the larger community and increase potential for implementing or sustaining rec-ommendations	The manuscript is more likely to reflect an accurate picture of the community environment of the study	Time consuming; requires extra mutual learning and negotiation

Source: Viswanathan, M., Ammerman, A., Eng, E., Gartlehner, G., Lohr, K. N., Griffith, D., Rhodes, S., Samuel-Hodge, C., Maty, S., Lux, L., Webb, L., Sutton, S. F., Swinson, T., Jackman, A., & Whitener, L. (July 2004), *Community-Based Participatory Research: Assessing the Evidence. Evidence Report/ Technology Assessment No. 99*, pp. 15–16. (Prepared by RTI-University of North Carolina Evidence-based Practice Center under Contract No. 290-02-0016.) AHRQ Publication 04-E022-2. Rockville, MD: Agency for Healthcare Research and Quality.

Although participatory research increases the level of involvement of the researched in the research process, it has limitations; it may ignore:

- The geopolitical power relations within which the research is conducted. In the previous chapters, for example, we noted the deficit and damage-focused research about the researched and how that fed into the research process.
- The significance that the researcher has placed on the knowledge that is produced. In the previous chapters, the role of the researcher in a postcolonial indigenous research paradigm was discussed and the importance of self-reflexivity noted.
- The consequence of power struggles on the generation of knowledge and the effect that local social differences, such as gender, age, wealth, and class, have on who has access to what sort of knowledge.

Table 8.1, for instance, emphasizes participation of community leaders and community members in the research process. There is no mention of community diversity and how local social differences, such as gender, age, race, ethnicity, ableness, wealth, and class, have informed and defined who represents the community. I will discuss the participatory transformative research approach as a methodological perspective that addresses most of the limitations outlined above.

Transformative Participatory Action Research

Hsiao-Chuan Hsia (2006) defines as *praxis-oriented research* a type of participatory research that combines an emphasis on participants as co-researchers with an emphasis on personal and social transformation, while Robert Chambers (1994) refers to this as *activist participatory research* and Donna Mertens (2009) calls it *transformative participatory action research*. The guiding principle in transformative participatory action research for personal and social transformation is purposive active engagement and political action by both the researched and the researcher. The researched and the researcher begin with a clear understanding that research is not neutral and that ideology determines the methodology of searching for knowledge and defining what can be known (Freire, 1973).

Activist participatory research grew out of the experiences and practices of conscientization in Latin America and from Paulo's Freire's work and inspiration, especially through his book *Pedagogy of the Oppressed* (1970). Freire's concept of conscientization plays an important part in political activism of the researched. A process that is part of Freire's liberatory education, conscientization helps the learner to move toward a new awareness of relations of power, myths, and oppression. In this context, the researched learn to perceive social, political, and economic contradictions and to take action to change the way they think and do things. The poor and the exploited are empowered to believe in themselves and to have the confidence and the will to conduct research on their own reality using their ways of knowing and to use the research findings to embark on positive social change. The most commonly cited definition of participatory action research with a transformative element first came from the Toronto Participatory Group after the Cartagena conference of 1977:

- Participatory research involves a whole range of powerless groups of people—exploited, the poor, the oppressed, and the marginalized;
- It involves the full and active participation of the community in the entire research process;

- The subject of research originates in the community itself, and the problem is defined, analyzed, and solved by the community;
- The ultimate goal is the radical transformation of social reality and the improvement of the lives of the people themselves. The beneficiaries of the research are members of the community;
- The process of participatory research can create greater awareness in the people of their own resources and mobilize them for self-reliant development;
- It is a more scientific method of research in that the participation of the community in the research process facilitates a more accurate and authentic analysis of social reality; and
- The researcher is a committed participant and learner in the process of research, that is, a militant rather than a detached observer (Hall, 1979, p. 5).

Participatory action research for personal and social transformation in the context of postcolonial indigenous research methodologies requires politically engaged methods. The following questions can guide the thought process of a researcher:

An activist researcher. How are the research questions asked? Are they deficit-based questions that rely on a deficit assumption about the researched, or do the questions focus on strengths and positive images of the researched? Why do I do research with the colonized and groups of people exploited and oppressed? Does the research have a clear stance against the political imperialism of its time? Does this research have a clear stance against marginalization and exploitation of the colonized that comes through either the research agenda pursued or the relationship of the researcher with the researched? Does the research address power struggles, oppression, and social differences such as race, gender, age, and class?

Geopolitical power relations. Does the research problematize and critique the tendency to make the researched speak through the voices, academic language, concepts, and theories of the West? Does the research problematize and critique Euro-Western archival knowledge and its exclusionary tendencies?

Reflexivity. Where do I stand with regard to the researched? Am I still the colonizer? Who are the researched? Are the researched still colonial subjects distinct from the colonizer because of their incapabilities, or are the researched active agents capable of generating solutions to their social challenges?

Change and transformation. Will this research bring about change? What theories and methods energize the researched to engage in a change process? Does this research change the way people think and do things? What theories and methods change the way people think and do things?

PARTICIPATORY RURAL APPRAISAL

One of the participatory methods to grow out of an attempt to address some of the questions raised above is the participatory rural appraisal (PRA). This is a term used to describe a family of approaches and methods that enable the disenfranchised, dispossessed communities in the third and fourth worlds to share and analyze their indigenous knowledge, life experiences, and conditions with the goal to plan and act. It began in the early 1970s and 1980s as a response to urban-based professionals' biased perceptions about the life experiences of the majority of the people in developing countries living in the rural areas and the defects of using large-scale surveys on these population groups. It is a people-centered methodology aimed at facilitating interaction between researchers and communities in urban and rural areas, so that researchers will better understand and learning from the researched. The goal is to initiate a participatory process that facilitates communities' ownership of the research process and outcomes (Mukherjee, 1997). PRA is widely practiced by a number of nongovernmental organizations and government departments in countries in Latin America, Canada, Australia, Asia, and Africa that are conducting research on and with the colonized Other. PRA methods are also increasingly being explored by university students and faculty carrying out research in various disciplines such as adult education, agriculture, gender studies, and so on. Three key principles are emphasized in PRA (Grenier, 1998, p. 42).

Culturally sensitive and responsive behavior and attitudes. PRA requires the researcher to be flexible, creative, patient, respectful, and willing to listen to and be taught by rural people.

Visual representation of information and ideas. PRA requires researchers to present information, ideas, or data in visual forms such as pictures, drawings, maps, charts, models, and graphs to increase participation by the illiterate, the poor, the exploited, disadvantaged women, children, and those with disabilities.

Multiple methods. PRA uses numerous research techniques that resonate with the colonized Other such as local histories, folklore, songs, poetry, dance, and so on. It also combines quantitative and qualitative methods to ensure meaningful participation of the researched in the inquiry process. For instance, PRA has been used to develop culturally appropriate survey questionnaires and to increase precision in sample surveys by engaging local people in the design. What follows is a discussion of some of the PRA techniques used with the survey method.

PRA Techniques and the Survey Method

We noted that the PRA methodology uses a combination of quantitative and qualitative methods. For example, it might use a survey questionnaire together with interview methods. PRA qualitative techniques can be used to inform the survey questionnaire and the sampling strategies in sample surveys. Most survey questionnaires are developed in the West using the Western languages and Western-based conceptual and theoretical frameworks. This approach, Gerard Gill (1993, cited in Mukherjee, 1997) argues, is like adopting an inappropriate technology from a developed country for use in developing countries. PRA methods can help improve the questionnaire-based methods in the following ways:

1. Visual techniques in the PRA method can help answer questions that would otherwise remain ineffectively communicated through the usual questionnaires.
2. Through its use of community-based data collection techniques, PRA allows participants to communicate from their frame of reference using their own vocabulary. In this way, PRA can be used to incorporate culture- and age-sensitive local words, terms, and concepts in the questionnaire.
3. PRA sessions in advance of a survey can assist in the framing of the questionnaire in terms of the perceived topics to be covered, the kind of questions, the importance of the questions, and the number of questions necessary in a questionnaire survey.
4. A distinct merit of PRA is the interaction with groups and communities based on topics facilitated by the outsider (Mukherjee, 1997). Questionnaire surveys can employ such group interactions to solicit group views in addition to individual responses.

Participatory Sampling Methods

PRA methods can also be used to indigenize the sampling strategies in the survey method. In a sample survey, the accuracy of the method to generalize from the sample to the population from which it is drawn depends on precision of the sampling strategies selected. These sampling methods rely on accurate descriptions of the population of study in order to determine the sampling strategy and the sample size appropriate for the study.

The characteristics used to describe the populations are usually limited to categories of analysis in conventional research such as age, education, and occupation. These categories exclude other categories of analysis informed by communities' value systems and ways of perceiving reality. For instance, a sample survey to determine the income profile or wealth of a community might use indicators of wealth that are not compatible with the way a given community categorizes the wealthy and the poor. Stratifying and sampling on the basis of these indicators will automatically bias the sample toward the researcher's perception of what it is to be wealthy or poor. Some African communities are also more likely to recognize group categories rather than individual characteristics. For instance, in some communities in Botswana, adults remember their age regiments rather than their own specific ages. In some villages, wards are organized in hierarchical structures that signify social status as well as wealth. These local variations are important if the researcher is to draw a sample that is representative of the population. Knowing the size of the population from which to draw the sample is also essential. This is not possible in many contexts because of poor record-keeping.

PRA techniques have been used to complement and improve conventional sampling procedures. PRA strategies such as village and social mapping can bring out characteristics of people in the community that can inform decisions on the sampling strategies to be used. Social maps might show, for instance, characteristics or indicators that distinguish individuals from one another and how people might be grouped according to their social status. Following is an illustration of how village mapping can inform sampling methods.

Village Mapping

A village map involves participants drawing their village and incorporating all the features that are important in understanding a problem of study. In this example, a village map is used to determine the size of a population so that representative samples can be drawn. Suppose that a researcher wants to identify a proportional representative sample of adults participating in a literacy program in a village made up of five wards. The researcher does not know the size of the population in each ward and is therefore unable to estimate the sample size from each ward. Here are some of the steps that the researcher could follow:

- Hold discussions with the community to explain the problem and identify community members from each ward who are interested in participating in the study
- Make plans for map drawing in each ward
- Make a list of what should be shown in the map that can assist in sample selection

The following can be indicated on the map:

- Each household
- The names of each household's head
- The number of family members in each household who attend literacy classes
- Separate symbols for recording females and males

The main advantage of this procedure of determining population size is that ward members know each other and are able to give accurate information on current situations in each household. The village map could be rechecked through discussions with different ward members.

⬤ OTHER METHODS

Participatory video and theater are additional data collection methods that open up communication channels with communities and research participants, promote dialogue and discussion, and set in motion dynamic exchange of views from one community to another and across communities in other countries. The participatory video is a set of techniques aimed at involving a group or a community of people in shaping and creating their own film (Lunch & Lunch, 2006). The development of participatory video is credited to the work of Don Snowden, a Canadian who in 1967 worked with fishing communities on the Fogo islands to pioneer the use of media to enable a people-centered development approach. Today, participatory video is used worldwide and applied in a diversity of situations ranging from documenting the research process, monitoring community activities and interventions, and sharing research findings from community to community to providing a healing and therapeutic environment to the disempowered or conducting a research process with a decolonization focus.

Nick and Chris Lunch (2006, p. 12) provide the following steps for using a participatory video:

- Participants learn how to use video equipment through games and exercises.
- Facilitators help groups to identify and analyze important issues in their community by adapting a PRA, for example, participatory methods used in prioritizing issues such as well-being rankings and direct-matrix pair-wise ranking and scoring.
- Short videos and messages are directed and filmed by the participants.

- Footage can be shown to the wider community at daily screenings.
- A dynamic process of community-led learning, sharing, and exchange is set in motion.
- Completed films can be used to promote awareness and exchange between various different target groups.
- Participatory video films or video messages can be used to strengthen communication with both decision makers and with other communities.

Activity 8.1

Read the study extract included here and answer the following questions:

1. Discuss the participatory action research techniques employed in the study.

2. Would you classify the study as a participant as co-researcher approach or as a transformative participatory action research approach? Support your view.

3. Did this study lead to personal and social transformation? Support your view.

4. Assess the extent of participation, decolonization, and indigenization of the research study using the evaluation questions listed in this chapter.

5. How are the research questions asked? Are they deficit-based questions that rely on deficit assumptions about the researched, or do the questions focus on strengths and positive images of the researched?

Source: J. J. Perkins, R. W. Sanson-Fisher, A. Girgis, and S. Blunden (1995), "The Development of a New Methodology to Assess Perceived Needs Among Indigenous Australians." *Social Science Medicine, 41*(2), 267–275. Used with permission of Elsevier Science LTD; permission conveyed through Copyright Clearance Center, Inc.

Despite the advantages of needs assessments that utilize surveys, this methodological approach has been criticized on a number of issues. . . . Given the shortcomings inherent in the use of survey methodologies of needs assessment, the aim of this study was to develop a new refined methodology. More specifically, this methodology aimed to classify perceived needs into general areas

(Continued)

(Continued)

or domains of needs, allow the identified needs to be prioritized, and finally to reduce the complexity of the assessment instrument so that those with limited formal education could indicate and prioritize their perceived needs.

Prior to the study, an extensive review of the needs assessment literature was undertaken to produce a listing of the existing strategies available to collect needs information. A consultative process was then established between community members living in the study communities, Aboriginal Medical Service staff, and Aboriginal representatives from State Health departments and Aboriginal researchers who had previously conducted needs assessment research. The outcome of this consultation process was the development of a new strategy which incorporated graphics to collect perceived community needs. . . . Overall, items were classified into 4 domains: health; education and employment; housing; and social issues and community facilities. Each item from the 4 domains was then given to Aboriginal artists who designed and illustrated the graphics.

A two stage process was adopted to administer the community perceived needs measure. In the first stage, Health Workers presented participants with the graphics from each of the domains, one domain at a time asked the question "Could you please look through these pictures and choose the three areas which you feel are of greatest need within your community. Choose the three that you would like something done about the most, and then rank these three in order of priority. The most important should be placed as number one and the least important as number three." To enhance the visual representation of the graphics, a magnetic display board was available for participants. This board allowed participants to display their choices of need and to re-organize the priority of needs on a visual basis. . . . At the end of Stage 1, each participant had selected 3 items of need from each of the 4 domains. These 12 items were then carried over into Stage 2 where they were removed from their respective display boards and presented to the participants again. Participants were then asked to look at these 12 items and to select the top five items of greatest need for their community, irrespective of the domain from which the items had originally been chosen. The top five items were then displayed and participants were asked to rank these items in order of priority. Again, the top as number one and the least important as number five. Overall, the process of administration took approx. 15 min. for each person.

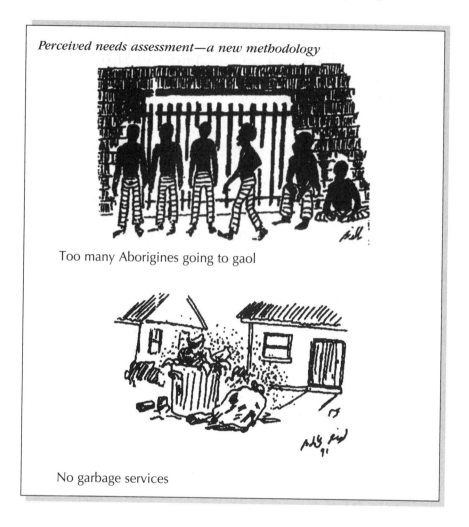

Perceived needs assessment—a new methodology

Too many Aborigines going to gaol

No garbage services

Appreciative Inquiry and Participatory Action Research

One of the criticisms addressed to participatory action research is that most of the approaches are problem focused, aiming at discovering communities' resource constraints, deficiencies, and unmet needs. Problem-focused modes of inquiry work with deficit questions and may serve only

> to contain conversations, silence marginal voices, fragment relationships, erode community, create social hierarchy, and contribute to cultural enfeeblement—thereby allowing scientific vocabularies of deficit to establish the very conditions they seek to eliminate. (Mertens, 2009, p. 184)

The end result is that people may see their communities as places full of problems and needs that can be solved only with the help of outsiders. Jim Ludema, David Cooperrider, and Frank Barrett (2006) recommend combining participatory action research with appreciative inquiry to change the mind-set of the researcher and the researched, inform the questions researchers ask and how they ask them, and ultimately create a research process that leads to social change and transformation.

Appreciative inquiry can be viewed as an approach to change-focused research (Reed, 2006). One of the challenges researchers face is moving away from the deficit-focused modes of inquiry using deficit-based questions (Ludema et al., 2006) to theoretical frameworks of positive psychology with emphasis on strengths and positive images of the researched. Appreciative inquiry is a change-focused research approach that is guided by affirmative assumptions about the researched people or communities. There are four phases to the approach:

> *Discovery*. During this phase, participants talk, discover and learn the best of the moments in the history of an organization or community. Participants tell stories of exceptional accomplishments and discuss the aspects of their history that they most value and want to enhance.

> *Dreaming*. During this phase, participants envision and imagine other possibilities for their organizations or communities. They may, for instance, use the positive stories to create a portrait of an organization or community's potential. Positive images grounded on extraordinary moments of a community's or organization's history are used to envision possibilities and suggest plans for the future.

> *Design*. In the design phase, participants dialogue on strategies to implement their dream.

> *Destiny*. This final stage involves delivery of new images of the future. During this stage, everyone realigns their activities with the positive image or ideal in a community or organization, and co-create the future.

An appreciative action research inquiry approach propels researchers to address the question: How are research questions asked, research objectives phrased, and questionnaire and interview guide questions framed? Sarah Michael (2005) used this approach as an interview tool to move her study from problem-focused to an appreciation-focused inquiry. Michael isolated the discovery stage from the dreaming, designing, and destiny phases of the full process and designed an interview protocol based on the discovery phase. The aim of Michael's research was to gain detailed understanding of the evolution of local nongovernmental organizations in Senegal, Tanzania, and Zimbabwe; their project and program experiences; and their relationships to their stakeholders. Michael decided to include in her research interview protocol questions centered on the best of what is within each NGO. Issues that needed to be covered were listed and then developed into appreciative questions. Michael lists these interview questions based on the discovery phase:

1. What's your favorite memory of working here?
2. What makes this NGO a good place to work?
3. What do you like best about your job?
4. Can you tell me about the history of your organization?
5. What first attracted you to work here?
6. What part of your work do you think your clients value most?
7. Can you describe the work of your organization?
8. What part of your work are you most proud of?
9. Which of your skills are you called on to use most often at your job?
10. How do you know when you have done a good job?
11. Can you tell me your favorite story about your clients?
12. What do you think attracts your clients to your organization?
13. What makes your organization special or different from other NGOs that you know?
14. What do you think is the heart of your organization's success?
15. What makes your relationship with your clients work?
16. Can you tell me about the groups or people that support your NGO and its work?
17. Can you tell me about the donor organization that you find to be the most supportive of your NGO?
18. What makes your relationship with them special?
19. Can you tell me about situations in which your NGO and the government have worked together?
20. If I came back to visit you in five years, what do you think your organization would look like?
21. What strengths and resources will best help you to achieve these goals?
22. If the director of an NGO that was just starting out wanted to learn from your experience, what's the best piece of advice that you could give them? (Michael, 2005, p. 225)

Using the interview questions listed, Michael conducted 60 appreciative inquiry interviews and noted that interviewees were eager to tell their stories; offered dynamic and unrehearsed information; and spoke more openly, with less defensiveness or fear of reprisal. You can also use appreciative questions in a focus group interview using indigenous social-justice methods like sharing circles.

You can employ, along with appreciative inquiry, desire-centered research frameworks (Tuck, 2009) to move research from focusing on deficit and damage. In a study on health, for instance, a researcher who incorporates a desire-centered framework in the research process would document the state and magnitude of a poor health system along with positive images of the health system that demonstrate hope, possibilities, and desire to change health system.

Eve Tuck (2009) illustrates a desire-centered method related to the exhibit, "Stereotypes vs. Human types: Images of Blacks in the 19th and 20th Centuries," at the New York Public Library in Harlem. She explains how the exhibit illustrates a research methodology that can name damage, only to refute it and paint another world that shows resistance, defiance, survivance, hope, desire, and possibilities. In this example, Tuck explains that the exhibit was divided into two rooms. The first room, which was the stereotypes side, showed negative images of Black Americans in advertising, entertainment, science, and education. The second room showed the "human types side," daguerreotype representations, "compelling, dimensional and nuanced images of African Americans" (Tuck, 2009, p. 417). These images were captured by U.S.- born Africans living in the 19th century who wanted to refute the prominent stereotype images in the first room. The images in the second room, Tuck explains, revealed complexity in who Black Americans believed they were and a further desire about what they can still be. This desire-centered method demonstrates the need to reflect on the theory of change that informs participatory research approaches, methods, and ethical frameworks employed in research with the colonized Other.

Healing Participatory Action Research Methods

In the previous chapters, it was noted that researchers and the researched needed to heal the wounds from a long history of the subjugation of postcolonial indigenous worldviews, ways of knowing, and indigenous knowledge systems and from the deficit theorizing about them that creates stereotypes of hopelessness and lack of agency.

Research with postcolonial subjects, indigenous peoples, and oppressed groups can be viewed as a "life changing ceremony" (Wilson, 2008, p. 61) in which indigenous practices of healing are incorporated in the research process through the use of various forms of symbols. Lynn Lavallée (2009) illustrates the use of the Anishnaabe symbol-based reflection method as an example of a participatory action research method that promotes healing and personal transformation.

Anishnaabe Symbol-Based Reflection

The Anishnaabe symbol-based reflection method is an arts-based method named after the Anishnaabe people, from whom the method was born (Lavallée, 2009). Lavallée incorporated the knowledge, values, and beliefs of the Ojibway, Algonquin, and Cree Nations in Canada to conduct an indigenous community-based research. The Anishnaabe symbol-based reflection method emerged from this community-based research. The method includes sharing circles (see explanation in Chapter 4) and symbols such as paintings, drawings, sculptures, crafts, songs, teachings, and stories. The Anishnaabe symbol-based reflection method was influenced by a participatory action research method called photovoice (Lavallée, 2009). In the photovoice research method, participants identify, represent, and enhance their community through photography. Photovoice is similar to participatory video. Participants are provided with cameras, which they use to capture stories, events, or practices that represent their voices on a given research issue. The three main goals that the photovoice and participatory video methods share with Anishnaabe symbol-based reflection method are:

- To enable people to record and reflect their community's strengths and concerns
- To promote critical dialogue and knowledge about personal and community issues through large and small group discussions of photographs, or symbols in the case of Anishnaabe symbol-based reflection method
- To enable dissemination of findings to policymakers

Activity 8.2

The extract below illustrates the execution of sharing circles and Anishnaabe symbol-based reflection method as healing and decolonizing participatory action research methods. Read the extract and discuss the following questions:

1. What were the benefits to participants of the methods used?

2. How are the symbols and songs used in the study, and what is their role in personal transformation of the participants?

(Continued)

(Continued)

3. What is the extent of voice, participation, decolonization, and indigenization of the research study using the evaluation questions listed in this chapter?

4. Would you classify the approach as deficit-, damage-, desire-based or appreciation-focused inquiry?

Source: L. F. Lavallée (2009), "Practical Application of an Indigenous Framework and Two Qualitative Indigenous Research Methods: Sharing Circles and Anishnaabe Symbol-Based Reflection," *International Journal of Qualitative Methods, 8*(1) 21–36. © 2009 Lavallée. Used by permission.

Introduction

The research topic focused on the physical, mental, emotional, and spiritual impacts of a physical activity program: a martial arts (tae kwon do) program offered to the Native Participants in this project were members of the Native Canadian Centre of Toronto, an Aboriginal cultural and recreation centre. The martial arts program had been part of the Native Canadian Centre since 1999. The program was equally a social, cultural, and spiritual program. The instructor, of Cree ancestry, brought his Aboriginal teachings into the classroom.

Conducting the sharing circles

Nine sharing circles with 16 people were carried out. The circles were scheduled at a convenient time for the participants, typically before or after a class. The smallest circle consisted of two people, and the largest had six. All circles included light snacks and beverages. I had prepared tobacco bundles prior to the sharing circles. . . . All 16 participants accepted the tobacco, including the non-Aboriginal participants.

Implementing Anishnaabe symbol-based reflection

At the end of the sharing circle, I introduced the second method: Anishnaabe symbol-based reflection. Doing this after the sharing circles allowed for examples to be used based on what was shared in the circles. I asked participants to think about a symbol or symbols that represented what and how they felt about the physical activity program and how it has influenced their lives, the lives of their families, and/or their community. I worked through some examples so that the participants could gain a deeper understanding of this method

Results

Aboriginal culture and tradition were interwoven in the teaching of the martial arts. The following stories reflect this.

I know that not all Native people are searching for their identity, but my life has been a lifelong journey of trying to understand who and what I am. This has caused problems for me. I understand now that the biggest problem was the sense of undeservingness I have. I don't think of it as a lack of self-esteem. Coming here is opening my eyes that I am deserving. I am deserving of my black belt, I am deserving of having people care about me and not hurt me. My Medicine Wheel with the hawk—my clan—symbolizes my healing journey and the growing understanding I have of myself as Anishnaabe. Kwe—As a woman. My undeservingness as a woman—I'm understanding through our informal healing circles in the bathroom and the strength that I get when I walk through these doors that my undeservingness is a symptom that comes from our long history and how we unlearned our ways to respect women. It comes from my Dad and his Dad and so on . . . and in turn the men I have selected because I'm comfortable with and expect to be treated unwell. So, my next symbol is The Strong Women's Song. The song that I know has brought me helpers to unlearn this lack of deserving. (Hawk)

THE PARTICIPATORY ACTION RESEARCH PROCESS

You have now learned about several research techniques that are used in indigenous participatory research approaches and how scholars have used some of the methods in their studies. I will discuss a recommended participatory action research approach that maximizes community involvement. The Trust for Community Outreach Education (2001, p. 89) in South Africa has recommended five steps that can be followed to ensure maximum participation of communities in research projects as follows:

1. Selecting a shared community problem and planning for the action research
2. Culturally sensitive and context-relevant gathering of information guided by group reflection
3. Continuous collection of data through fieldwork
4. Community-informed analyzing and interpretation of data
5. Planning and taking action

The *PRA Field Handbook* produced by Egerton University (2000, p. 14) in Kenya augments the above process by adding eight steps:

1. Site selection
2. Preliminary visits
3. Launching
4. Data gathering
5. Data synthesis and analysis
6. Preparation of community action plan (CAP)
7. Adoption of the CAP and strategies for its implementation
8. Participatory monitoring and evaluation

Imagine that you wanted to engage a community in a process of collective inquiry that would empower them to make certain decisions about some aspects of their life, for example, health.

Preparation

Your first step would be to decide on what shall make up a community and then to select a site. The next step is to select a person in the health field, for example, a health worker who is known to the community, to share with you the community culture and issues of concern and to introduce you to community leaders. At this initial stage, meetings should be devoted to building trust and rapport with the community.

Once introduced, the researcher takes time to know the community by appearing in public gatherings, reading local literature, and participating in public events where permitted. This process should be followed by a meeting with community leaders with the intention to recruit some of them as research partners who should assist in selling the research idea to the community. The assembled team should be representative in terms of gender, ethnicity, ableness, and all other social categories intended to benefit from the research.

Throughout the book, I have emphasized the importance of training the researched to be co-researchers in the inquiry. Once the research team is formed, members should be trained on goals, methods, and principles of change-focused research approaches such as appreciative inquiry (Ludema et al., 2006), and desired-based research approaches (Tuck, 2009). Training should be followed by defining the research questions and identifying issues of greatest importance to the community, keeping in mind that the research design and data-gathering techniques should be informed by change theories that move away from deficit- and damage-focused modes of inquiry to research guided by affirmative assumptions about the researched communities. A structure to guide decision making should also be discussed and agreed upon, for example, a consensus on the operational ethical principles. This should be followed by allocation of roles and responsibilities.

Launching

In the second stage, community leaders who are also part of the research team inform the whole community about the research idea through public meetings. The research should be as inclusive as possible and thus the research project should reach all the segments of the community. It is important that the research team identify strategies for community mobilization that ensure maximum community participation. For instance, leaders of the various community organizations such as church leaders, youth organizations, women's organizations, and so on may be requested to launch the research project in their organization. Members of the research team have to be present at all the community mobilization and launch ceremonies.

Data Collection

Field data can be clustered into spatial, temporal, social, and technical data. It is important to use methods that ensure maximum participation of community members as well as maximum use of local knowledge and resources.

Spatial data. Data collection starts with a map of what the community perceives to be its community space (Egerton University, 2000). With some training, community members use local materials such as sticks, stones, foliage, and so on to create landmarks identifying facilities, distribution of various resources, social set-ups, community constraints, strength in their community, and so on. This can be followed by transect walks and guided field walks where the researcher and community co-researchers conduct a walking tour through areas of interest to observe, to listen, to identify different zones or conditions, and to ask questions to identify problems and possible solutions. Roles are reversed; community co-researchers are the experts, and the researcher listens and learns as much as possible from them.

Time-related data. You have learned about the importance of a people's history in the research process. Participatory action research recognizes the importance of recording significant events in the life of a community that may influence attitudes and behavior. PRA uses time lines to list and date major historical community events, past trends, events, disasters, tragedies, challenges, opportunities, and achievements. The time line is created by holding discussions with groups of all ages and sectors of the community. The information can help the community to understand the underlying causes of its challenges, envision solutions based on past experiences, and focus on future actions and information requirements. Also included under time-related data are seasonal calendars and daily activity profiles. Seasonal calendars record monthly activities and highlight particular peak times in the community that may constrain, delay, or facilitate the implementation of a research project. For instance, it may not be ideal to start a community project that involves mothers during a harvesting period because most of them might be away in the fields. Daily activity profiles of men, women, youth, and elders give the research team data on the amount of time community members can devote to the project.

Social data. Household interviews collect data about activities of each member of the household and household resources as well as a record of the household's local folklore, songs, dance, and poetry that provide insight into values, history, practices, and beliefs of the community. Household histories or stories of community challenges and how they were resolved are recorded to provide insightful descriptions of characteristic problems and how they are dealt with. Intriguing practices and beliefs based on myth are also recorded. Practices that are unusual or do not fit into the conventional scientific thinking are explored for as long as they are meaningful to local people (Grenier, 1997).

Technical data. Technical data may include survey data required to complement local data generated by the community. At this point, the researcher should reach a consensus with the co-researcher on the type of expert data needed to supplement community-produced data. As a researcher, you could still involve the community in village mapping, for instance, to determine the size of the population in the site of study.

Data Analysis

Community members who were involved in the data collection should also participate in the analysis and interpretation of the findings and in identifying data-informed challenges and solutions in the community. In this way, the researcher is less likely to be criticized for limited insight or cultural insensitivity. An effective way to engage the community in the data analysis is to create thematic groups. Each group explores a theme using the available data; identifies the challenges, causes of problems, and opportunities; envisions and imagines other possibilities; and suggests solutions and plans for the future. The researcher facilitates group discussions and decision making by drawing the community's attention to issues of sustainability, productivity, equitability, costs, technical feasibility, sociocultural acceptance, time scales, and human resources.

Those involved in the data analysis should be encouraged to present their findings to the rest of the community. Presentation formats could include exhibition of diagrams, maps, charts, and photos of the research activity in public places or at selected community gatherings. Sharing information facilitates discussions and provides an additional cross-checking device, while exhibitions can inspire other community members to take part in research activities. Once the groups are through with the analysis, they can come together to prioritize the issues and agree on a community action plan. Participatory methods used in prioritizing issues could include wealth and well-being rankings and direct-matrix pair-wise ranking and scoring (Grenier, 1997). In wealth and well-being ranking, for example, people are asked to sort cards (or slips of paper) representing individuals or households from rich to poor or from sick to healthy. This technique can be used for cross-checking information and for initiating discussions on a specific topic, for example, poverty. The technique can also be used to produce a benchmark against which future development interventions can be measured or evaluated. With indirect-matrix pair-wise ranking and scoring, people rank and compare individuals, items, or resources using their own categories and criteria by raising hands or placing representative objects on a board. The Perkins et al. (1995) study discussed in Activity 8.1 illustrates some of the ranking procedures. Once completed, the community action plan should also be shared with the rest of the community using some of the PRA methods discussed in this chapter.

Creating a Community Action Plan (CAP)

The community action plan will show the goal of the research project, the objectives to be achieved, strategies to achieve the objectives, time frame, persons responsible, resources required, and a monitoring and evaluation framework.

Implementation, Monitoring, and Evaluation

Once the research process is completed, the researcher's role should be that of ensuring that tasks listed in the plan are completed on time, community members take up their roles and responsibilities, and a monitoring and evaluation framework is in operation. A final participatory phase is that of community involvement in the monitoring and evaluation of the activities in the CAP. Evaluation should be carried out by a team from within the community. Involving the community in the monitoring and evaluation process ensures that they continue to use local indigenous knowledge methods to track progress and actions related to the implementation of the CAP. It is good practice to form an evaluation committee made up of community members. The committee should agree on what formative evaluation methods are to be, how results will be reported to the community, when reports should be made, and how evaluation reports should be used. For instance, photovoice videos and films can be used to report on significant achievements as well as weaknesses that need to be addressed. The reports keep the community informed of their activities and enable the community to revise their implementation strategy before it is too late. Clearly, then, the PRA approach places the entire research process and implementation of the research findings in the hands of the community.

▌ SUMMARY

This chapter has discussed two types of participatory action research approaches: the participants as co-researchers only focus and transformative participatory action research approaches that have been used with oppressed groups and postcolonial subjects. The PRA methodology was discussed as an action research approach that was developed to maximize participation of marginalized communities and oppressed groups and the colonized Other in general, in the research process and in resolving challenges in their communities. The need was also noted to combine participatory action research methods that are problem focused with appreciative-inquiry and desired-focused approaches to facilitate healing and social transformation. The chapter emphasizes the need to change the mindset of the researcher and the researched.

KEY POINTS

- Action research aims at demystifying the research process so that it does not remain solely in the hands of experts.
- The key to action research is participation of the researched as co-researchers and the empowerment and social transformation of the colonized Other.
- Participatory action research approaches use a combination of methods to facilitate appreciative-inquiry and desire-focused approaches, leading to healing of the researched and a wider scope of representation for the voices of the dispossessed, disenfranchised colonized Other in the research process.
- Participatory action research approaches assume that the researched are best placed to identify and address their challenges and that their local indigenous knowledge can inform interventions to address community challenges.

Activity 8.3

Read the case study below and answer the following questions:

1. How were the co-researchers selected?

2. How were decisions concerning the project made?

3. Who designed the project objectives and the research design?

4. Who designed the research instrument and collected and analyzed the data?

5. Who prepared the research report?

6. What were the benefits of the project to the community and to the co-researchers?

7. Assess the extent of participation, decolonization, and indigenization of the research study using the evaluation questions listed in this chapter.

(Continued)

(Continued)

Source: Louise Grenier (1998), *Working With Indigenous Knowledge: A Guide for Researchers,* International Development Research Centre, Ottawa. Used by permission.

A case study from Ecuador

IK research has often been carried out by outsiders for other outsiders, with the result that the content, language, and storage location of the data made the research findings inaccessible to the local communities. By way of contrast, this Ecuadorian case study (Kothari, 1995) is an account of how local people compiled a book of their oral knowledge of medicinal plants.

It took 10 months to complete the book (3 months to do the research; 7 months to prepare the book). An NGO representing 18 communities from the region provided administrative support. Following the presentation of the project objectives, the 18 communities were formally invited to participate in the project. Each community was asked to select two literate participants, one female and one male. The project coordinators (three NGO members, a locally respected healer, and the author) offered 10 USD per month to attract participants; the total budget was 2,000 USD. Six of the 18 communities expressed an interest, but initially the majority was unable to find a female participant. In some cases, the younger women's parents or husbands worried about mixed-gender issues. Older women did not meet the literacy requirement, but they willingly participated once the literacy requirement was relaxed. Ultimately, the project team included the project coordinators and six men and six women from various villages.

The coordinators developed a short, bilingual questionnaire to obtain the following information about the medicinal plants and their uses: symptoms and causes of illness, the corresponding plant remedy, a description of the plant and its habitat, its local name(s), the method for preparing and administrating the remedy, and the plant's nonmedical uses. Other questions helped to identify the traditional healers. The coordinators trained the 12 participants to administer the questionnaire by pairing them up and asking them to interview and document one another's knowledge of medicinal plants. This pretested and improved the wording of the questionnaire. Most important, it provided the participants with an opportunity to gain hands-on experience with an unfamiliar exercise, both as interviewers and interviewees. Following the training session, the participants selected the interviewees, usually from their own community, and completed the questionnaires in their preferred language.

All the participants met once a week to discuss their experiences and to review the completed questionnaires. Important project decisions, such as addressing individual concerns, planning the direction of the project, dealing with financial matters, and setting a target number of questionnaires to be completed per week, were made collectively. At the end of the interviewing phase, the budget was exhausted. Seven of the initial participants (five of them women) continued with the project. In the post interview phase, the collected information was sorted by plant species. If there was consensus on a particular plan remedy, the participants summarized the data. Remedies for which there was no consensus were laid aside for further investigation

Kothari designed the book for the villagers. The information is presented in a structured but simple format, in both Spanish and the local language. The book presents the preparation and administration of each remedy in written and pictorial form. A drawing of the plant and its local name are also given. Four hundred copies of the book were presented to the participating communities. The intent is to have all proceeds from the sale of the book support related activities.

SUGGESTED READINGS

Chambers, R. (1994). Participatory Rural Appraisal (PRA): Challenges, potentials, and paradigm. *World Development, 22*(10), 1437-1454.

Grenier, L. (1998). *Working with indigenous knowledge: A guide for researchers.* Ottawa: International Development Research Centre.

Lavallée, L. F. (2009). Practical application of an indigenous framework and two qualitative indigenous research methods: Sharing circles and Anishnaabe symbol-based reflection. *International Journal of Qualitative Methods, 8*(1) 21-36.

Ludema D. J., Cooperrider, D. L., & Barrett, F. J. (2006). Appreciative inquiry: The power of the unconditional positive question. In P. Reason & H. Bradbury (Eds.), *Handbook of action research* (pp.155-165). Thousand Oaks, CA: Sage.

Lunch, N., & Lunch, C. (2006). *Insights into participatory video: A handbook for the field.* Sevierville, TN: Insight Publishing.

Michael, S. (2005). The promise of appreciative inquiry as an interview tool for field research. *Development in Practice, 15*(2), 222-230.

Perkins, J. J., Sanson-Fisher R. W., Girgis, A., & Blunden, S. (1995). The development of a new methodology to assess perceived needs among indigenous Australians. *Social Science Medicine, 41*(2), 267–275.

RTI International. (2004). *Community-based participatory research: Assessing the evidence* (AHRQ Publication, No. 04-E022–2). Chapel Hill: University of North Carolina.

CHAPTER **9**

POSTCOLONIAL INDIGENOUS FEMINIST RESEARCH METHODOLOGIES

Women in colonized spaces not only suffer the yoke of colonial oppression, but also endure the burden of two patriarchal systems imposed on them.

Musa Dube (2000, p. 20)

If we fail to recognize the ways in which subjective factors such as race, class, and gender influence the construction of knowledge, we are unlikely to interrogate established knowledge which contributes to the oppression of marginalized and victimized groups.

Patience Elabor–Idemudia (2002, 230)

OVERVIEW

The chapter highlights attempts to decolonize Euro-Western methodologies from the perspective of non-Western marginalized feminisms. The argument is that women in non-Western societies have been marginalized and their voices distorted by Western patriarchies, third world patriarchies, colonialism, imperialism, and globalization, as well as by Western feminist theory and research. The chapter is devoted to defining postcolonial Indigenous feminists' methodologies; the worldviews, perspectives, and epistemologies that inform these methodologies; and research methods that privilege non-Western women. The chapter further describes healing research methods that have emerged from research with women as they encounter multiple oppressions and dominations. As much as possible, I use excerpts to illustrate what scholars say they do when they conduct research and write about what they call third world feminisms, African feminisms, Black feminisms, borderland-Mestizaje feminisms, or marginalized feminisms.

LEARNING OBJECTIVES

By the end of this chapter, you should be able to:

1. Distinguish between postcolonial indigenous feminist theory and Western feminist theory, as well as recognize the complementary nature of Western feminist theory and research perspectives to postcolonial indigenous feminist perspectives
2. Understand some of the misconceptions in Western feminist theory and literature in relation to non-Western women in the third world and the African Diaspora and women in the First Nations.
3. Identify and describe postcolonial indigenous feminist epistemologies and methods that privilege non-Western women's voices
4. Describe healing methods used in research with women

Feminism is "a movement and a set of beliefs that problematizes gender inequality" (DeVault, 1999, p. 27). There are many feminisms, each distinguished according to its emphasis and aims. For instance, for African feminisms, the deconstruction of Western concepts, theories, categories of analysis, and knowledge production about Africa, Africans, and African women is a vital step toward producing knowledge that expresses the lived experiences of women. Feminism, nevertheless, expresses a concern with the neglect of women and the inevitable male bias in the structures of academic disciplines, the theoretical frameworks that inform research practices, the methodologies, the methods, the fieldwork, the analytical frameworks, and the reporting strategies. In this chapter, the emphasis is on how research is theorized and practiced from the perspective of non-Western, marginalized feminisms.

POSTCOLONIAL INDIGENOUS FEMINIST THEORY AND RESEARCH METHODOLOGIES

The term *postcolonial indigenous feminist research methodologies* is used here to refer to the process of critique, decolonization, and indigenization of Euro-Western methodologies and the theorizing of methodologies that are informed by the theoretical perspectives and the worldviews of third world feminisms, African feminisms, Black feminisms, borderland-Mestizaje feminisms, and all the marginalized non-Western feminisms. Shailaja Fennell (2009) has outlined four contested themes that come from a comparison of gender theory from Western Europe and America with those from locations within Africa and South Asia. The first theme is an argument by non-Western feminists for a deconstruction of universalization within gender theory. Scholars are, for instance, expressing their criticism about deficit theories of non-Western societies and omissions of their worldviews and the oral literatures that inform their frames of reference. There is, for instance, a discontent among non-Western feminists, who believe that some Western feminisms have used Western female-based structures of language, concepts, theories, models of reality, and worldviews as criteria against which experiences of all non-Western women and non-Western men can be known and written about. Fennell and Madeleine Arnot (2009) note that the result of universalized Western gender theory is that the diversity of experiences of girls and women in non-Western societies, their struggles, negotiations, and resistance to different forms of patriarchal oppression and domination, as well as imperial domination, are most likely to go unrecognized. A postcolonial indigenous feminist perspective moves out of the cage of universalized Western gender theory and employs postcolonial and indigenous perspectives to reveal local standpoints that express girls' and women's agency and resistance to oppression.

The second theme centers on the denial by Western feminists of non-Western women's power within indigenous relational worlds that celebrate motherhood, sisterhood, and friendship. In Africa, for example, a variety of African feminisms emphasize the centrality of motherhood in African households and family organizations and the agency and power of mothers as the source of solidarity. Among the Tswana-speaking people in Botswana, the following proverbs (Chilisa, 2002) illustrate woman-centered, mother-centered feminism:

Ngwana wa mosadi ga a wele mo isong.	A woman's child does not fall into the fire due to exhaustion.
Ngwana wa mosadi ga a ke a bopama ka na aswa.	A woman's child does not get lean or die from starvation.
Mosadi mooka o anya le mariga.	A woman will always provide even during difficult times.
Mmagwana ke yoo tswarang thipa kafa bogaleng.	A mother carries all the burdens of her children (Chilisa, 2002).

The argument is that the Othering of motherhood and the denial of the importance of African relational gender roles have relegated African women to subject/victim and further concealed how girls and women have used these roles as sites for resistance and sources of empowerment. These perspectives demonstrate the continued need for marginalized feminisms to theorize gender analysis from the perspectives, worldviews, and lived experiences of non-Western women.

The third theme is how non-Western feminists and postcolonial Indigenous feminists have used poststructural deconstruction methods to voice their discontent with the hegemonic intellectual apparatus. These writers have reworked the underlying concepts of structure and agency to privilege both contextual and indigenous meanings. Patricia Hill Collins (2000), writing about Black feminism, argues that knowledge is socially situated because it is based on experiences and different situations. This approach is supported by African feminists, who argue that oppressed groups can learn to identify distinct opportunities to turn their condition of marginalization into a source of critical insight about how the dominant society thinks and is constructed. Carole McCann and Seung-Kyung Kim (2003) also observe that this self-reflection and self-actualization have the potential to develop a feminist theory of knowledge that delineates a method for constructing effective knowledge from the insights of women's experiences.

The last theme is how African and Asian feminists and other non-Western feminists aim to move gender research toward postcolonial and indigenous approaches and how they construct knowledge derived from the experiences of girls and women in their specific locations and histories. Non-Western feminisms call for the critique, decolonization, and indigenization of Euro-Western methodologies as well as the literature and theory about the Other. They propose and describe ways to read literature, employ theory, and conduct research while resisting all forms of patriarchal and imperial oppression (Dube, 2000). They also urge scholars to "find and highlight theory and theorizing in spaces perhaps not deemed theoretical from a Western academic perspective" (Saavedra & Nymark, 2008, p. 258); to employ theoretical frameworks that are eclectic and combine theories and techniques from disparate disciplines and paradigms to construct their own paradigms (Sandoval, 2000); and to demonstrate "what indigenous cultures can offer in terms of concrete ways to read/re-read our current situations in the world" (Dillard 2008, p. 278). Catherine Marshall and Michelle Young (2006) argue that we must view gender research as a revolution and that methodology used to investigate gender issues must involve "assertive question shifting, redefinition of issues, sharp attention to the power of dominant values, and vigilant monitoring of how questions are asked and how research is used" (p. 65).

The aims of research in the context of postcolonial indigenous feminist frameworks are to

1. Address "the complex matrix of power generated by a patriarchal, colonialist Eurocentrism that attempted to eliminate all remnants of cultures that were multifocal or egalitarian; or that represented a challenge to European male power" not usually addressed (Cannella & Manuelito, 2008, p. 48). For instance, Ifi Amadiume (1987), in her book, *Male Daughters, Female Husbands*, shows how patriarchal tendencies introduced by colonialism changed a somewhat flexible gender system that did not totally marginalize women into a more entrenched patriarchal system that is still evident today.

2. Challenge the Western feminist construction of universal female experiences, replacing it with the recognition of "specifically situated women" located within varying complex systems of power. The argument is that Western feminisms have used Western women's experiences as the norm and basis for the construction, analysis, and evaluation of the Other non-Western women's experiences. This Othering of non-Western women has resulted in the creation of stereotypes and images that portray non-Western women as oppressed, uneducated, and passive. For instance, there is a tendency to portray Muslim women as oppressed and to use their veil-wearing as a measure of their oppression (Mohanty, 1991) or to use the practice of clitorectomy in third world countries as a symbol of oppression. Consequently, it is argued that Western feminist theories impose their goals and aspirations on non-Western women and advocate for the eradication of all cultural practices that are oppressive from the standpoint of Western culture. Postcolonial indigenous feminist research requires researchers to bring into the research framework issues of class, ethnicity, and agency of non-Western women and to recognize that the expressions and experiences of patriarchy vary from one context to another (Lunden, 2006).

3. Challenge researchers to identify with the colonized and historically oppressed peoples of the world and women and to design and adopt research methodologies that reject essentializing but instead engage in intersectional analyses of all forms of erasure, domination, and exclusion. Collins's (2000) matrix of domination is an example of methodologies that engage in intersectional analyses of all forms domination and exclusion.

4. Challenge researchers to theorize research methods, analysis frameworks, and reporting strategies from bottom up, using the experiences of women and the diversity of indigenous knowledge systems and epistemological standpoints of women. The endarkened feminist epistemology and healing methodologies (Dillard, 2008) are examples of research perspectives that emerge from the indigenous knowledge, wisdom, and experiences of research participants.

5. Reject simplistic and dualistic research endeavors and appropriately renegotiate and reconcile Western feminisms and non-Western feminisms to create coalitions of knowledge systems, hybridity, alliances of worldviews (Cannella & Manuelito, 2008), and transformative methods that build bridges across theories, disciplines, paradigms, and strategies for globalizing resistance from bottom up. This chapter presents borderland-Mestizaje feminism as an example of a framework that enables researchers to use what they need in order to be heard and understood (Saavedra & Nymark, 2008).

6. Challenge researchers to be radical activists who involve women and marginalized peoples in participatory transformative action research and who challenge the Eurocentric error that assumes that only "scientists have the 'right' (and ability) to intellectually know, interpret, and represent others" (Cannella & Manuelito, 2008, p. 49)

Researchers can use the following questions to assess the extent to which a postcolonial indigenous feminist perspective is present in the research studies they read or plan to conduct:

• Do the literature, theory, and research methods expose and show non-Western women's resistance to the multiple patriarchal systems that oppress women, to Western feminist theory that marginalizes non-Western women, and to imperialism and imperializing literatures? What alternative theory, literature, and research methodologies are proposed?

• Does this research demonstrate a genuine search for alternative research methodologies that promote interdependence between worldviews, knowledge systems, nations, races, ethnicities, and gender and sexual orientations? How does it achieve this objective?

- How does this research employ indigenous knowledge and literature to reject empire and envision alternative methodologies that rename the experiences of non-Western women from their standpoint, namely, the standpoint theory? How does it envision other ways of representing voices of women and other oppressed groups in research reports?
- Is the research action-oriented and values-oriented?

To fully understand how you can evaluate the dominance of Euro-Western methodologies and Western feminist theory in research on non-Western women and how you can translate the perspectives of postcolonial Indigenous feminists into your own research work, it is important to gain a basic understanding of feminist theory, Western feminisms, and how they evolved. I will highlight the generic meaning of feminist theory and how feminists problematize theory and the meaning of Western feminisms.

Jane Flax (1993) discusses the purpose of feminist theory:

1. To understand the power differential between men and women; how it came into being; what maintains it and how the power relations between men and women affect other power relations—for instance, race, ethnicity, class, ableness; and how patriarchy reinforces other oppressive power structures.
2. To understand women's oppression, how it evolved, how it changes over time, how it is related to other forms of oppression; and finally, how to change the oppression of women.

But then, what is theory? Should women theorize? What are the implications if women do not theorize? Alison Jaggar and Paula Rothenberg (1993) note:

A theory, in the broadest sense of the word offers a general account of how a range of phenomena are systematically interconnected by placing individual items in a larger context; it increases our understanding of the whole and the parts constituting that whole. Because people always want to make sense of their worlds, for the sake of intellectual satisfaction as well as practical control, every human society develops theories designed to organize reality in ways that make it intelligible. (p. 75)

While it may appear that theories are necessary for understanding and critiquing research methods that are oppressive to women, they have also been discredited by some feminists who charge theory itself with being "elit-ist," "totalizing," "arrogant," and even "terroristic" and privileging the realities of a few (Jaggar & Rothenberg, 1993, p. 76). Feminist liberal, radical Marxist, socialist, and postmodernist theories, for example, have been seen to origi-nate from the West and to be associated with white middle-class women. These theories also mark the differences in Western feminisms.

The views on the place of theory in women's work are varied. Arguing for theory, Flax (1993) maintains that for women to reject theory in their work is "to internalize the cultural prescription that women are unable to think abstractly" (p. 80). Women thus need to engage in theory to remedy the biases, omissions, and marginalization that come with male-oriented social science theory and to chart ways to end the subordination and oppression of women. Others (Saavedra & Nymark, 2008) propose a bottom-up approach to theorizing as a project that is "immediately active" allowing researchers to build "theory from the lives of ordinary women and from spaces unimagined in mainstream theorizing" (Dillard, 2008, p. 278). Postcolonial indigenous feminist theorizing on feminisms arises from the worldviews and lived experiences of non-Western women. Thus, we have African feminisms theo-rizing the experiences of women of African descent or borderland-Mestizaje feminisms theorizing from the perspectives of, for example, Chicana women. Western and non-Western feminisms are discussed to illustrate the differ-ences and similarities in these feminisms.

⬛ WESTERN FEMINISMS

According to Chandra Mohanty (1991) all Western feminist theories take the West as the norm. Drawing from J. Gaby Weiner (1995), feminisms that arise from these theories can be summarized as follows:

Liberal (or Bourgeois or Individualistic) Feminism

Liberal feminism focuses on the subordination of women through unequal opportunities that are institutionalized through the legal, political, social, and economic structures. The various versions of liberal feminism insist that women's opportunities should be equal with men's. The quest for equal opportunities for women and men have led to the development of gender planning and analysis tools that require policymakers and research-ers to assess whether different roles and needs of women are equally rep-resented in any given development activity. Most research sponsors today insist that women and other marginalized groups are included in a research study and that research findings are disaggregated by gender. Donna Mertens (2009) critiques a variety of gender analysis frameworks that are used in international development studies for sensitivity to cultural and contextual factors that define the lived experiences of women. She concludes that "simply adding gender as a variable to the inquiry without considering the cultural and contextual factors that surround gender does not yield transformative potential that is required" (p. 254) for marginalized groups. Most non-Western feminisms, for instance, emphasize the interdependence between men and women, noting that men are their partners in the struggle against oppression. There is, thus, a continued need for marginalized feminisms to theorize gender analysis from the perspectives, worldviews, and lived experiences of non-Western women.

Radical Feminism

Radical feminism focuses on the equal but different biological and psychological characteristics of men and women and insists that, although men and women are different, their characteristics have equal value. Radical feminists insist, for example, that the nurturing, intuition, and caring attributes of women should find space in knowledge production as much as the supposedly objective-oriented and abstract thinking of men. In social science research, for example, feminists have advanced care-based research ethics as an alternative to the duty ethics principles, with their emphasis on research driven by universal principles, and the utilitarian ethics of consequences, which prioritizes the goodness of research outcomes (Edwards & Mauthner, 2002). Postcolonial Indigenous feminists complement the ethics of care principle by recognizing a relational ethical framework where the researcher is a transformative healer actively involved in healing, building communities, and promoting harmony.

The Marxist Socialist Feminist Theory

Socialist feminist theory uses Marxist concepts of production, capitalism, class, race, ethnicity, and disability to explain women's marginalization and oppression. Socialist feminisms give researchers a framework to understand how different groups of women have different experiences that are affected by oppression rooted in class, race, ethnicity, or disability. Postcolonial indigenous feminist research emphasizes the contextual and cultural complexity in which women are situated and how these intersect with class, race, ethnicity, age, or ableness and with colonialism and imperialism to produce different forms of oppression.

POSTCOLONIAL INDIGENOUS FEMINISMS

What is clear, therefore, is that postcolonial indigenous feminist theories do not necessarily reject Western feminist theories but appropriate them to critique all forms of patriarchal oppressions and, in addition, critique Western feminisms for marginalizing the voices of non-Western women. The excerpt in Activity 9.1 illustrates research that resists Western feminist theory and literature that portray non-Western women as lacking agency. It shows the shortcomings of Western feminist theory as the universal point of reference in researching women's experiences.

Activity 9.1

Read the study extract included here and answer the following questions:

1. What features of Lunden's thesis make it postcolonial indigenous feminist research?

2. Review the role of postcolonial theory in research discussed in Chapter 2 and discuss its application to indigenous feminist research in this excerpt.

Source: E. Lunden (2006), *Postcolonial Theory Challenging Mainstream Feminist Perspectives*, Lund, Sweden: Lund University, Department of Political Science. Used by permission.

Postcolonial theory challenging mainstream feminist perspectives statement of purpose

Lunden (2006) discussed how the concept of empowerment could be understood within Western mainstream feminist theory and postcolonial/postmodern feminist theory. The aim was to challenge the mainstream feminist view of empowerment, which is hegemonic within the discourse of development. Lunden wanted to show that many assumptions made by Western mainstream feminist theory are not always universally true but that there are other ways of thinking about women and empowerment. The intention was more about contrasting the perspectives, rather than determining which understanding of empowerment is better.

Research questions

How does Western mainstream feminist theory conceptualize the Third World woman?

How does postcolonial feminist theory conceptualize the Third World woman?

How can empowerment be conceptualized from a Western mainstream feminist perspective?

How can empowerment be conceptualized from a postcolonial feminist perspective?

To what extent do the strategies used by the Garmeen Bank and SEWA to empower poor women reflect a Western mainstream feminist view of empowerment?

Conclusion

It was concluded that the theoretical discussion revealed that the different feminist approaches understand the Third World Woman in very different ways, or at least focus on different aspects. Mainstream feminism highlights the oppression of women by their husbands and by patriarchal structures, while postcolonial and postmodern feminists put emphasis on Third World women's ability to organize and to act in their own interests. It was also concluded that mainstream feminism tends to see economic advancement and development as the principal solution to women's subordination while postcolonial/postmodern perspectives require the poor women to decide what empowerment should entail.

In what follows, perspectives and worldviews on research methodologies from borderland-Mestizaje feminisms and Chicana feminist epistemologies, as well as African feminisms and endarkened feminist epistemology, are presented as examples of a growing distinctive body of literature about research practice and epistemologies emanating from non-Western feminisms. You are encouraged to identify other non-Western feminisms and the epistemologies, worldviews, and research practices emanating from those feminisms.

You will recognize ideas that were also discussed in previous chapters, such as self-determination in research, relational ways of existence and knowing, and the role of an activist researcher, participatory-transformative research methods, and healing participatory action research methods. This is because postcolonial indigenous feminist methodologies have a particular resonance with postcolonial indigenous research methodologies as they both challenge dominant Western methodologies and interrogate the role of colonialism and imperialism in the construction of knowledge. Postcolonial indigenous feminist research, in addition, seeks to make visible non-Western women's resistance to the multiple patriarchal systems that oppress women, to rename the experiences of non-Western women from their standpoints, and to envision other ways of representing voices of women and other oppressed groups in research. Feminist research in postcolonial contexts is more sensitive to the inclusion of gender, age, class, race, ethnicity, and disability in the research process and it takes a stand on behalf of building coalitions of knowledge systems.

Borderland-Mestizaje Feminism

Borderland-Mestizaje feminism is a hybrid and multidimensional mode of thinking that emerges from the work of scholars who center Chicana feminist perspectives and cultural practices in their inquiries, examinations, and analyses. It is "a tool, methodology, and an epistemology" (Saavedra & Nymark, 2008, p. 257). As a tool, Ellen Demas and Cynthia Saavedra (2004) note, "La mestiza deconstructs oppressive colonizing traditions and constructs new metaphors; she unlearns patriarchal assumptions and engages in a transnational feminist struggle; she interprets history and writes new myths; she tears down category and invites ambiguity" (p. 218). This method "entails grappling with multiple epistemologies and rejecting binary, simplistic, and deterministic ways of theorizing and researching" (Saavedra & Nymark, 2008, p. 257). Borderland-Mestizaje feminism "resist[s] the symbolic barriers that divide communities along race, class, gender, and sexual orientation lines, academic disciplines, political ideologies and organizational structures" (Elenes, 2005, p. 1). It seeks transformation for all whose voices have been silenced and "for those bodies that have been policed, regulated and medicalized (Saavedra & Nymark, 2008, p. 256). It seeks to highlight methodologies and methods of postcolonial indigenous societies that have been suppressed by dominant epistemologies. Borderland-Mestizaje feminism is an example of third-space methodologies. It theorizes a mosaic, rhizomatic, and integrative framework for synthesizing postcolonial indigenous methods, Western methodologies, and emergent methods and methodologies. A mosaic approach implies collecting, analyzing, and interpreting many pieces of data that voice people's experiences, ways of knowing, and worldviews in ways that are inclusive of all knowledge systems and that value diversity and promote democracy and self-determination for all. A rhizomatic approach implies a way of viewing knowledge as dynamic, heterogeneous, and nondichotomous and thus an approach that views post-colonial indigenous research methodologies as legitimate.

Multiple Epistemologies

An important characteristic of borderland-Mestizaje feminism is that it engages with multiple epistemologies. One of the most widely documented is the Chicana feminist epistemology. Dolores Delgado Bernal (1998) describes:

> A Chicana feminist epistemology must be concerned with the knowledge about Chicana—about who generates an understanding of their experiences, and how this knowledge is legitimized, or not legitimized. It questions objectivity, a universal foundation of knowledge, and the Western dichotomies of mind versus body; subject versus object; objective truth versus subjective emotion; and male versus female. In this sense, a Chicana feminist epistemology maintains connections to indigenous roots by embracing dualities that are necessary and complementary qualities and by challenging dichotomies that offer opposition without reconciliation. This notion of duality is connected to Leslie Marmon Silko's (1996) traditional Native American way of life: "In this universe, there is no absolute bad; there are only balances and harmonies that ebb and flow." (p. 64)

Four sources of cultural intuition are the foundation of a Chicana feminist epistemology: one's personal experience, the existing literature, one's professional experience, and the analytical research process.

Personal experience. Derived from the background that the researcher brings to the study, personal experience is shaped by family values and identities and knowledge of the community that is passed from generation to generation through oral traditions.

Existing literature. This consists of technical literature on a topic, such as theoretical or philosophical writings, and nontechnical literature, which includes biographies, public documents, person documents, and cultural studies writings.

Professional experience. This refers to cultural intuition that comes through long experience of working in a particular field or on a topic.

Analytical research process. Delgado Bernal suggests including Chicana participants in an interactive data analysis as a strategy that contributes to the researcher's cultural intuition. This is in addition to making comparisons, asking additional questions, thinking about what one is hearing and seeing, sorting data, developing a coding scheme, developing themes, and engaging in concept formation (Delgado Bernal, 1998).

Activity 9.2

The extract below illustrates Delgado Bernal's application of the Chicana feminist epistemology to educational research. Read it and do as follows:

1. List all the methods used in the article and suggest additional indigenous methods that you might use.

2. Delgado Bernal notes, "In the future, we must look for additional strategies that provide opportunities for Chicanas and are dedicated to achieving social justice." What are some of the indigenous focus group methods dedicated to achieving social justice discussed in this book?

3. Discuss the use of multiple methods and multiple theoretical perspectives in non-Western feminist research.

Source: Adapted from D. Delgado Bernal (1998), "Using a Chicana Feminist Epistemology in Educational Research," *Harvard Educational Review, 68*(4), 555–582. Copyright © by the President and Fellows of Harvard College. All rights reserved. For more information, please visit www.harvardeducationalreview.org.

Introduction

My historical-sociological case study, informed by my own achieved cultural intuition and a Chicana feminist epistemology, posed the following research question: How does pivoting the analysis onto key Chicana participants provide an alternative history of the 1968 Blowouts? This research question itself is distinctively Chicana, especially when compared to previous research that has examined the Blowouts. Chicano and White males have studied the event from a perspective of protest politics (Puckett, 1971); a spontaneous mass protest (Negrete, 1972); internal colonialism (Munoz, 193); the Chicano student movement (Gomez-Quinones, 1978);

and a political and social development of the wider Chicano movement (Rosen, 1973). Indeed, none of their historical accounts locate Chicanas in a central position in the research, or address the many factors that restricted or enabled Chicana students to partici-pate. My study in contrast, examined how women interpret their participation in the Blowouts nearly thirty years later, and how their participation is important to an understanding of transforma-tional resistance, grassroots leadership, and an alternative history of the Blowouts (Delgado Bernal, 1997, 1998).

Methodology

To gain new perspectives and interpretations of the 1968 Blowouts and Chicana school resistance, my primary methods of data col-lection were in-depth, semi-structured oral history interviews, with eight key female participants from the Blowouts, a two-hour semi-structured focus group interview, and phone interview. Following a network sampling procedure (Gandara, 1995), I interviewed eight women who were identified by other female participants or resource individuals as "key participants" or "leaders" in the Blowouts. In scheduling these interviews, I allowed ample time, realizing that the length of each interview would vary. The interviews took place when and where it was most convenient for each woman—in their homes, their mother's home, or at work. I created an interview protocol with open ended questions in order to elicit multiple levels of data that would address my research questions. Though the interview protocol was used as a guide, I realized that as the women spoke of very per-sonal experiences, a less-structured approach allowed their voices and ways of knowing to come forth. I also asked probing questions to follow up on responses that were unclear or possibly incomplete in order to understand how the women interpreted the reasons and ways in which they participated in the Blowouts.

Data analysis

After conducting individual oral history interviews, I corre-sponded with each woman twice. The first time I sent a complete copy of the interview transcript with a letter describing their role in the analysis of the data.

I now realize that the focus group process seemed natural to me, partially because of the cultural intuition I brought to the research project. I was used to my grandmother's storytelling in

(Continued)

which absolute "Truth" was less important to me than hearing and recording their life experiences. It was my familiarity with, and respect for ancestral wisdom taught from one generation to the next, and a regard for collective knowledge that allowed me to approach the research project with complete respect for each woman's testimony of school resistance. Indeed, the women shared their community knowledge through a form of storytelling in which all the women talked about their resistance by invoking stories about their families, quoting their parents, and mentioning where their parents were born. To make a point about democratic ideals and their right to question authority, Rosalinda contrasted her upbringing and socialization with that of her mother's generation earlier.

Conclusion

How educational research is conducted significantly contributes to what and whose history, community, and knowledge is legitimated. A Chicana feminist epistemology addresses the failure of traditional research paradigms that have distorted or omitted the history and knowledge of Chicanas. Though similar endarkened feminist epistemologies exist in specific segments, women's studies and ethnic studies acknowledging Chicana segments of women's studies, and ethnic studies acknowledging a Chicana feminist epistemology in educational research are virtually unprecedented. And yet, a disproportionate number of all Chicana and Chicana Ph.D.s received their doctoral degrees in the field of education, these scholars are restricted by cultural hegemonic domination in educational research.

A Chicana feminist epistemology gives Chicana and Chicano education scholars some freedom to interpret their research findings outside of existing paradigms, and hopefully develop and propose policies and practices that better meet the needs of Chicanas and Chicanos.

A major tenet of cultural intuition and a Chicana feminist epistemology is the inclusion of Chicana research participants in the analysis of data. This allows Chicana participants—whether they are students, parents, teachers, or school administrators—to be speaking subjects who take part in producing and validating knowledge. A focus group interview is one data collection strategy that helps Chicana scholars and non-Chicana scholars include the epistemology of their research participants in the analysis of data. The example I provide in this article demonstrates how focus groups can be paired with an oral history methodology to include Chicana participants in the interpretation of data. In addition, it seems that focus groups can be effectively used with other qualitative and quantitative research methods and methodologies, such as school ethnography, student interviews, survey research, and classroom observations. In the future, we must look for additional strategies that provide opportunities for Chicanas and are dedicated to achieving social justice. Hopefully, "an analysis of the Chicana/o experience can assist us in forging a new epistemological approach to academic life and can help us uncover a methodology that is true to and helpful in the struggle of these people as it 'creates' a new knowledge base" (Pizarro, 1998, p.72).

African Feminisms and Black Feminisms

Mekgwe (2003) defines African feminism as a discourse that

takes care to delineate those concerns that are peculiar to the African situation. It also questions features of traditional African cultures without denigrating them, with the understanding that these might be viewed differently by the different classes of women. (p. 7)

The following principles guide African feminisms and inform African feminist research practice:

Contextual and cultural complexity. African feminisms critique and reject dominant narratives that generalize, homogenize, and essentialize the conditions of African women, men, and children; instead, it seeks awareness of specific contexts, cultures, and peoples. Such an approach requires describing particular national or regional trends, while simultaneously raising awareness of contextual variations within broader trends. Some African feminists, for instance, prefer the term *womanism*, arguing that the term *feminism* is associated with Western ideologies. From this womanism perspective arose the term *Africana womanism* to describe the particular experiences of people of African origin, both diasporic and indigenous. I have noted that African feminisms, in contrast to other feminisms, emphasize the centrality of motherhood in African households and family organizations and the agency and power of mothers as the source of solidarity.

Comprehensiveness. This principle of African feminism emphasizes the interrelationships, interconnectedness, and interdependence between women, men, and children and between the living and the nonliving. Research and theorizing relies on understanding the complex and comprehensive parameters of the women's lives. Unlike Western feminism, for example, African feminisms recognize men as partners in the struggle against gender oppression. This desire not to separate women's issues from the male struggle is a significant departure from Western feminism, where male gender power relations are central to the feminist position (Reed, 2001).

Self-determination and liberation. This principle emphasizes the power and agency of Africans and African women in particular to theorize from their cultures and lived experiences, to produce knowledge that is contextually relevant, and to build relationships and heal the self, the community, and the larger sociocultural context. Africana womanism, for instance, claims that the solutions to gender inequality should be found in African philosophy. Explaining the Africana womanism position, Pamela Hudson-Wees (cited in Reed, 2001) notes, "Essentially, the Africana womanism position is that the framework for a world free of oppression already exists within traditional African philosophical worldview, if only the Africana woman will claim it" (p. 175).

The philosophical worldview of the Bantu of southern Africa is that a being is because of others. "I am we; I am because we are; we are because I am"; a person is through others. Refer back to Chapter 4. It was also noted there that existence-in-relation and being-for-self-and-others sum up the African conception of life and reality. Black feminists share similar views about relational existence. For example, in writing about African American women's collective voice experiences, Collins (2000) states, "The voice that I know is both individual and collective, personal and political, reflecting the intersection of my unique biography within the larger meaning of my historical times" (p. vi). Along similar lines, Cynthia Dillard (2008) describes an endarkened feminist epistemology that she argues is informed by African philosophical worldviews. An endarkened feminist epistemology describes

how reality is known when based in the historical roots of Black feminist thought, embodying a distinguishable difference in cultural standpoint located in the intersection/overlap of the culturally constructed socializations of race, gender and other identities; and the historical and contemporary contexts of oppressions and resistance of African ascendant women. (p. 280)

The emphasis is on disrupting the Euro-Western research paradigm, theorizing research from the lives of women and indigenous knowledge, and engaging in a transformative research process where the researcher is a supportive and reflective activist in the community. An endarkened feminist epistemology is guided by three key concepts that emerge from an African-based cosmology: spirituality, community, and praxis.

Spirituality. Dillard (2008) notes, no matter where they reside, spirituality is "the very essence" of African people. "It is a kind of cosmological spirituality that holds central the notion that all life is sacred and the moral virtue of individuals and that of the community is the same" (p. 278).

Community. An endarkened feminist epistemology emphasizes connectedness with the community through relations, language, and cultural ways of celebrating identities, including rituals to honor the living and the nonliving. In this context, research should become a participatory activity that involves the community and serves the ideals of the community.

Praxis. This principle emphasizes action-oriented research that serves the needs of the community. In the context of an endarkened feminist epistemology, the thoughts and actions of researchers should be informed by an African worldview.

The assumptions and key concepts in the endarkened feminist epistemology give rise to a healing methodology, which Dillard (2008) defines as follows:

Healing methodology is both a verb and a noun. Healing is as healing does. As a noun, healing methodology [includes] the indigenous practices/pedagogies that explicitly engage and enact the cultural knowledge, historical and traditional wisdom, politics, and ever-present spiritualities of Africa and her diaspora. It is a "dynamic spirituality that does not allow for fixed or definite theory that can be applied at all times and in all places" (Gutierrez, 2003, p. xii), but it is a form of struggle against domination and is "consistent with the profound indigenous pedagogical tradition of excellence in the history of African people" (King, 2005a, p. 15). Healing methodology as spirituality, then, is deeply rooted in the Creator's presence within history and within the lives of African ascendant people. (p. 286)

Spirituality and transformation are central to healing methodologies and require centering methods in unconditional love, compassion, reciprocity, ritual, and gratitude. Dillard (2008) describes these five principles.

Love entails an effort "to engage love as the experience that creates more reciprocal and thus more just sites of inquiry" (p. 287). It also includes carefully seeking understanding of the needs, aspirations, and sufferings of community members as people that the researcher loves.

Embracing compassion as a methodology suggests that researchers can help communities to relieve their suffering through the process of activist research without being crushed by the weight of suffering.

Seeking reciprocity refers to a researcher's intention and capacity to see human beings as equal. That requires shedding all discrimination and prejudice and removing all boundaries between the researcher and the researched.

Ritual becomes part of the research process. African life experiences embrace the need to appreciate the web of connections and relations that people have with each other, with the environment, with the land, and with nature. The research process should accommodate rituals that enable the researched to recognize, renew, and sustain their relationships with each other and with nature, the environment, the living, and the ancestral spirits. Talking circles methods—for example, the use of magic wooden spoons and baskets in focus groups interviews—demonstrate the application of rituals in indigenous research.

Gratitude involves the need to be thankful for the work of research as spiritual methodology and as a healing process for researchers and others. Engaging in the methodologies in the spirit of gratitude responds to the researcher's need to "remember to put back together the fragments of cultural knowledge of Africa and her Diaspora in ways that give thanks for all who have witnessed and worked on behalf of the humanity of Black people; and the inclusion of our wisdom in the world's grand narrative" (Dillard, 2008, 289).

African feminisms, Africana womanisms, Black feminisms, and Dillard's endarkened epistemology share similarities with African perspectives on relational indigenous methodologies, which were discussed in Chapter 4 in this context:

- A relational existence where the emphasis is on an "I am because we are" principle that encourages respect and honoring of all members of the human community as part of the research act.
- An I/we connection as a relational existence that is spiritual and promotes love and harmony.
- A relational way of knowing where the researched are knowers, and knowledge has a connection with the knowers.

- A relational ethical framework where the researcher is a transformative healer actively involved in healing, building communities, and promoting harmony.

Healing Methodologies

A common thread that cuts across African feminisms and Dillard's endarkened feminist epistemology is the emphasis on healing methods as necessary research tools for life-enriching and transformative experiences, as well as the spiritual growth of women suffering multiple oppression and domination and of researchers as well. To be a reflective activist, a postcolonial Indigenous feminist researcher must listen with compassion and love to women and make visible the healing methods that women employ when they communicate their life experiences. In many instances, the research topic may trigger painful memories for participants. Research on gender violence or research in post-conflict settings, for instance, often triggers memories of pain, suffering, and even anxiety. An activist researcher, it was noted in Chapter 8, aims at engaging in participatory action research that brings about change: both personal and social transformation. Carrying out research in settings where there is conflict or war and work on gender violence, for instance, requires participatory methods that bring about change, personal and social transformation, and healing for individuals and communities.

I highlight participatory healing methods that are built on African feminisms of relationships and interconnectedness, showing how these methods can heal, encourage innovative thinking about the world, and assist participants in envisioning strategies that bring about personal and social transformation. As already noted, African approaches to epistemology are characterized by understanding of interconnectedness, the relationship and interdependence captured in the concept of *ubuntu,* which recognizes that individual identity is possible only in community with others and nature. "I am because you are." Without relationship with the other, and without reference to the other, the individual cannot be. One cannot have a sense of "me without a sense of "we." Methods from a feminist and African perspective include interactive small-group work, role-plays, art-based methodologies, body sculpture, song, and storytelling. The methods can also draw from cultural practices such as drum circles and rituals.

During the sharing of life experiences, for instance, women may engage in rituals using stones, which they bring to the circle, place in a basket, encircle, and retrieve when they tell a story of their life's experiences. These stones become symbols of shared knowledge that can be built on for collective understanding. During sharing, stories are not debated, nor are interpretations argued. Participants listen without framing a counter-response in their minds while stories are told, looking for patterns and threads. There is no attempt to arrive at a correct answer. Rather, all stories are considered to carry a part of the solution or truth.

One method for understanding the nature of conflict, its impact on people, and ways to heal from conflict is writing down the conflict issues and their personal effects on a sheet of paper. The sheet of paper is then torn into pieces and used to build a vessel. This vessel carrying one's pain is exchanged. The vessel is a reminder of each other's pains and makes one mindful of one's actions toward others. The vessel creates the impetus for generating options that take the other into account (Lazarus, 2000). The bowl of pain becomes a vessel that demonstrates the ability to transform individual and community lives into creative and positive living. The methods move the research from damage-focused research to appreciative and desire-focused inquiries. Such methods make it difficult for retribution and revenge to become entrenched but instead allow healing to take place and balance to be created. Some examples of how knowledge can be accessed through rituals are discussed in the next section.

▌ INDIGENOUS FEMINIST PARTICIPATORY METHODS IN PRACTICE

In Chapter 7, it was noted that rituals and sacred objects can be used in research to express equality among participants and their connection to each other and to the living and the nonliving; it can also be a way of appreciating the collective construction of knowledge. Here are some examples of how women are resisting conventional methods of communicating their life experiences in preference for indigenous methods that are participatory, make use of objects, and show love and respect to all the participants through rituals. In unpublished research notes from a case study on female leadership and empowerment in Botswana, Gabo Ntseane (2009) describes the researched women's use of utensils and the meanings attached to their use.

Focus Group and the Use of a Magic Wooden Spoon

In one of the focus group discussions, the women insisted that they use a wooden spoon to guide the discussions instead of a focus group moderator. The focus group started with one of the women saying: "To ensure that we all contribute let us use this magic stick to help process our thoughts and contribute when it is appropriate." The researcher was also requested to be part of the focus group because as one put it, "As a woman like us, you also have to share the wisdom that you have. The spoon says you have to eat something (no matter how small) from the same pot with us, but also put in something even if it is just one firewood or a drop of water. Every one is capable of doing something, thus the spoon has to go round and not skip anybody." The use of a spoon symbolizes collective decision making (i.e., the idea that no one person can know it all, but several scoops of wisdom from other members help shape and refine an idea to make it a useful decision).

The Use of a Basket

In another focus group, a woman suggested that the host put a basket in the middle of the focus group. Asked what the role of the basket was, this is how one responded. "When women commit to coming together, it is because they want to collect something that will contribute to the welfare of their children or community. We see your study as giving you, us, and the other women in the other three countries participating in the study [the will] to contribute to a bigger purpose." The basket represents a "vision or goal"; thus to successfully implement the goal each individual's contribution and participation is required. Having the basket in the middle of the focus group is a reminder and motivation for contribution. In fact, this is how one respondent kept using the basket to encourage the group to think hard about the issues, "this basket is half full, or is almost full. We can't take it to other women in Africa not full. What will they think of us and our society?"

Using Song as a Resistance Voice and a Healing Method

In Chapter 5, songs were discussed as part of the oral literature that communicates the historical information about resistance to colonialism and colonial ideology, as well as historical information on events, practices, values, and so on. In two studies on women, poverty, and resource development in the villages of Transkei in South Africa, Nhlanhla Jordan (2005) describes how songs were used as a feminist research method that revealed women's resistance to patriarchy and also served as a source of healing. The studies, she asserts, were conducted from the women's perspective and from an Indigenous Afrocentric standpoint. Jordan reveals that an analysis of the songs showed how women have found creative ways to resist patriarchal domination by their men and to heal by using song as voice. The song and dance allowed women to relive their experiences and to get in their worlds and express their innermost feelings. Singing together also allowed them to collectively share the pain of patriarchal oppression and to heal through the knowledge that they collectively resist the dominance. In research with women, listening to their songs is a method that approaches the researched in a comfortable and nonthreatening manner and also allows the researcher to start from the researched point of reference. Ntseane (2009) also argues that, at times, women insist that their stories be heard through the songs they have composed. She notes:

> Instead of using the interview guide that the researcher had prepared for data collection, some groups requested that the researcher listen to songs about their leader's attributes; stories about the leadership nicknames of female leaders/leadership; and traditional words that adequately describe the power of female leadership. A group of women belonging to an opposition political party, for example, suggested that they sing a song. This song did not only narrate the story of their leader, but also gave them an opportunity to physically demonstrate her power and authority through the way she walks, talks and demonstrates respect in her dealings with all politicians. The rich and detailed description embedded in the song included this, *Kwankwetla ya rona e gata e gatoga, fa a tsena ko Khaseleng ka wa bo a botsholetse ditsompelo le bokgone jo Batswana ba bothokang* meaning, "When our capable one walks to council for a meeting, you can't miss her humbled confidence and preparedness as demonstrated by her non-verbal communication actions." (p. 10)

It is clear that images of non-Western women as passive and lacking agency are not always true. Women in Ntseane's study are shown resisting conventional focus group interviews and becoming active participants who bring indigenous methods to the research with women. These context-specific and indigenous data collection methods still have to be documented and used in research. Ntseane (2009) concluded that the women's resistance to her conventional focus group techniques in preference for indigenous approaches is a wakeup call to those who still think other cultures/groups/gendered ways of research can continue to be marginalized.

Healing From Patriarchal Oppressive Ideologies: Small-Group Methods

Feminist methods are action oriented, involve group work, and seek healing by naming oppression and engaging in a change process. Ami Nitza, Bagele Chilisa, and Veronica Makwinja-Morara (2010) describe a participatory group method that they call the *Mbizi group model*, which was used to empower Batswana adolescent girls to overcome the gender inequality that puts women at increased risk of HIV infection. The *Mbizi* group model was used in an intervention to assist group members in naming the barriers created by restrictive and oppressive gender context, to show how these barriers impact their lives in general and group members as individuals, and finally, to assist group members in developing and implementing collective and individual strategies for overcoming the barriers. The *Mbizi* group model involved heightening girls' awareness of the social contexts in which they live and how these contexts influence their behavior. The specific objectives of the Mbizi group method were to assist group members to (a) examine and deconstruct dangerous cultural practices and traditions that influence girls' sexual decision making (b) develop collective efficacy, skills, and strategies for dealing with barriers that impede members' success; and (c) develop a supportive peer network with more positive norms regarding gender roles.

Stage 1: Goals, Interventions, and Strategies for the Initial Stage of the Group

The first step toward achieving these goals is the development of an empowering group climate, which includes free expression and exchange of opinions and ideas, a strong sense of cohesion and support, and a collaborative, nonauthoritarian relationship between members. In addition to creating the conditions necessary for the rest of the group process to be effective, the development of a safe, cohesive, and empowering group climate will directly promote the goals of the group. That is, being given the opportunity to speak one's mind and to have one's opinions and ideas heard and valued will begin to promote a sense of empowerment. The talking circle technique can be employed at this stage. In the talking circle, the group member holding a symbolic object chosen by the group is allowed to speak his or her mind without interruption or comment from members or the leader. Initially, the talking circle can be used to have each person state his or her name or respond to a simple question; after members are comfortable with this practice, the talking circle can be used to encourage deeper levels of sharing. Finally, nonverbal and movement activities allow members to begin the process of sharing without having to speak verbally in front of the group.

Stage 2: Makungulupeswa: Riddles

As noted in Chapter 5, myths, stories, songs, and proverbs can promote male domination in most aspects of daily life, including promoting sexual submission of girls and women to men. The *Mbizi* group method heightens awareness of these messages among women and girls, their collective impact on girls and women, and their impact on group members themselves. An activity titled *makungulupeswa* is used to begin the development of heightened awareness. In this activity, facilitators request group members to name and write cultural messages (myths, proverbs, song lyrics, etc.) that are disempowering to women on strips of paper, which are then placed into a basket in the center of the group. Group members take turns drawing out a slip of paper and reading the message aloud. Each message is critically examined, using questions such as: What is the message being communicated? What purpose did/does the message serve? In what ways is the message limiting, restrictive, or otherwise harmful to girls and women? Following an examination of these individual messages, facilitators lead a discussion on the themes or ideas that arise from the activity. Facilitators should help members consider the social construction of gender roles, how they may have internalized the sexist messages transmitted by the culture, and how this may have limited them, hindered them, or otherwise shaped their behavior in terms of their friendships, intimate relations, and sexuality.

Stage 3: Storytelling and Mbizi

Following this collective exercise, the subsequent activities of the working phase are intended to help members reflect more deeply on their own experiences with sexism and gender discrimination and to identify changes they would like to make or strengths they have that they can apply to address challenges that they will face. Storytelling and the Mbizi technique are used to help group members share experiences of sexism, gender discrimination, or abuse. Using the talking circle, each group member is given an opportunity, at her own discretion, to share a story or give voice to her own lived experience. Once all members have had the opportunity to tell a story without interruption, facilitators give members a chance to respond to each other's stories. Facilitators then build on members' stories and responses to facilitate a discussion that promotes universality, cohesion, support, and empowerment.

Following the sharing of stories, an activity is introduced that encourages group members to begin to consider how they can use their own internal and external strengths and resources to take action to overcome barriers and challenges that have been identified through the previous activities and discussions. Using an adaptation of *A Garden as a Metaphor for Change in Group* (DeLucia-Waack, 2008), the metaphor of *Mbizi* is used. *Mbizi* is an *Ikalanga* term that refers to the tradition of neighbors cooperating to work together, particularly to share workloads. Using a *Mbizi* story group, members are encouraged to identify barriers they would like to remove from their lives, skills and strategies they would like to develop, and support or assistance they need to share to achieve these goals.

Stage 4: Skill-Building

Based on members' stories, the next sessions are used to provide knowledge or to promote skill development tailored to the specific needs of the group. Consistent with the goal of empowering group members, the knowledge and skills introduced must be driven by the expressed needs of the members themselves and not imposed by group leaders.

Stage 5: Continuation of Relationships and Beyond

The goals of the final stage are consistent with those of any group and include helping members to reflect on their learning and growth in the group, making plans for applying the learning to life outside of the group, and bringing closure to the group experience and the relationships developed within it. In addition, the group goal of developing a supportive peer network and positive norms regarding gender roles can be reinforced and solidified during this stage. Activities used in this stage provide the opportunity for both collective and individual reflection and consolidation. On a collective level, members work together to write or rewrite a proverb, story, or song that represents the awareness, new ideas, and beliefs about gender roles that were developed in the group. Alternatively, adapting the *Closing: What Have We Learned About Ourselves?* described by Janice DeLucia-Waack (2006), group members can work together to write a letter to other girls, sharing what they have learned in the group.

At the individual level, members identify areas of growth, new knowledge and skills developed, and ways they have utilized their strengths to assist others in the group. Members should be asked to predict specific challenges and barriers they may face in the future; the group can then work together to consider how to apply member strengths or new skills developed in the group to address these potential barriers.

An important final consideration in the *Mbizi* group method is the continuation of relationships beyond the life of the group. Ample attention is given to reflecting on the relationships developed in the group. Group members should be allowed ample opportunity to give each other feedback about their own strengths and the ways they have affected others in the group. Plans for maintaining their relationships and support for each other should be discussed. The *Mbizi* method embraces the I/we principle of *ubuntu* where relationships and connectedness to one another are valued and continue beyond life. It is a method that gives the researched and the researcher opportunities to establish proposed long-lasting relationships that go beyond the project (Getty, 2010; Lavallée, 2009; Pryor et al., 2009).

▌ SUMMARY

Western feminisms have contributed enormously to our understanding of male bias in the literature, theoretical frameworks that inform research practices, and biased methods that distort women's experiences or exclude their voices from the research agenda. The problem is that often, Western feminisms have used Western women's experiences as the norm and basis against which all other non-Western women's life experiences are judged. Non-Western feminisms problematize Western feminisms and at the same time present alternative non-Western feminisms within the realities of life experiences that come with ongoing colonialism, imperialism, racism, and patriarchal oppression. There are many non-Western feminisms. The chapter highlighted the principles underlying borderland-Mestizaje feminism, African feminisms, a Chicana feminist epistemology, and an endarkened feminist epistemology; it showed how these inform feminist research methods. The chapter demonstrated that non-Western feminist research employs indigenous participatory methods and healing methods that promote collective thinking, resistance to oppression, personal and social transformation, and healing.

KEY POINTS

• Postcolonial indigenous feminist theories do not necessarily reject Western feminist theories but appropriate them to critique all forms of patriarchal oppression and in addition Western feminisms for muting the voices of non-Western women.

- Research with non-Western women is revealing social justice research methods that promote social transformation, spiritual growth, and healing.
- Women's indigenous healing methods, such as the use of utensils, song, and dance, need to be documented and made visible.

Activity 9.3

Read the extract on Activity 2.1. In what ways does Kaomea's theoretical and interpretive framework reflect the principles of non-Western feminism's research aims and practice?

Read the extract in Activity 9.1 and do the following:

- Imagine you are replicating the study and answer the following:

    1. Theoretical framework: Describe and discuss the feminisms and theories that inform your study.

    2. Literature review: What will constitute the literature to be reviewed?

    3. Methodology:

- What research approach will you use? The researched as active participants, or researched as co-researchers?
- What data gathering methods will you use?
- What will be your strategy for data analysis?

SUGGESTED READINGS

Chilisa, B., & Ntseane, P. (2010). Resisting dominant discourses: Implications of indigenous African feminist theory and methods for gender and education research. *Gender and Education, 22*(6), 617–631.

Collins, P. H. (2000). *Black feminist thought: Knowledge consciousness and politics of empowerment.* New York: Routledge.

Delgado Bernal, D. (1998). Using a Chicana feminist epistemology in educational research. *Harvard Educational Review, 68,* 555–582.

Dillard, C. M. (2009). When the ground is black, the ground is fertile: Exploring Endarkened feminist epistemology and healing methodologies of the spirit. In N. K. Denzin, Y. S. Lincoln, & L. T. Smith L. (Eds.), *Handbook of critical and indigenous methodologies* (pp. 277–291). Thousand Oaks CA: Sage.

Dube, M. (2000). *Postcolonial feminist interpretation of the Bible.* St Louis, MO: Charles Press.

Fennell, S. (2007). Contested gender frameworks: Economic models and provider perspectives in education. In S. Fennell & M. Arnot (Eds.), *Gender education and equality in a global context* (pp. 35–55). Abingdon, VA: Routledge.

Fennell, S. (2009). *Decentralizing hegemonic gender theory: The implications for educational research* (RECOUP Working paper No. 21). Cambridge, UK: Cambridge University, Development Studies and Faculty of Education.

Hudson-Weems, C. (1998). African womanism. In O. Nnanemeka (Ed.), *Sisterhood, feminisms, and power: From Africa to the diaspora* (pp. 149–162). Trenton, NJ: Africa World Press.

Marshall, C., & Young, M. (2006). Gender and methodology. In C. Skelton, B. Francis, & L. Smulyan (Eds.), *The Sage handbook of gender and education.* London: Sage.

Mekgwe, P. (2003). *Theorizing African feminisms: The colonial question.* Paper presented at the University of Botswana, Department of English Seminar Series.

Mohanty, C. (1991). Under Western eyes: Feminist scholarship and colonial discourses. In C. Mohanty, A. Russo, & L. Torres (Eds.), *Third world women and the politics of feminism* (pp. 51–80). Bloomington: Indiana University Press.

Nitza, A., Chilisa, B., & Makwinja-Morara, V. (2010). Mbizi: Empowerment and HIV/AIDS prevention for adolescents girls in Botswana. *The Journal of Specialists in Group Work, 35*(2), 105–114.

Nnameka, O. (Ed.). (1997). *The politics of mothering: Womanhood, identity, and resistance in African literature.* London: Routledge.

Ntseane P. G. (2009). *Community leadership and empowerment: Botswana case study.* Kampala, Uganda: Institute of Social Transformation.

Reed, P. Y. (2001). African womanism and African feminism: A philosophical, literacy, and cosmological dialect on family? *Western Journal of Black Studies, 25,* 168–176.

Saavedra, C. M., & Nymark E. D. (2008). Borderland and Mestiszaje feminism: The new tribalism. In N. K. Denzin, Y. S. Lincoln, & L. T. Smith (Eds.), *Handbook of critical and indigenous methodologies* (pp. 277–291). Thousand Oaks, CA: Sage.

CHAPTER 10

BUILDING PARTNERSHIPS AND INTEGRATING KNOWLEDGE SYSTEMS

Every research activity is an exercise in research ethics; every research question is a moral dilemma, and every research decision is an instantiation of values.

Joshua Clegg and Brent Slife (2009, p. 24)

Researchers are knowledge brokers, people who have the power to construct legitimating arguments for or against ideas, theories or practices. They are collectors of information and producers of meaning which can be used for, or against indigenous interests.

Fiona Cram, Adreanee Ormond, & Lynette Carter (2004, p. 158)

I see having some version of self-reflective practice as a necessary core for all inquiry. For example, anyone engaging in collaborative research needs robust self-questioning disciplines as their base.

Judi Marshall (2001, p. 433)

OVERVIEW

This chapter draws from discussions in the book to synthesize working relations and partnerships between researchers and the researched; partnerships between institutions and communities; and ways of integrating indigenous knowledge methods and techniques into the global knowledge economy. The chapter further outlines a matrix for planning research from a postcolonial indigenous research perspective.

LEARNING OBJECTIVES

By the end of the chapter, you should be able to:

1. Describe working relationships and partnership approaches that support research with a postcolonial indigenous perspective
2. Debate questions that arise when one plans a research study with a postcolonial indigenous research perspective
3. Outline a research plan for a study with a postcolonial indigenous perspective

Before You Start

1. List and discuss some of the strategies for decolonizing and indigenizing Western-based research methodologies discussed in this book
2. List and discuss postcolonial indigenous methods, techniques, and methodologies discussed in the book
3. Summarize indigenous reporting and dissemination of findings strategies discussed in the book
4. Discuss research approaches that can promote social action, change, and transformation in communities

The focus in this book has been to complement the debate on the call for decolonization of research methods by highlighting strategies for decolonization; integrating knowledge systems; and discussing how to address power, a key factor in the planning of the research, the literature review, the formulation of the research questions, and the choice of research techniques in conducting research. I have also described postcolonial indigenous research methodologies as a framework that brings together methods, techniques, and methodologies used by global postcolonial and indigenous scholars as they conduct research with postcolonial subjects and indigenous communities. I defined postcolonial indigenous research methodologies as covering a wide spectrum of approaches that range from those that decolonize and indigenize Western research methodologies to those that emanate from the worldviews of postcolonial subjects and indigenous peoples. Throughout the book, I illustrated studies that decolonize and indigenize the Western research methodologies approach, as well as studies that use the worldviews of postcolonial subjects and indigenous people as a starting point to plan and execute the research process. What is still needed, however, is a framework for planning a postcolonial indigenous research study. What follows is a discussion of partnerships and working relationships between researchers and the researched and between communities and research institutions; cross-cultural partnerships and partnerships between knowledge systems; and a framework for planning and executing a postcolonial indigenous research study.

POSTCOLONIAL INDIGENOUS AND SOCIAL JUSTICE 🪨 WORKING RELATIONSHIPS

As I conclude this book, the sayings common to the Tswana-speaking people of southern Africa on relationships and working together come to my mind and inevitably inform my conceptualization of this chapter.

Mmua lebe oa bo a bua la gagwe.	Everyone has a right to a say, for even what might appear like a bad suggestion helps people to think of better ideas.
Mongwe le mongwe o latlhela thware legonyana.	Everyone throws in a word or brings a perspective.
Mafoko a kgotla a mantle otlhe.	Every voice has a value in a gathering.
Setshware ke ntsa pedi ga se thata.	Together we can succeed.
Dilo makwati dikwatololwa mo go babangwe.	We learn from others.

All these sayings promote respect for voice in dialogues, conversations, and discussions in any forum intended to build knowledge irrespective of race, gender, ethnicity, or ability. I will begin with a discussion of postcolonial indigenous and social justice working relationships between the researchers and the researched.

Researcher–Researched Relationships

Methods of gathering data can either give or deny the researched the authority to speak from their perspective. Within postcolonial indigenous methodologies, talking circles and sharing cycles (Lavallée, 2009) and use of utensils (Ntseane, 2009) are examples of social justice methods "in which all participants including the facilitator are viewed as equal, and information, and, spirituality and emotionality are shared" (Lavallée, 2009, p. 29). Refer to Chapters 7 and 9. Numerous sources of tension between the researchers and the researched remain, and these compel social science researchers to work jointly to promote

an integrative coming together of world-views in a way that is not just pluralistic tolerance, respect and co-existence, but goes beyond that to effect transformation in the sense of the emergence of a new synthesis that incorporates the existing diversity of world-views. (Fatnowna & Pickett, 2002, p. 258)

A sharing circle or talking circle research technique does not necessarily ensure that the researched share information on every topic of interest to the researcher. Sharing knowledge on some topics may be regarded as violating the cultural norms and exposing the researched, as well as their families or communities, to harm. In an interview with researchers, Lee Anne Nichols, a Cherokee woman, notes that the reason many Native Americans may be reluctant to talk about or record healing practices, for example, is that "when tribes made treaties with the Whiteman, the Whiteman did not honor their written word; so tribes now are hesitant to trust the written word" (Struthers, Lauderdale, Nicholas, Tom-Orme, & Strickland, 2005, p. 194). Also, "an Indian person may be willing to share stories about healing practices, but may not be willing to have the story audio taped because it is not the traditional way of passing history to others." Healers, she notes, "select to pass on their knowledge to specially selected persons or apprentices." Other reasons for the reluctance to enter into a discussion may stem from a feeling that they are not taken seriously and that non-Indians may be looking for entrepreneurial opportunities.

Recently, a group of high school drama students in Botswana were brought before the village chief and punished for singing an initiation song in their drama performance. The song, it was explained, can be sung only at the initiation ceremony by the initiates. Singing the song, it was argued, was an indication of intentions to marginalize, disrespect, and demonize the culture. In Chapter 6, songs were discussed as possible sources of historical information and a commentary on political and social values, with the potential to bring to the knowledge production discourse topics and concepts nonexistent in Western literature. It is clear from these examples that there is tension about what can be said or written and by whom. The Western academic discourse has its own rules on what can be said and written, how it can be said and written, where it can be written, by whom, and for whom. Similarly, from the researched's perspective, postcolonial indigenous discourses on the production of knowledge have their own rules on what can be said, who is allowed to say it, where and when it can be said, whether it can be written, by whom, and for what purpose. The end result is two parallel knowledge systems, each with the power to filter knowledge that eventually reaches the public domain. There is no doubt that what we know based on the research we carry out with postcolonial subjects and indigenous peoples is a product of the power struggle between the two knowledge systems, with each using its power to control and shape what is eventually said. What is the role of academic institutions in integrating these parallel knowledge systems?

The literature includes many stories about how some dissertation topics, theoretical frameworks, methods of collecting data, ethical protocols, data analysis procedures, and modes of reporting—those emanating from a postcolonial indigenous perspective—were found unacceptable to the students' supervisors, dissertation committees, and university and college ethics review boards. Polly Walker (2001) relates her experience with her university:

> When I began my doctoral thesis, I was concerned about how to truthfully express my experiences and those of many of my Indigenous colleagues who speak freely of spiritual experiences as an integral part of our research process, while quite aware that such expressions are held suspect within Western Academia. When I discussed my concerns regarding the articulation of the spiritual aspects of research with the supervisors of my PHD research, they told me that I could not mention spiritual experience within my thesis. They explained that if I did, it would not be considered valid social science research. (p. 18)

It is also evident that the researched can either refuse to cooperate with the researched by holding back the information that is required, by deliberately giving misleading information, or by not turning up for appointments with the researcher. What follows are suggestions on working toward a social justice relationship between academic institutions and the researched.

Institutional Ethics Protocols and the Researched

Most universities have ethics review boards and standardized research clearance forms that researchers complete when they apply for a permit to conduct their studies. In some universities, this application clearance form reflects a quantitative approach and is consequently limiting in its applicability to postcolonial indigenous research methods, which cover a rich diversity of qualitative methods (Hodge & Lester, 2006). In some cases, even when the application clearance form is inclusive of qualitative approaches, there is a tendency to legitimize only conventional qualitative methods such as the interview method.

Universities' ethics application forms related to human subjects should give equal status to quantitative and indigenous qualitative methods, with their emphasis on relational methods that recognize spirituality as a way of knowing. Additional questions that give legitimacy to postcolonial indigenous methods need to be asked. University research ethics application forms should, for instance, ask about the researcher's intentions to decolonize and indigenize Western-based methods and to indicate indigenous methods to be used in the study.

Overcoming Researcher-Centric Research Projects

Most students' research projects, theses, and dissertations are designed to meet the perceived needs of the student. The choice of the research topic and the conceptualization and the implementation of the study are, in most cases, predetermined by the students, working within the boundaries of academic institutions' standard procedures and regulations for research projects and thesis writing (Hodge & Lester, 2006). Such practices undermine attempts to decolonize research to ensure that fundamental issues such as research ownership and benefits of the research to communities are addressed. Paul Hodge and John Lester propose linking researched communities' priorities to research and coursework as a way to promote social justice relations between the researcher and the researched and to reduce colonizing tendencies of academic research. The procedure involves a research unit or department working with the communities to draw a list of research topics and prioritizing the list according to communities' issues of concern. The research unit then attaches the topics to courses and students according to student level. Some topics, for instance, may be appropriate for courses, research projects, and theses at undergraduate level, while others may be suitable for graduate-level courses and students. The next step is to draw a research unit plan that factors in the amount of time students are likely to spend negotiating their research activities with the community and strategies for interaction between the community and the research unit or department and students. The research unit facilitates the discussions with communities and, as much as possible, works out a flexible time frame that allows community members to participate as co-researchers in students' research projects, where the design requires a participatory approach with community members as co-researchers.

Roles and Responsibilities of Researchers and Community Partners

Throughout the book, the working relationships between the researcher and researched are discussed, along with the roles and responsibilities of researchers and their partners. Numerous ethics protocols guide research with postcolonial and indigenous communities. The execution of social justice research will, however, depend on the extent to which researchers take their roles and responsibilities seriously.

Researchers are called on to:

- Employ the worldviews, values, and cultures of indigenous peoples of the world, the formerly colonized, and historically marginalized communities to inform research methodologies.
- Envision research methodologies built on worldviews that emphasize connectedness and the cyclical nature of human experiences.
- Assume roles of transformative healers.
- Resist colonizer/colonized relationships that embrace deficit theorizing and damage-focused research about the Other.
- Promote a relational approach to research where consent to do research is sought at individual, community, and group levels and where consent is collective.
- Practice researcher reflexivity informed by an "I/we" relationship.
- Embrace ethical protocols that draw from cultural practices informed by connectedness and a web of relationships.

These roles and responsibilities could form the basis for initiatives from which to draw research guidelines and contract agreements that facilitate social justice working relationships between the researchers and the researched, with the living and the nonliving, and between institutions and communities. Refer to Chapter 4 for a discussion of researcher responsibilities.

CROSS-CULTURAL PARTNERSHIP RESEARCH AND COLLABORATION BETWEEN ACADEMICS AND DONORS

Decolonization of research methodologies requires all those involved in research with postcolonial subjects in Africa, Asia, and Latin America and among indigenous peoples in Australia, New Zealand, Canada, and the United States to interrogate the "captive mind" that sees the world in one color. Decolonizing methodologies do not apply only to research "exclusively in contexts where geopolitical experience of colonization happened," but also "among groups where colonizing research approaches are deployed" (Swadener & Mutua, 2008, p. 35). In this context, partners in research include researched communities marginalized by colonial research paradigms, research funding agencies, Indigenous researchers, and international and transnational researchers committed to research that promotes social justice, human rights, and democracy. Of note are the differences in interest, motivation for research, and worldviews between Western researchers and Indigenous researchers and between the funding agencies and the researchers, as well as the multiple power dimensions among them (Bresciani, 2008; Chilisa, 2005; Moseley, 2007; Pryor et al., 2009). Chapter 3 illustrated some of the differences in worldviews and power dynamics at play in collaborative research. I conclude the book with the following suggestions on partnerships.

Partnerships between funding agencies, researchers, and communities. A postcolonial indigenous research perspective seeks to establish long-lasting relationships among partners involved in a research process. For this to become a reality, researchers must decide if they will work repeatedly in the same set of communities over an extended period of time. That will require that they develop a field or topic of research interest with defined communities and plan their research career around those research interests and the communities identified. Funding agencies should, in turn, commit to funding community participatory research studies for a reasonable time to allow relationships with all partners to evolve and be sustained. Long-lasting relationships between researchers and communities are possible. William Moseley (2007) for example, reports an ongoing research relationship with a community in Mali (Africa) that started in 1987.

Partnerships between Western and non-Western researchers from developed and developing countries. Collaborative research between Western and non-Western researchers creates agency and the decolonization of research methodologies as well as possible coalitions committed to multidimensional borrowing and lending from all cultures to envision methodologies that resist domination and promote and respect human rights, social justice, democracy, and healing. Scholars (Bresciani, 2008; Pryor et al., 2008) point to power dynamics that hinder healthy working relationships. It is thus crucial that collaborators devote time to articulating their worldviews. Postcolonial indigenous relational axiology that informs the four Rs of relational accountability, respectful representation, reciprocal appropriation, and rights and regulation can guide the working relationships between research-ers. The *ubuntu* worldview of "I am because we are" can help researchers to see themselves as one humanity working for a common goal. The decolo-nization of the working relationships between Westerns and non-Western researchers should strive for *ubuntu*'s principle of resistance to dominance and spirit of respect, love, compassion, and honoring of all members of the human community as part of the research act. Researchers must also apply themselves to the relational ethics that they will employ with the researched.

Partnership of Knowledge Systems

There is also a need for partnership of knowledge systems. Postcolonial indigenous techniques are predominantly qualitative. Practices and proce-dures are communicated orally and stored in songs, dance, artistry, cultural taboos, and so on. Partnerships of parallel knowledge systems alluded to in this book could involve designing equivalent quantitative measures of indig-enous procedures and practices that communicate postcolonial subjects and indigenous people's worldviews and integrating them into the global knowledge economy. Hester du Plessis and Gauhar Raza (2004) show how indigenous knowledge methods and techniques can be integrated into the global knowledge economy. They conducted a research project that involved documenting, studying, and understanding the extent to which indigenous knowledge systems are used in the traditional manufacturing process of practicing artisans and crafts persons in India and South Africa; they sought to establish how these processes could be integrated with global science in multiscale assessment. They demonstrate the method of integrating the two knowledge systems by noting:

> When the artisan was asked how he knows when temperature of the kiln is at maximum, the (unexpected) answer is that it is indicated by the sound of the first pot cracking in kiln. Some variants on this ques-tion included answers regarding the color observed in the firing pro-cess that gives an indication of the temperature level. In our scientific terms, that crucial moment can be measured with a thermometer and translated into the exact scientific terms. (p. 6)

The process clearly demonstrates how indigenous knowledge used in the traditional manufacturing process of practicing artisans was transformed to a measurement scale that could be communicated internationally. There are many opportunities for such partnerships. In the health sciences, for instance, there is growing evidence that many instruments have not been adequately validated for use in diverse settings; one example is the World Health Organization Self-Report Questionnaire, which is the most widely used psychiatric case-finding questionnaire in Africa (Patel et al., 1997). In response to this challenge, the Shona Symptom Questionnaire, an indigenous measure of common mental disorders, was developed in Zimbabwe (Patel et al., 1997). In Chapter 4, an example of an assessment scale to measure Afrocentrism was presented. Partnerships of knowledge systems will require the integration of indigenous measures of human behaviors with measures developed in other cultures to enable communication between researchers in different culture and with the researched in frameworks, concepts, and languages that they understand.

¶ PLANNING RESEARCH FROM A POSTCOLONIAL INDIGENOUS RESEARCH PERSPECTIVE

After reading this book, do you wish to carry out a study that draws from the multiple epistemologies and worldviews of postcolonial subjects and indigenous peoples? Planning a research study begins with a thinking process in which decisions are made on four main areas: orienting decisions, research design and methodology, data analysis, and presenting and reporting the results (Cohen, Manion, & Morrison, 2007).

Orienting Decisions

These are strategic decisions that frame the general nature of the research. The first set of questions requires the researcher to clearly define the research agenda and the role of the researched in framing the research agenda. Questions could include the following:

- Why do I do research with the formerly colonized, the oppressed, and the disempowered?
- Will the research bring about change and transformation?
- Will the research have a clear stance against the political, academic, and methodological imperialism of its time?
- Will the research take a stance against Western archival knowledge and its colonizing and Othering ideologies?

A researcher who wishes the researched to participate in the identification of the issue of study, the research design, analysis, and reporting, for instance, should have a strategy for building a partnership with the researched community. The feasibility of research with such an approach will also depend on a number of factors, among them research report completion time and a host of academic requirements, including a statement of originality and the way an institution defines it and the willingness of the institution, the department, and the dissertation committee to accommodate decolonizing research approaches and indigenous knowledge-centered research approaches. These questions also require researchers to define their roles and responsibilities and to arrive at a clear, conscious definition of the self in relation to the researched. Table 10.1 shows the main questions subissues and decisions that the researcher needs to consider.

Research Design and Methodology

Strategic orienting decisions establish what is feasible and how the researcher addresses the practicalities of the research. Political decisions are consciously addressed throughout the planning of the study. Political and practical decisions have to be made on the following questions:

- Will the research take a stance against methodological imperialism?
- What is the main research approach? Is it a decolonization of Western-based methodologies, for example, indigenizing a qualitative research, quantitative survey, ethnographic study, or participatory action research study, or is it an indigenous knowledge-centered research approach?
- What is the purpose of the study, and what are the research questions emanating from the purpose of the study?
- What worldviews and theories frame the purpose of the study, research questions, and methods of data collection?
- What type of data will be required to address the research questions?
- What techniques or methods of gathering data will the study use?
- Who will carry out the study?

The purpose of the research, the research questions to be addressed, and the researcher's commitment to a politically engaged research will to a large extent determine the main research approach. Once the main research approach is chosen, the researcher can then select the data-gathering methods and validity and reliability approaches that are compatible with the political stance of the research, the purpose of the study, and the research questions the study seeks to address. In Chapter 6, it was noted that a growing number of methodologies draw from the philosophical and theoretical assumptions of postcolonial indigenous worldviews, such as the Kaupapa

(text continues on page 306)

Table 10.1 Research Planning Matrix

Questions	Subissues	Decisions
Why do I do research with the formerly colonized, third world, fourth world, or developing countries?	Whose research is it? Who owns it? Whose interest does it serve? Who will benefit from it? Who will design its questions and form its scope? Who will carry it out? Who will write it up? How will its results be disseminated? Will the research address power relations, inequalities, and injustices, such as those based on race, gender, age class?	Find out if your institution or the department has a working relationship with the community in which the study is conducted and how you can plan your study with the community. If your research topic is researcher-centric, decide on the role and level of participation of the researched. Estimate the amount of time you need to conduct the research with either a community-centric research approach or a researcher-centric approach that has a defined level of researched participation. Decide whether one of your aims is to build research capacity in the community. Determine whether the researched will be co-researchers and co-authors of the research report and if your institution has provision for your intentions.
Will the research bring about change and transformation?	What theory and methods energize the researched to engage in a change process? Will this research change the way people think and do things? What theory and method change the way people think and do things?	Decide on the theory and method that is likely to ignite a change and transformation process.

Will the research have a clear stance against the political and academic imperialism of its time?	Which worldviews inform perceptions of reality? Where is the place of indigenous knowledge systems in the production of knowledge? What counts as knowledge? What is the place of indigenous knowledge in the produced knowledge? How will global science be used to further the development of indigenous knowledge systems?	Decide whether your research approach is that of decolonizing and indigenizing Western-based methodologies (that is, inserting an indigenous perspective into one of the major paradigms) or whether you will draw from indigenous knowledge systems to conduct research informed by a postcolonial indigenous research paradigm.
Will the research take a stance against Western archival-knowledge and its colonizing and "othering" ideologies?	Will the research problematize and critique the Euro-Western archival-knowledge, and its exclusionary tendencies? Will the research challenge literature that perpetuates victim-blaming, deficit-based theories and analysis? Will the research name White privilege and racism in the literature?	Decide on a strategy for the review of the literature and consider using the following as a guide: Determine the assumptions, prejudices, stereotypes that inform the literature you review. Determine and expose the way the literature and theories reviewed portray the researched. Determine and expose any deficit thinking or theorizing in the literature reviewed. Identify the evidence that is there to be used to bring to question the literature reviewed. Determine the gaps in the literature. Determine the body of indigenous knowledge of the researched that you will utilize to counter theories and the body of knowledge that cause humiliation and embarrassment to the researched. Decide on the theories and indigenous knowledge that will guide your critique of the archival knowledge. Define literature from an indigenous perspective. For instance, literature as language, cultural artifacts, legends, stories, practices, songs, rituals poems, dances, tattoos, lived experiences, personal and community stories told in weddings, funerals, celebrations, and wars. Find which of this literature can be accessed and written about.

(Continued)

Table 10.1 (Continued)

Methodology and design questions	Subissues	Decisions
Will the research take a stance against methodological imperialism	*Paradigm:* What paradigm informs your methodology? Is it the postpositivist paradigm, interpretive paradigm, transformative paradigm, or a postcolonial indigenous paradigm? *Theoretical Framework:* What informs the choice of your research topic; the research questions you ask; the literature reviewed; data collection methods, analysis and interpretation? Is it an indigenous knowledge-based knowledge and theory; postcolonial theory; critical race-based theory; feminist theory; critical theory or a combination of some of the above? *Research Approach:* Is it a quantitative participatory approach study, for instance, a survey? Is it a qualitative participatory approach study, for instance, an ethnographic study? Is it a combination of qualitative and quantitative participatory approach study? *Data collection:* What assumptions about the nature of reality, knowledge and values inform your data collection methods? Are you, for instance, adopting a decolonization of methods approach that inserts an indigenous data collection method into a study guided by a Euro-Western based paradigm? Or is it a decolonization approach within a postcolonial indigenous research paradigm? What assumptions guide the choice of selection	Decide on the role and place of critique, decolonization, indigenization and dreaming and envisioning of new indigenous methods in the research study? Decide on the dominant worldview and how other world views will compliment the dominant world view. Decide on the theories that will inform the conceptual and theoretical framework of the study. Decide on the research approach.

Data Analysis Questions	Subissues	Decisions
	of participants in the study (sampling); the setting of the study, and the techniques of data collection? What role does the following play in your choice of data collection and sampling of research participants' procedures? ethno-philosophy; philosophic sagacity; cultural artifacts; and decolonization of interviews. Are you using any of the following: proverbs and metaphors as conceptual frameworks; storytelling methods; songs and poems; talk circles, or indigenous-knowledge based interview guides? See chapters 5 and 7 for a discussion of these strategies.	
What type of data will be required?	Does the research need qualitative data, quantitative type of data, or both? Who will own the data?	Decide on the most appropriate data required for the research questions to be addressed. Ensure that issues on ownership of data are addressed.
What techniques or methods of gathering data will the study use?	Will the research critique, decolonize, and indigenize conventional methods? Will indigenous methods be used? Will the study invoke the histories, world views and indigenous knowledge systems to imagine and suggest new indigenous methodologies? What methods do I use to accurately generate and record marginalized voices and indigenous and local knowledge predominantly excluded through Euro-Western conventional methodologies?	Decide on the conventional methods that are suited for the research questions to be addressed and how they will be indigenized. Decide on the indigenous methods that will be used. Decide whether the study will explore possibilities of emergent methods emanating from interaction with the research and informed by participants world views.

(Continued)

Table 10.1 (Continued)

Data Analysis Questions	Subissues	Decisions
What ethical principles guide the study?	How will the research process build relational accountability, respectful representation, reciprocal appropriation, and rights and regulation? How will reflexivity be addressed?	Find out about your Institutional Review Board and whether it will accommodate the researcher's ethical protocols. Find out if the researched have a community review board that will inform your relationship with the researched. Use the following as a guide to definition of self in relation to the researched: What is my relationship with the researched? Is it involved or detached? Is it that of a person who knows more than the researched? Be aware of the community value systems that guide your interaction with the researched and one's treatment of the data. Decide how the methods you use will help to build respectful relationships between yourself, the researched, and the topic that you are studying. How can I relate respectfully to the other participants involved in this research so that together we can form a stronger relationship with the idea that we will share? Decide on your roles and responsibilities as a researcher and the relationships you wish to create. Decide on what you are contributing or giving back to the relationship?

How will data be analyzed?	Is the data to be analyzed quantitative or qualitative? Classify data according to that which used conventional methods and that which used indigenous methods.	If your research approach is that of inserting an indigenous perspective into one of the major paradigms, determine the conventional analysis methods in the study and the complimentary indigenous perspectives to be used.
	Will the study use indigenous analytical frameworks? Will conventional analytical frameworks be used? Will the research problematize and critique the tendency to make the researched speak through the voices, academic language concepts, and theories of the West? With what and whose theories do you use to conceptualize and analyze data?	If the study draws from an indigenous knowledge system framework, decide on the indigenous analytical framework to be used and complementary conventional approaches to be used.
How will the research report be written and research findings disseminated?	Who will write the research report and for whom? Will different constituencies require different forms of reporting and disseminating research findings? Will the researched co-author the report? Will bilingual texts be used for the analyses and presentation of data? Will research results be available, accessible, and unusable for both the researched and the international community of scholars?	Ensure that there is a procedure to address co-authorship issues. Decide on indigenous methods of disseminating and reporting findings. Determine whether your institution or research committee accommodates the use of bilingual texts in the analysis and presentation of data. Determine if the research report will be simultaneously written in two languages.
By what and whose standards are the design, data collection, and analysis and interpretation of research findings deemed valid and reliable?	Will the study adopt positionality or standpoint judgments in framing validity? Will the study use specific communities and research sites as arbitrators of validity standards?	Decide on the role of the researched in validating the study.

Maori research, Afrocentric methodologies, and methodologies based on the Medicine Wheel. The emphasis in Chapter 6 was on methodologies that emanate from the values and cultures of the researched. Some of the methods discussed in this book include the following: interview methods based on the medicine wheel; talking circles and sharing circles methods; Anishnaabe symbol-based research; Mmogo method; participatory rural appraisal methods; methods based on philosophic sagacity; storytelling methods; and language, metaphorical sayings, songs, and artifacts as sources of data.

Data Analysis

Postcolonial indigenous research methodologies emphasize research *with* people rather than research *on* people. Practical and politically engaged questions on analysis have to be answered:

- How will the data be analyzed, and who will analyze it?
- Will the study use indigenous analytical frameworks?
- Will conventional analytical frameworks be used?
- Will the research problematize and critique the tendency to make the researched speak through the voices, academic language, concepts, and theories of the West?
- Whose worldviews and theories will be used to conceptualize and analyze the data?
- Who will verify and validate the data and the way it is interpreted?
- Whose data is it? Who will own and store it?

Presenting and Reporting Results

In Activity 4.2, an extract from Wilson (2008) on a style of writing a dissertation from an indigenous perspective was presented. An argument was made for writing a dissertation in story form. The role of language in research was discussed in Chapter 6, along with strategies for presenting texts—for example, the use of bilingual texts in the analysis and presentation of data—and simultaneously writing the report in two languages. Forms of disseminating research findings to the researched include poetry, theater, art, seminars, and discussion forums. Politically engaged questions on presenting and reporting results include:

- Who will write the research report, for whom, and in what language?
- Will different constituencies require different forms of reporting and disseminating research findings?

- Will the researched co-author the report?
- Will bilingual texts be used for the analyses and presentation of data?
- Will research results be available, accessible, and usable for both the researched and the international community of scholars?

Addressing the politically engaged and practical questions and taking decisions on them ensure that the research is aligned with the intentions of postcolonial indigenous research methodologies and that the coherence and practicability of the planned study are addressed in an ethically defensible context.

SUMMARY

We are in an era that promotes multiplicity and difference. The worldviews from postcolonial and indigenous communities add to the rainbow of diversity. This chapter highlighted the role of academic institutions, institutional structures such as departments, academics, students, and researchers in recognizing the legitimacy of postcolonial indigenous research methodologies. The goal is to make them visible and integrate them in the academic discourse and the global knowledge economy.

KEY POINTS

- The mind-set of academics and their institutions must change so that they can see the researched postcolonial subject and indigenous peoples not only as sources of data and sites for application and development of new theories, but also as sources of their own stories, their own theories, and constructive critiques on Western academic discourse; the researched are gatekeepers of their indigenous knowledge.
- There is a need to build partnerships to translate research results into action and to integrate knowledge systems such that indigenous knowledge methods and techniques are part of the current discourses on research methodologies and the global knowledge economy.
- Indigenous research methodologies require diverse partnership relations that need to be negotiated, agreed on, and acted on by the partners.
- Social justice working relationships between researchers and participants or communities as partners require a commitment of researchers to guiding principles on their roles and responsibilities.

Activity 10.1

1. Review ethics protocols and application clearance forms in your institutions and debate if they accommodate the use of postcolonial indigenous research methodologies.

2. Read through the matrix on Table 10.1 and draw a plan for a research study in which you make decisions regarding the following:

- *Research theoretical and conceptual framework:* Decide whether your research approach is that of decolonizing and indigenizing Western-based methodologies (that is, inserting an indigenous perspective into one of the major paradigms) or whether you will draw from indigenous knowledge systems to conduct research informed by a postcolonial indigenous research paradigm. Decide if you will plan the research with the community or if your study will be researcher-centric.
- *Literature review:* Decide if the research will problematize and critique the Euro-Western archival knowledge and its exclusionary tendencies.
- *Methodology and design:* Decide on the dominant worldview and how other worldviews will complement the dominant worldview. Decide the most appropriate data required for the study, indigenous methods that will be used, or conventional methods that will be indigenized and how they will be indigenized.
- *Data analysis:* Decide if the research will use indigenous analytical frameworks, conventional analytical frameworks, or both. Decide if the participants will be involved in the analysis and interpretation of the research findings.
- *Dissemination of research findings:* Decide who will write the research report and for whom and if different constituencies will require different forms of reporting and dissemination strategies.

SUGGESTED READINGS

Bresciani M. (2008). Exploring misunderstanding in collaborative research between a world power and a developing country. *Research and Practice Assessment,* *2*(1), 1–11.

Hodge, P., & Lester J. (2006). Indigenous research: Whose priority? Journeys and possibilities of cross-cultural research in geography. *Geographical Research,* *44*(1), 41–51.

Moseley W. G. (2007). Collaborating in the field, working for change: Reflecting on partnerships between academics, development organizations and rural communities in Africa. *Singapore Journal of Tropical Geography, 28,* 334-347.

Pryor, J., Kuupole, A., Kutor, N., Dunne, M., & Adu-Yeboah, C. (2009). Exploring the fault lines of cross-cultural collaborative research. *Compare, 39*(6), 769-782.

Struthers R., Lauderdale J., Nicholas L. N., Tom-Orme L., & Strickland C. J. (2005). Respecting tribal traditions in research and publications: Voices of five Native American nurse scholars. *Journal of Transcultural Nursing, 16*(3), 193-201.

REFERENCES

Aboriginal Research Centre. (2005). *Mi'knaw research centre and protocols.* Available at http//mrc.uccb.ns.ca/prinpro.html

Abt Associates. (2001). *The impact of HIV/AIDS on the education sector in Botswana.* Johannesburg, South Africa: Author.

Adair, J. G., Puhan, N. B., & Vohra, N. (1993). Indigenization of psychology: Empirical assessment of progress in Indian research. *International Journal of Psychology, 28*(2), 149–169.

Akbar, N. (1991). Paradigms of African American research. In R. L. Jones (Eds.), *Black psychology* (pp. 709–772). Berkeley, CA: Cobb & Henry.

Alagoa, E. J. (1968). The use of oral literary data for history: Examples from Niger Delta proverbs. *Journal of American Folklore, 81,* 235–242.

Alatas, S. H. (2004). The captive mind and creative development. In P. N. Mukherji & C. Sengupta (Eds.), *Indigeneity and universality in social science: A South African response.* New Dehli: Sage.

Allan, K., & Burridge, K. (1994). *Euphemism and dysphemism: Language used as shield and weapon.* New York: Oxford University Press.

Amadiume, I. (1987). *Male daughters, female husbands: Gender and sex in African society.* London: Zed Books.

American Psychological Association. (2002). *Guidelines on multicultural education, training, research practice, and organizational change for psychologists.* Washington, DC: Author.

Arnot, M. (2009). Gender voices in the classroom. In C. Skeleton, B. Francis, & L. Smulyan (Eds.), *The SAGE handbook of gender and education* (pp. 405–421). Thousand Oaks, CA: Sage.

Aroztegui Massera, C. (2006). *The calabozo: Virtual reconstruction of a prison cell based on personal accounts.* Unpublished doctoral dissertation, Texas A&M University, College Station.

Asante M. K. (1988a). *The Afrocentric idea.* Philadelphia: Temple University Press.

Asante, M. K. (1988b). *Afrocentricity.* Trenton, NJ: Africa World Press.

Asante, M. K. (1990). *Kemet, Afrocentricity and knowledge.* Trenton, NJ: Africa World Press.

Ashcroft B., Griffiths G., & Tiffin, H. (1991). *The empire writes back.* London: Routledge.

Ashcroft B., Griffiths, G., & Tiffin, H. (2000). *Post-colonial studies: The key concepts.* London: Routledge.

Atkinson, R. (1998). The life story interview as a bridge in narrative inquiry. In D. J. Clandinin (Ed.), *Handbook of narrative inquiry: Mapping a methodology* (pp. 224–245). Thousand Oaks: Sage.

Bailey, K. D. (1994). *Methods of social research.* New York: Free Press.

Battiste, M. (2000). *Reclaiming indigenous voice and vision.* Vancouver: UBC Press.

Baugh, E. J., & Guion, L. (2006). Using culturally sensitive methodologies when researching diverse cultures. *Journal of Multidisciplinary Evaluation, 4,* 1–12.

Bell, L. A. (2001). *Self-awareness and social justice pedagogy.* Paper presented at the National Conference on Race and Ethnicity in Higher Education, Seattle, WA.

Benham, M. K. P. (2007). Mo'olelo: On culturally relevant story making from an indigenous perspective. In D. J. Clandinin (Ed.), *Handbook of narrative inquiry: Mapping a methodology* (pp. 512–533). Thousand Oaks, CA: Sage.

Bennell, P. S., Chilisa, B., Hyde, K., Makgothi, A., Molobe, E., & Mpotokwane, L. (2001). *The impact of HIV/AIDS on primary and secondary schooling in Botswana: Developing a comprehensive strategic response.* London: Department of International Development.

Benton-Banai, E. (1988). *The Mishomis book: The voice of the Ojibway.* Hayward, WI: Indian Country Communications.

Bhabha, H. (1994). *The location of culture.* New York: Routledge.

Bishop, R. (2008a). Freeing ourselves from neo-colonial domination in research: A Kaupapa Maori approach to creating knowledge. In N. K. Denzin & Y. S. Lincoln (Eds.), *The landscape of qualitative research* (3rd ed., pp. 145–183). Thousand Oaks, CA: Sage.

Bishop, R. (2008b). Te Kotahitanga: Kaupapa Maori in mainstream classrooms. In N. K. Denzin, Y. S. Lincoln, & L. T. Smith (Eds.), *Handbook of critical and indigenous methodologies* (pp. 439–458). Thousand Oaks, CA: Sage.

Blaut, J. M. (1993). *The colonizer's model of the world: Geographical diffusionism and Eurocentric history.* New York: Guilford Press.

Bogdan, R. C., & Biklen, S. K. (1982). *Qualitative research for education: An introduction to theory and methods.* Boston: Allyn & Bacon.

Bopp, J., Bopp, M., Brown, L., & Lane, P., Jr. (1989). *The sacred tree.* Twin Lakes, WI: Lotus Light.

Botswana Institute for Development Policy and Analysis (BIDPA). (2000). *Microeconomic impacts of the HIV/AIDS epidemic in Botswana.* Gaborone, Botswana: Author.

Brabeck, M., & Brabeck, K. (2009). Feminist perspectives on research ethics. In D. M. Mertens & P. E. Ginsberg (Eds.), *The handbook of social research ethics* (pp. 39–53). Thousand Oaks, CA: Sage.

Bresciani, M. (2008). Exploring misunderstanding in collaborative research between a world power and a developing country. *Research and Practice Assessment, 2*(1), 1–11.

Brown, P., & Levison, S. (1987). *Politeness: Some universals in language usage.* Cambridge, UK: Cambridge University Press.

Cannella, G. S. (1997). *Deconstructing early childhood education: Social justice and revolution.* New York: Peter Lang.

Cannella, G. S., & Manuelito, K. (2008). Feminisms from unthought locations: Indigenous worldviews, marginalized feminisms, and revisioning an anticolonial social science. In N. K. Denzin, Y. S. Lincoln, & L. T. Smith (Eds.), *Handbook of critical and indigenous methodologies.* Thousand Oaks, CA: Sage.

Caracciolo D., & Mungai, A.M. (Eds.). (2009). *In the spirit of ubuntu: Stories of Teaching and research.* Rotterdam, The Netherlands: Sense Publishers.

Carter, M. (2003). Telling tales out of school: "What's the fate of a black story in a white world of white stories?" In G. R. Lopez & L. Parker (Eds.), *Interrogating racism in qualitative research methodology* (pp. 29-48). New York: Peter Lang.

Castells, M. (1993). *Economy and the new international division of labor.* In M. Carnoy, M. Castells, S. S. Cohen, & H. Cordons (Eds.), *The new global economy in the information age.* London: Macmillan.

Central Statistics Office. (1997). *Literacy survey report.* Gaborone, Botswana: Government Printers.

Cha, A. E. (2006). Protests by prostitutes in Cambodia ended Tenofovir testing. *Washington Post.*

Chambers, R. (1994). Participatory Rural Appraisal (PRA): Challenges, potentials, and paradigm. *World Development, 22*(10), 1437-1454.

Chambers, R. (1997). *Whose reality counts? Putting the first last.* London: International Technological Publications.

Chilisa, B. (2002). National policies on pregnancy in the education system in sub-Saharan Africa: A case of Botswana. *Gender and Education Journal, 14*(1), 21-35.

Chilisa, B. (2005). Educational research within postcolonial Africa: A critique of HIV/AIDS research in Botswana. *International Journal of Qualitative Studies, 18*(6), 659-684.

Chilisa, B. (2006). Decolonising ethics in social science research: Towards a framework for research ethics. In A. Rwomire (Eds.), *Challenges and responsibilities of doing social research in Botswana: Ethical issues* (pp. 199-207). Nairobi: OSSREA.

Chilisa, B. (2009). Indigenous African-centered ethics: Contesting and complementing dominant models. In D. M. Mertens & P. E. Ginsberg (Eds.), *The handbook of social research ethics* (pp. 407-425). Thousand Oaks, CA: Sage.

Chilisa, B., Bennell, P. S., & Hyde, K. (2001). *The impact of HIV/AIDS on the University of Botswana: Developing a strategic response.* London: Department for International Development.

Chilisa, B., Malinga, T., & Mmonadibe, P. (2009, September 22-25). *Predictors of abstinence among 10-18 year adolescents in Botswana: Application of the theory of planned behaviour.* Paper presented at the AIDS Impact Conference, Gaborone, Botswana.

Chilisa, B., & Ntseane, P. (2010). Resisting dominant discourses: Implications of indigenous African feminist theory and methods for gender and education research. *Gender and Education, 22*(6), 617-631.

Chilisa, B., & Preece, J. (2005). *Research methods for adult educators in Africa.* Cape Town, South Africa: Pearson.

Christian, B. (2000). *The race for theory.* In J. James & T. Denean Sharley-Whitting (Eds.). *The black feminist reader* (pp. 11–23). Malden, MA: Blackwell.

Church, A. T., & Katigbak M. S. (2002). Indigenization of psychology in the Phillipines. *International Journal of Psychology, 37,* 129–148.

Clegg, W. J., & Slife, B. D. (2009). *Research ethics in the postmodern context.* In D. M. Mertens & P. E. Ginsberg (Eds.), *The handbook of social research ethics.* Thousand Oaks, CA: Sage.

Cohen, L., Manion, L., & Morrison, K. (2007). *Research methods in education.* London and New York: Routledge Falmer.

Collins, P. H. (2000). *Black feminist thought: Knowledge, consciousness, and the politics of empowerment.* New York: Routledge.

Commey, P. (2003, December). New scramble for Africa. *The New African.* Available at http://www.africasia.com/newafrican/na.php?ID=253&back_month=24

Commeyras, M., & Chilisa, B. (2001). Assessing Botswana's first national survey on literacy with Wagner's proposed schema for surveying literacy in the Third World. *International Journal of Educational Development, 21*(5), 433–446.

Commeyras, M., & Montsi, M. (2000). What if I woke up as the other sex? Botswana youth perspectives on gender. *Gender and Education, 12,* 327–346.

Coombe, C. (2000). *Managing the impact of HIV/AIDS on the education sector* (Briefing paper prepared for Africa Development Forum). Pretoria, South Africa: UNECA.

Cram, F. (2004a, October 13–15). *Evidence in an indigenous world.* Paper presented at the Australasian Society 2004 International Conference, Adelaide, Australia.

Cram, F. (2004b). *Theories, practices, models, analyses.* Paper presented at the Evaluation workshop in Hawai`i.

Cram, F. (2009). Maintaining indigenous voices. In D. M. Mertens & P. E. Ginsberg (Eds.), *The handbook of social research ethics* (pp. 308–322). Thousand Oaks, CA: Sage.

Cram, F., Ormond, A., & Carter, L. (2004, June 10–12). *Researching our relations: Reflections on ethics and marginalization.* Paper presented at the Kamhameha Schools Research Conference on Hawai`ian Well-being, Honolulu, HI.

Creswell, J. W. (2009). *Research design: Qualitative, quantitative, and mixed approaches* (3rd ed.). Thousand Oaks, CA: Sage.

Creswell, J. W., & Clark, V. L. P. (2011). *Designing and conducting mixed methods research.* Thousand Oaks, CA: Sage.

Cross, T., Earl, K., Echo-Hawk Solie, H., & Mannes, K. (2000). *Cultural strength and challenges in implementing a system of care model in American Indian communities* (Systems of care: Promising practices in children's mental health, Vol. 1). Washington, DC: American Institutes for Research, Center for Effective Collaboration and Practice.

Delgado Bernal, D. (1998). Using a Chicana feminist epistemology in educational research. *Harvard Educational Review, 68,* 555–562.

Deloria V. (1995). *Red earth, white lies: Native Americans and the myth of scientific fact.* New York: Scribner.

DeLucia-Waack, J. L. (2006). Closing: What have we learnt about ourselves? In J. L. DeLucia-Waack, H. K. Bribord, J. S. S. Kleiner, & A. Nitza (Eds.), *Group work experts share their favorite group activities: A guide to choosing, planning, conducting, and processing* (pp. 152-154). Alexandria, VA: Association for Specialists in Group.

DeLucia-Waack, J. L. (2008). A garden metaphor for change in group. In L. L. Foss, J. Green, K., Wolfe-Stiltner, & J. L. DeLucia-Waack (Eds.), *School counsellors share their favorite group activities: A guide to choosing, planning, conducting, and processing* (pp. 161-163). Alexandria, VA: Association for Specialists in Group Work.

Demas, E., & Saavedra, C. M. (2004). (Re)conceptualizing language advocacy: Weaving a postmodern Mestizaje image of language. In K. Mutua & B. B. Swadener (Eds.), *Decolonizing research in cross-cultural contexts* (pp. 215-233). Albany: State University of New York Press.

Denzin N. K. (1992). *Symbolic interactionism and cultural studies: The politics of interpretation.* Oxford, UK: Blackwell.

Denzin, N. K., & Lincoln, Y. S. (1998). *Collecting and interpreting qualitative materials.* London: Sage.

Denzin, N. K., & Lincoln Y. S. (Eds.). (2005). *The SAGE handbook of qualitative research.* Thousand Oaks, CA: Sage.

Denzin, N. K., Lincoln, Y. S., & Smith, L. T. (Eds.). (2008). *Handbook of critical and indigenous methodologies.* Thousand Oaks, CA: Sage.

Department for International Development. (2001). *Research on gendered school experiences: The impact on retention and achievement in two countries.* London: DFID.

DeVault, M. L. (1999). *Liberating method: Feminism and social research.* Philadelphia: Temple University Press.

Dillard, C. M. (2008). When the ground is black, the ground is fertile: Exploring endarkened feminist epistemology and healing methodologies of the spirit. In N. K. Denzin, Y. S. Lincoln, & L. T. Smith. (Eds.), *Handbook of critical and indigenous methodologies* (pp. 277-291). Thousand Oaks, CA: Sage.

Diop, C. (1978). *The cultural unity of black Africa.* Chicago: Third World Press.

Drescher, M. (2009). Contextualizing local knowledge: Reformulations in HIV/AIDS prevention in Burkina Fasso. In C. Higgins & B. Norton (Eds.), *Language and HIV/AIDS: Say no to AIDS* (pp. 197-219). Bristol, UK: Multilingual Matters.

Dube, M. W. (2000). *Postcolonial feminist interpretation of the Bible.* St. Louis, MO: Chalice Press.

Dube, M. W. (2001). Divining Ruth for international relations. In M. W. Dube (Ed.), *Other ways of reading the Bible* (pp. 179-198). Geneva: WCC.

Dube, M. W. (2002). Postcoloniality, feminist spaces, and religion. In L. E. Donaldson & P. Kwok (Eds.), *Postcolonialism, feminism, and religious discourse* (pp. 100-122). New York: Routledge.

Du Plessis, H., & Raza, G. (2004, March 17–20). *Linking indigenous knowledge with attitudes towards science among artisans in India and South Africa: A collaborative cross-cultural project.* Paper presented at the conference on Bridging Scales and Epistemologies, Alexandria, Egypt.

Easterbrooks, S. R., Stephenson, B., & Mertens, D. (2006). Master teachers' responses to twenty literacy and science/mathematics practices in deaf education. *American Annals of the Deaf, 151*(4), 398–409.

Economic and Social Development Department. (2006). *Building on gender, agrobiodiversity, and local knowledge: A training manual.* Rome: Food and Agriculture Organization of the United Nations.

Edwards, R., & Mauthner, M. (2002). Ethics and feminist research: Theory and practice. In M. Mauthner, M. Birch, J. Jessop, & T. Miller (Eds.), *Ethics in qualitative research* (pp. 14–31). Thousand Oaks CA: Sage.

Edwards, S., McManus, V., & McCreanor, T. (2005). Collaborative research within Maori on sensitive issues: The application of Tikanga and Kaupapa in research on Maori sudden infant death syndrome. *Social Policy Journal of New Zealand, 25,* 88–104.

Egerton University. (2000). *Egerton PRA field handbook for participatory rural appraisal practitioners* (3rd ed). Njoro, Kenya: Author.

Eichelberger, R. T. (1989). *Disciplined inquiry: Understanding and doing educational research.* New York: Longman.

Elabor-Idemudia, P. (2002). Participatory research: A tool in the production of knowledge in development discourse. In K. Saunders (Ed.), *Feminist post-development thought: Rethinking modernity, postcolonialism, and representation* (pp. 227–242). London: Zed Books.

Elenes, C.A. (2005, April). *Decolonizing educational research and practice: Chicana feminism, border theory, and cultural practices.* Paper presented at the AERA annual meeting, Montreal, Canada.

Ellis, J. B., & Earley, M. A. (2006). Reciprocity and constructions of informed consent: Researching with indigenous populations. *International Journal of Qualitative Methods, 5*(4), 1–13.

Emagalit, Z. (2001). *Contemporary African philosophy.* Available at http://homepages.acc.msmc.edu/faculty/lindeman.af.htmls

Escobar, A. (1995). *Encountering development.* Princeton: Princeton University Press.

Fanon, F. (1967). *Black skin, white masks: A dying colonialism: and towards African revolution.* New York: Grove.

Fatnowna, S., & Pickett, H. (2002). The place of indigenous knowledge systems in the post-post modern integrative paradigms shift. In C. O. Hoppers (Ed.), *Indigenous knowledge and the interaction of knowledge systems* (pp. 257–285). Cape Town, South Africa: New Africa Books.

Fennell, S. (2009). *Decentralizing hegemonic gender theory: The implications for educational research* (RECOUP Working paper No. 21). Cambridge, UK: Cambridge University, Development Studies and Faculty of Education.

Fine, M. (1994). Dis-stance and other stances: Negotiations of power inside feminist research. In A. Gitlin (Ed.), *Power and method: Political activism and educational research* (pp. 13–35). New York: Routledge.

Fitznor, L. (1998). The circle of life: Affirming aboriginal philosophies in everyday living. In D. C. McCance (Ed.), *Life ethics in world religions*. Atlanta, GA: Scholars Press.

Flax, J. (1993). Women do theory. In M. A. Jaggar & P. S. Rothenberg (Eds.), *Feminist framework* (pp. 80–85). New York: McGraw-Hill.

Fontana, A., & Frey, J. (2005). The interview: From political stance to political involvement. In N. K. Denzin & Y. S. Lincoln (Eds.), *The SAGE handbook of qualitative research* (pp. 695–727). Thousand Oaks, CA: Sage.

Foucault, M. (1977). *The archeology of knowledge*. London: Tavistock.

Freire, R. (1970). *Pedagogy of the oppressed*. New York: Continuum.

Freire, P. (1973). *Education for critical consciousness*. New York: Seabury Press.

Gegeo, D. W., & Watson-Gegeo, K. A. (2001). "How we know": Kwara'ae rural villagers doing indigenous epistemology. *The Contemporary Pacific, 13*, 55–88.

Gerard A. (1970). Preservation of tradition in African creative writing. *Research in African Literatures, 1*(1), 35–39.

Getty, G. A. (2010). The journey between Western and indigenous research paradigms. *Journal of Transcultural Nursing, 21*(1), 5–14.

Gill, G. J. (1993). *OK, The data's lousy, but it's all we've got (being a critique of conventional methods)*. London: International Institute for Environment and Development.

Gillan, R. (1993). *Feminism and geography: The limits of geographical knowledge*. Minneapolis: University of Minnesota Press.

Gilligan, C. (1982). *In a different voice: Psychological theory and women's development*. Cambridge, MA: Harvard University Press.

Glover M. (1997). *Kaupapa Maori health research: A developing discipline*. Paper presented at the Hui Whakapiripiri, Whaiora.

Goduka, I. N. (2000). African or indigenous philosophies: Legitimizing spiritually centered wisdoms within the academy. In P. Higgs, N. C. G. Vakalisa, T. V. Mda, & N. T. Assie-Lumumba (Eds.), *African voices in education* (pp. 63–83). Lansdowne, South Africa: Juta.

Gonzalez, G., & Lincoln Y. (2006). Decolonizing qualitative research: Nontraditional forms in the academy. *Forum: Qualitative Social Research, 7*(4).

Gonzalez, M. C. (2000). The four seasons of ethnography: A creation-centered ontology for ethnography. *International Journal of Intercultural Relations, 24*, 623–650.

Grande, S. (2000). American Indian identity and intellectualism: The quest for a new red pedagogy. *Qualitative Studies in Education, 13*, 343–359.

Grenier, L. (1998). *Working with indigenous knowledge: A guide for researchers*. Ottawa: International Development Research Centre.

Guba, E. G., & Lincoln, Y. S. (1989). *Fourth-generation evaluation*. Newbury Park, CA: Sage.

Guba, E., & Lincoln, Y. (2005). Paradigmatic controversies, contradictions, and emerging confluences. In N. K. Denzin & Y. S. Lincoln (Eds.), *Handbook of qualitative research* (pp. 191–215). Thousand Oaks, CA: Sage.

Guralnik, B. D., & Solomon, S. (Eds.). (1980). *Webster's new world dictionary* (2nd ed.). Cleveland, OH: William Collins Publishers.

Hall, S. (1992). The west and the rest: Discourse and power. In S. Hall & B. Gieblin (Eds.), *Formations of modernity* (pp. 276-320). Cambridge, UK: Polity Press.

Henry, E., & Pene, H. (2001). Kaupapa Maori: Locating indigenous ontology, epistemology, and methodology in the academy. *Organization, 8,* 234-242.

Hitchcock, G., & Hughes, D. (1995). *Research and the teacher: A qualitative introduction to school-based research.* London: Routledge.

Hodge, P., & Lester, J. (2006). Indigenous research: whose priority? Journeys and possibilities of cross cultural research in geography. *Geographical Research, 44*(1), 41-51.

Holloway, I., & Wheeler, S. (1996). *Qualitative research for nurses.* Oxford, UK: Blackwell Science.

hooks, b. (1990). *Yearning: Race, gender, and cultural politics.* London: Turnaround.

Hope, S., & Gaborone, S. (1999). *HIV/AIDS in the Kweneng West Sub-district in Botswana: Situation and response analysis.* Gaborone, Botswana: UNDP.

Hoppers, C. A. (2002). *Indigenous knowledge and the integration of knowledge systems.* Cape Town, South Africa: New Africa Books.

Hornby, A. S. (Ed.). (1994). *Oxford advanced learner's dictionary of current English.* Oxford, UK: Oxford University Press.

Hsia, H.-C. (2006). Empowering foreign brides through praxis-oriented research. *Societies Without Borders, 1,* 93-111.

Huber, M. (1993). Mediation around the medicine wheel. *Medicine Quarterly, 10*(4), 355-365.

Irwin, K. (1994). Maori research methods and processes: An exploration. *Sites Journal, 28,* 25-43.

Jack, A., Seloilwe, E., Mokoto, M., Letshabo, K., Veskov, D., Kobue, M., et al. (1999). *A study of knowledge, attitude, and behavioral aspects of HIV/AIDS among students of the University of Botswana.* Gaborone: University of Botswana, Botswana Ministry of Health, and World Health Organization.

Jaggar, A. M., & Rothenberg, P. (1993). *Feminist frameworks: Alternative theoretical accounts of the relations between women and men.* New York: McGraw-Hill.

Jensen, K. (2007). Routine HIV testing. *Bulletin of the World Health Organisation, 85*(5).

Jordan, N. (2005). *Feminist methodology and research among rural African women in Transkei.* South Africa: University of the Transkei.

Jussim, L. (2002). Intellectual imperialism. *Dialogue, 17*(1), 18-20.

Kaomea, J. (2003). Reading erasures and making the familiar strange: Defamiliarising methods for research in formerly colonized and historically oppressed communities. *Educational Researcher, 32*(2), 14-25.

Kaphagawani, D. N. (2000). What is African philosophy? In P. H. Coetzee & A. P. J. Roux (Eds.), *Philosophy from Africa* (pp. 86-98). Oxford, UK: Oxford University Press.

Kaphagawani, D. N., & Malherbe, J. G. (2000). African epistemology. In P. H. Coetzee & A. P. J. Roux (Eds.), *Philosophy from Africa* (pp. 205-216). Oxford, UK: Oxford University Press.

Kaplan, M. (2002). Employing proverbs to explore intergenerational relations across cultures. In M. Kaplan, N. Henkin, & A. Kusano (Eds.), *Linking lifetimes: A global view of intergenerational exchange* (pp. 39-64). Lanham, MD: University Press of America.

Kemmis, S., & McTaggart, R. (2000). Participatory action research. In N. K. Denzin & Y. S. Lincoln (Eds.), *Handbook of qualitative research* (2nd ed., pp. 567-605). Thousand Oaks, CA: Sage.

Kincheloe, J. L., & Steinberg, R. S. (2008). *Indigenous knowledges in education. Complexities, dangers, and profound benefits.* Thousand Oaks, CA: Sage.

King, M. L. (1958). *Stride toward freedom.* New York: Harper & Row.

Koro-Ljungberg M. (2010). Validity, responsibility, and aporia. *Qualitative Inquiry, 6*(8), 603-610.

Krefting, L. (1991). Rigor in qualitative research: The assessment of trustworthiness. *American Journal of Occupational Therapy, 45*(3), 214-222.

Kuhn, T. (1962). *The structure of scientific revolutions.* Chicago: University of Chicago Press.

Kvale, S. (1996). *Interviews: An introduction to qualitative research interviewing.* Thousand Oaks, CA: Sage.

Ladd, P. (2003). *Understanding deaf culture: In search of deafhood.* Tonawanda, NY: Multilingual Matters.

Laenui, P. (2000). Processes of decolonization. In M. Battiste (Ed.), *Reclaiming indigenous voice and vision* (pp. 150-160). Toronto: UBC Press.

Laible, J. (2000). A loving epistemology: What I hold critical in my life, faith, and profession. *Journal of Qualitative Studies in Education, 13*(6), 683-692.

Lane H. L. (1999). *The mask of benevolence: Disabling the deaf community.* San Diego, CA: Dawn Sign Press.

Lather, P. (1991). *Getting smart: Feminist research and pedagogy with/in the postmodern.* New York: Routledge.

Lavallée, L. F. (2009). Practical application of an indigenous framework and two qualitative indigenous research methods: Sharing circles and Anishnaabe symbol-based reflection. *International Journal of Qualitative Methods, 8*(1), 21-36.

Law, J. (2004). *After method: Mess in social science research.* London: Routledge.

Lawson, R. (1995). Critical race theory as praxis: A view from outside to the outside. *Harvard Law Journal, 38,* 353-370.

Lazarus, A. (2000). African and feminist approaches to peace education: Meeting on the margin. *Conflict Prevention Newsletter, 3*(2), 10-12.

Lester-Irabinna, R. (1997). Internalisation of an indigenous anti-colonial cultural critique of research methodologies: A guide to indigenous research methodologies and its principles. *Journal of American Studies, 14*(2), 109-122.

Liamputtong P. (2010). *Qualitative cross cultural research.* Cambridge, UK: Cambridge University Press.

Liddell, C., Barrett, L., & Bydawell, M. (2006). Indigenous beliefs and attitudes to AIDS in a rural South Africa community: An imperial study. *Annals of Behavioral Medicine, 23*(3), 218-225.

Lincoln, Y. (2009). Ethical practices in qualitative research. In D. M. Mertens & P. E. Ginsberg (Eds.), *The handbook of social research ethics* (pp. 150-169). Thousand Oaks, CA: Sage.

Lincoln, Y. S., & Gonzalez, G. (2008). The search for emerging decolonizing methodologies in qualitative research: Further strategies for liberatory and democratic inquiry. *Qualitative Inquiry, 14*(5), 784-805.

Lincoln, Y. S., & Guba, E. A. (1985). *Naturalistic inquiry.* Beverly Hills, CA: Sage.

Louis, R. P. (2007). Can You hear us now? Voices from the margin: Using indigenous methodologies. *Geographic Research, 45*(2), 130-139.

Louw, D. J. (1994). Metaphorical truth, conflict, and truth-experience: A critique of Vincent Brummer. *South African Journal of Philosophy, 13*(2), 58-65.

Louw, D. J. (2001). *Ubuntu: An African assessment of the religious other.* Available at http://www.bu.edu/wcp/Papers/Afri/AfriLouw.htm

Ludema, D. J., Cooperrider, D. L., & Barrett, F. J. (2006). *Appreciative enquiry: The power of the unconditional positive question.* In P. Reason & H. Bradbury (Ed.), *Handbook of action research* (pp. 155-165). Thousand Oaks, CA: Sage.

Lunch, N., & Lunch, C. (2006). *Insights into participatory video: A handbook for the field* [in five languages]. Available at http://insightshare.org/resources/pv-handbook

Lunden, E. (2006). *Postcolonial theory challenging mainstream feminist perspectives.* Lund, Sweden: Lund University, Department of Political Science.

Macleod, C., & Bhatia, S. (2008). *Postcolonialism and psychology.* London: Sage.

Makgoba M. W., Shope, T., & Mazwai, T. (1999). Introduction. In M. Makgoba (Ed.), *African renaissance: The new struggle* (pp. vii-xx). Cape Town: Mafube Publishing and Tafelberg Publishing.

Manuelito, K. (2004). An indigenous perspective on self-determination. In K. Mutua & B. Swadener, (Eds.), *Decolonizing research in cross-cultural contexts: Critical personal narratives* (pp. 235-253). Albany: State University of New York Press.

Marshall, C., & Young, M. (2006). Gender and methodology. In C. Skelton, B. Francis, & L. Smulyan (Eds.), *The SAGE handbook of gender and education* (pp. 63-78). London: Sage.

Marshall, J. (2001). Self-reflective inquiry practices. In P. Reason & H. Bradbury (Eds.), *Handbook of action research* (pp. 433-439). London: Sage.

Mazrui, A. (1990). *Cultural forces in world politics.* London: James Currey.

Mazrui, A. (1992). Towards diagnosing and treating cultural dependency: The care of the African University. *International Journal of Educational Development, 12*(2), 95-111.

McCann, C., & Kim S. (2003). *Feminist theory reader: Local and global perspectives.* New York: Routledge.

Mekgwe, P. (2003). *Theorizing African feminism: The "colonial" question.* Paper presented at the University of Botswana, Department of English Seminar Series.

Merriam, S. B., & Simpson, E. L. (2000). *A guide to research for educators and trainers of adults.* Malabar, FL: Krieger.

Mertens, D. M. (2009). *Transformative research and evaluation.* New York: Guilford.

Mertens, D. M. (2010a). *Research and evaluation in education and psychology: Integrating diversity with quantitative, qualitative and mixed methods.* Thousand Oaks, CA: Sage.

Mertens, D. M. (2010b). Transformative mixed methods research. *Qualitative Inquiry, 16*(6), 469-474.

Metz, M. (2001). Intellectual border crossing in graduate education: A report from the field. *Educational Researcher, 30*(5), 12-18.

Michael, S. (2005). The promise of appreciative inquiry as an interview tool for field research. *Development in Practice, 15*(2), 222-230.

Miles, M., & Huberman, A. (1984). *Qualitative data analysis: A sourcebook of new methods.* Thousand Oaks, CA: Sage.

Ministry of Health. (1992-2000). *HIV Sentinel Surveillance in Botswana.* Gaborone, Botswana: AIDS/STD Unit.

Ministry of Social Development. (2004). *Ngau Ara Tohutohu Rangahau Maori Guidelines for research and evaluation with Maori.* Pokapu, New Zealand: Centre for Social Research and Evaluation with Maori, Te Pokapu, Rangahau Arotake Hapori.

Mishra, S. (2000). Haunted lines: Postcolonial theory and the genealogy of racial formations in Fiji. In D. Brydon (Eds.), *Postcolonialism: Critical concepts in literacy and cultural studies.* London: Routledge.

Mkabela, Q. (2005). Using the Afrocentric method in researching indigenous African culture, *The Qualitative Report, 10*(1), 178-189.

Mohanty, C. (1991). Under Western eyes: Feminist scholarship and colonial discourses. In C. Mohanty, A. Russo, & L. Torres (Eds.), *Third world women and the politics of feminism* (pp. 51-80). Bloomington: Indiana University Press.

Moquin, H. (2007). *Postcolonial reflections on research in a Inuit community: Learning in community.* Proceedings of the joint international Adult Education Research Conference and the Canadian Association for the Study of Adult Education, University of Glasgow, Scotland.

Moseley W. G. (2007). Collaborating in the field, working for change: Reflecting on partnerships between academics, development organizations, and rural communities in Africa. *Singapore Journal of Tropical Geography, 28,* 334-347.

Mukherjee, N. (1997). *Participatory rural appraisal and questionnaire survey.* New Delhi: Concept Publishing.

Mukherji, P. N. (2004). Indigeneity and universality in social science. In P. N. Mukherji & C. Sengupta (Eds.), *Indigeneity and universality in social science. A South African response.* New Delhi: Sage.

Mumby, D. K. (1993). *Narrative and social control: Critical perspectives* (Sage series in communication research). Newbury Park, CA: Sage.

Musyoka, M., & Mertens, D. M. (2007). Making research and evaluation our own: Ethical implications for strengthening the foundations for Africa-rooted and Africa-led inquiry. *Mosenodi, 15,* 104-113.

Mutua, K., & Swadener, B. (2004). *Decolonizing research in cross-cultural contexts.* Albany: State University of New York Press.

Nader, R. H. (2005). *Cultural impacts on public perceptions of agricultural biotechnology: A comparison of South Korea and the United States.* Unpublished doctoral dissertation, Texas A&M University, College Station.

Namuddu, K. (1989, June 26–30). *Problems of communication between northern and southern researchers in the context of Africa.* Paper presented at the Seventh World Congress, Montreal.

Neuman, W. L. (1997). *Social research methods.* Boston: Allyn & Bacon.

Neuman, W. L. (2003). *Social research methods: Qualitative and quantitative approaches* (5th ed.). Boston: Allyn & Bacon.

Neuman, W. L. (2010). *Social research methods: Qualitative and quantitative approaches* (7th ed.). Boston: Allyn & Bacon.

Ngugi wa Thiong'o. (1986a). *Decolonizing the mind: The politics of language in African literature.* London: James Currey.

Ngugi wa Thiong'o. (1986b). *Writing against neo-colonialism.* London: Vita Books.

Ngugi wa Thiong'o. (1993). *Moving the centre: The struggle for cultural freedoms.* London: James Currey.

Nitza, A., Chilisa, B., & Makwinja-Morara, V. (2010). Mbizi: Empowerment and HIV/AIDS prevention for adolescent girls in Botswana. *The Journal of Specialists in Group Work, 35*(2), 105–114.

Ntseane, P. G. (2009). *Community leadership and empowerment: Botswana case study.* Kampala, Uganda: Institute of Social Transformation.

O'Brien, J. (2006). Some ethical consideration in selecting research methods. In A. Rwomire (Ed.), *Challenges and responsibilities of doing social research in Botswana: Ethical issues* (pp. 101–108). Nairobi, Kenya: OSSREA.

Oliver A. C. (1934). Mental tests in the study of the African. *Journal of the International African Institute, 7*(1), 40–46.

Omolewa, M., Adeola, O. A., Adekanmbi, G. A., Avoseh., M. B. M., & Braimoh, D. (1998). *Literacy, tradition, and progress: Enrolment and retention in an African rural literacy programme.* Hamburg, Germany: UNESCO Institute for Education.

Onyewumi, O. (1998). Deconfounding gender: Feminist theorizing and Western culture. *Signs: Journal of Women in Culture and Society, 23*(4), 1049–1062.

Oruka, O. (1998). *Sage philosophy: Indigenous thinkers and modern debate.* Nairobi, Kenya: Nairobi University Press.

Page, R. (2001). Reshaping graduate preparation in educational research methods: One school's experience. *Educational Researcher, 30*(5), 19–25.

Pallas, A. (2001). Preparing education doctoral students for epistemological diversity. *Educational Researcher, 30*(5), 6–11.

Parr, R. (2002). *Te Matahauariki methodology: The creative relationship framework* (Te Matahauariki Institute Occasional Paper Series). Hamilton, New Zealand: University of Waikato.

Patel, V., Simunyu E., Gwazura, F., Lewis, G., & Mann, A. (1997). The Shona symptom questionnaire: The development of an indigenous measure of common mental disorders in Harare. *Acta Psychiatr Scand, 95*(6), 469–475.

Patton, M. Q. (2002). *Qualitative evaluation and research methods.* Newbury Park, CA: Sage.

Pelletier, S. R. (2003). Indigenous research in social work: The challenge of operationalizing worldview. *Native Social Work Journal, 5,* 117-139.

Perkins J. J., Sanson-Fisher, R. W., Girgis A., & Blunden S. (1995). The development of a new methodology to access perceived needs among indigenous Australians. *Social Science Medicine, 41*(2), 226-275.

Peshkin, A. (2000). The nature of interpretation in qualitative research. *Educational Researcher, 30*(9), 5-9.

Pillow, W. (2003). Race-based methodologies: Multicultural methods or epistemological shifts? In G. R. Lopez & L. Parker (Eds.), *Interrogating racism in qualitative research methodology* (pp. 181-202). New York: Peter Lang.

Porsanger, J. (2004). An essay about indigenous methodology. *NORDLIT, 15,* 105-120.

Prah, K. K. (1999). African renaissance or warlordsm? In M. Makgoba (Ed.), *African renaissance: The new struggle* (pp. 1-12). Cape Town, South Africa: Mafube Publishing and Tafelberg Publishing.

Pryor, J., Kuupole, A., Kutor, N., Dunne M., & Adu-Yeboah, C. (2009). Exploring the fault lines of cross-cultural collaborative research. *Compare, 39*(6), 769-782.

Ramasilabele, B. T. (1999). *The views of people about HIV/AIDS patients at Kgale View in Gaborone* (Research project in partial fulfillment of the Degree of Home Economics). Gaborone: University of Botswana.

Ramsey, G. (2006). Ethical responsibilities of an African-centered research. In R. Apollo & F. B. Nyamnjoh (Eds.), *Challenges and responsibilities of social research in Africa: Ethical issues* (pp. 167-171). Addis Ababa, Ethiopia: OSSREA.

Reed, J. (2006). *Appreciative inquiry: Research for change.* Thousand Oaks, CA: Sage.

Reed, P. Y. (2001). African womanism and African feminism: A philosophical, literacy, and cosmological dialect on family? *Western Journal of Black Studies, 25,* 168-176.

Reinharz, S. (1992). *Feminist methods in social research.* New York: Oxford University Press.

Reviere, R. (2001). Toward an Afrocentric research methodology. *Journal of Black Studies, 31*(6), 709-727.

Rigney, L. (1999). Internationalization of an indigenous anticolonial culture critique of research methodologies. *Wicazo Sa Review, 14*(2), 109-121.

Roe, E. (1995). Development narratives or making the best of blueprint development. *World Development Narratives, 19*(6), 1065-1070.

Roos, V. (2008). The Mmogo method: Discovering symbolic community interactions. *Journal of Psychology in Africa, 18*(4), 659-668.

Saavedra, C. M., & Nymark, E. D. (2008). Borderland and Mestizaje feminism: The new tribalism. In N. K. Denzin, Y. S. Lincoln, & L. T. Smith (Eds.), *Handbook of critical and indigenous methodologies* (pp. 277-291). Thousand Oaks, CA: Sage.

Said, E. W. (1993). *Culture and imperialism.* London: Vintage.

Sandoval. C. (2000). *Methodology of the oppressed.* Minneapolis: University of Minnesota Press.

Scheurich, J. (1997). *Research method in the post-modern.* London: Falmer Press.

Scheurich, J. J., & Young, D. M. (1997). Coloring methodologies: Are our research epistemologies racially biased? *Educational Researcher, 26*(4), 4–16.

Schipper, M. (2003). Tree trunks and crocodiles in the ocean of reciprocal knowledge. *Etudes maliennes, 57,* 48–65.

Schmitt, R. (2005). Systematic metaphor analysis as a method of qualitative research. *The Qualitative Report, 10*(2), 358–394.

Schumaker, L. (2001). *Fieldwork, networks, and the making of cultural knowledge in Central Africa.* Durham & London: Duke University Press.

Sefa Dei, G. J. S. (2002). African development: The relevance and implications of "indigenousness." In G. J. Sefa Dei, B. L. Hall, & D. G. Rosenberg (Eds.), *Indigenous knowledges in global contexts: Multiple readings of our world* (pp. 70–86). Toronto: University of Toronto Press.

Senghor, L. (1966). Negritude. *Optima, 16,* 1–8.

Sharra, S. (2009). Towards an African peace epistemology: Teacher autobiography and uMunthu in Malawian education. In D. Caracciolo & A. M. Mungai (Eds.), *In the spirit of ubuntu: Stories of teaching and research* (pp. 23–50). Rotterdam: Sense Publishers.

Sindane, J. (1994). *Ubuntu and nation building.* Pretoria, South Africa: Ubuntu School of Psychology.

Skutnabb-Kangas, T. (2000). *Linguistic genocide or worldwide diversity and human rights.* Hillsdale, NJ: Lawrence Erlbaum.

Smith, G. H. (1990). *Research issues related to Maori education.* Paper presented to NZARE Special Interest Conference, Massey University, reprinted in 1992, The Issue of Research and Maori, Research Unit for Maori Education, The University of Auckland.

Smith G. H. (2000). Protecting and respecting indigenous knowledge. In M. Battiste (Ed.), *Reclaiming indigenous voice and vision* (pp. 207–224). Vancouver, Canada: University of British Columbia Press.

Smith, L. T. (1999). *Decolonizing methodologies: Research and indigenous people.* London: Zed Books.

Smith, L. T. (2008). On tricky ground: Researching the native in the age of uncertainty. In N. K. Denzin & Y. S. Lincoln (Eds.), *The landscape of qualitative research* (3rd ed., pp. 113–143). Thousand Oaks, CA: Sage.

Solórzano, D. G., & Yosso, T. J. (2001). Critical race and LatCrit theory and method: Counter-storytelling, Chicana and Chicano graduate school experiences. *International Journal of Qualitative Studies in Education, 14*(4), 471–495.

Spivak, G. C. (1988). Can the subaltern speak? In N. Cary & L. Grossberg (Eds.), *Marxism and the interpretation of culture.* Urbana: University of Illinois Press.

Spradley, James P. (1979). *The ethnographic interview.* New York: Holt, Rinehart and Winston.

Struthers, R., Lauderdale, J., Nicholas, L. N., Tom-Orme, L., & Strickland, C. J. (2005). Respecting tribal traditions in research and publications: Voices of five Native American nurse scholars. *Journal of Transcultural Nursing, 16*(3), 193–201.

Sutton, C. (1999). *Helping families with troubled children: A preventive approach.* Chichester, UK: John Wiley.

Swadener, B. B., & Mutua, K. (2008). Decolonizing performances: Deconstructing the global postcolonial. In N. K. Denzin, Y. S. Lincoln, & L. T. Smith. (Eds.), *Handbook of critical and indigenous methodologies* (pp. 31–43). Thousand Oaks, CA: Sage.

Swanson D. M. (2009). Where have all the fishes gone? Living ubuntu as an ethics of research and pedagogical engagement. In D. Caracciolo & A. M. Mungai (Eds.), *In the spirit of ubuntu: Stories of teaching and research* (pp. 3–21). Rotterdam: Sense Publishers.

Symonette, H. (2004). Walking pathways towards becoming a culturally competent evaluator: Boundaries, borderlands, and border crossings. In M. Thompson-Robinson, R. Hopson, & S. SenGupta (Eds.), *In search of cultural competence in evaluation: Toward principles and practices* (pp. 95–110). San Francisco: Willey.

Teffo, L. J. (2000). Africanist thinking: An invitation to authenticity. In P. Higgs, N. C. G., Vakalisa, T. V. Mda, & N. T. Assie-Lumumba, *African voices in education* (pp. 103–117). Lansdowne, South Africa: Juta.

Tetreault, M. K. (1993). Classroom for diversity: Rethinking curriculum and pedagogy. In J. A. Banks & C. A. Banks (Eds.), *Multicultural education: Issues and perspectives.* Boston: Allyn & Bacon.

Teunis, N. (2001). Same-sexuality in Africa: A case study from Senegal. *AIDS and Behavior, 5*(2), 173–182.

Thayer-Bacon, B. (2003). *Relational epistemologies.* New York: Peter Lang.

Thompson, A., & Gitlin, A. (1995). Creating spaces for reconstructing knowledge in feminist pedagogy. *Educational Theory, 45*(2), 125–150.

Tlou, S. D. (2001). *Menopause, health, and productivity.* A paper presented at a seminar organized by the Gender Network. Gaborone: University of Botswana.

Tournas, S. A. (1996). From sacred initiation to bureaucratic apostasy: Junior secondary school-leavers and the secularization of education in southern Africa. *Comparative Education, 32*(1), 10–17.

Trust for Community Outreach and Education (TCOE). (2001). *Participatory action research: A facilitator's manual.* Cape Town, South Africa: Author.

Tshireletso, B. (2001). *The Mazenge spirit.* Unpublished thesis in partial fulfillment of the requirement of the degree of Bachelor of Arts in Theology, University of Botswana.

Tsuruta, T. (2006). African imagination of moral economy: Notes on indigenous economic concepts and practices in Tanzania. *African Studies Quarterly, 9*(1-2), 104–121.

Tuck, E. (2009). Suspending damage: A letter to communities. *Harvard Educational Review, 79*(3), 409–427.

Tutu, D. M. (1999). *No future without forgiveness.* New York: Doubleday

UNAIDS. (2000). *Report on the global HIV/AIDS epidemic, 2000.* New York: United Nations.

United Nations Educational, Scientific and Cultural Organization (UNESCO). (1996). *The declaration of adult education and lifelong learning* (An African position paper presented at the African regional consultation on adult and continuing education and the challenges of the 21st century). Dakar, Senegal: UNESCO.

Van Dijk, T. A. (1993). *Elite discourse and racism.* Newbury Park, CA: Sage.

Van Schaik J. L. (1998). *Bagololo ba re.* Pretoria, South Africa: Van Shaik.

Vargas, L. R. S. (2003). *Critical race theory in education: Theory, praxis, and recommendations.* In G. R. Lopez & L. Parker (Eds.), *Interrogating racism in qualitative research methodology.* New York: Peter Lang.

Viruru, R., & Cannella, G. (2006). A postcolonial critique of the ethnographic interview: Research analyses research. In N. Denzin & M. Giardina (Eds.), *Qualitative inquiry and the conservative challenge* (pp. 175–192). Walnut Creek, CA: Left Coast.

Viswanathan, M., Ammerman, A., Eng, E., Gartlehner, G., Lohr, K. N., Griffith, D., Rhodes, S., Samuel-Hodge, C., Maty, S., Lux, L., Webb, L., Sutton, S. F., Swinson, T., Jackman, A., & Whitener, L. (2004). *Community-based participatory research: Assessing the evidence* (Evidence Report/Technology Assessment No. 99 (Prepared by RTI-University of North Carolina Evidence-Based Practice Center under Contract No. 290-02-0016, AHRQ Publication 04-E022- 2). Rockville, MD: Agency for Healthcare Research and Quality.

Vizenor, G. (1994). *Manifest manners: Post Indian warriors of surveillance.* Middleton, CT: Wesleyan University Press.

Walker, P. (2001). Journeys around the medicine wheel: A story of indigenous research in a Western University. *The Australian Journal of Indigenous Education, 29*(2), 18–21.

Wardhaugh, R. (1989). *An introduction to sociolinguistics.* New York: Blackwell.

Weber-Pillwax, C. (2001). What is indigenous research? *Canadian Journal of Native Education, 25*(2), 166–174.

Weiner, J. (1995). *Feminism and education.* Buckingham, UK: Open University Press.

Whyte, W. F. (1991). *Participatory action research.* Newbury Park, CA: Sage.

Wilson P., & Wilson, S. (2000). Circles in the classroom: The cultural significance of structure. *Canadian Social Studies, 34*(2), 11–12.

Wilson, S. (2008). *Research is ceremony: Indigenous research methods.* Manitoba, Canada: Fernwood.

Winter, R. (1996). Some principles and procedures for the conduct of action research. In O. Zuber Skerritt (Ed.), *New directions in action research* (pp. 13–27). London: Falmer Press.

World Health Organization. (2004). *UNAIDS/WHO policy statement on HIV testing.* Geneva: Author.

Yang, X. (2005). *Institutional challenges and leadership competencies in Chinese ministry of education-directed universities in implementing the 1999 Chinese action scheme for invigorating education towards the 21st century.* Unpublished doctoral dissertation, Texas A&M University, College Station.

Young, L. (2001). Border crossing and other journeys: Re-envisioning the doctoral preparation of educational researchers. *Educational Researcher, 30*(5), 3–5.

Youngman, F. (1998). *Old dogs and new tricks? Lifelong education for all the challenges facing adult education in Botswana.* Inaugural lecture, University of Botswana, Gaborone.

Yusuf, Y. K., & Mathangwane, J. T. (2003). Proverbs and HIV/AIDS. *Proverbium, 20.*

INDEX

SAGE Research Methods Online

The essential tool for researchers

**Sign up now at
www.sagepub.com/srmo
for more information.**

An expert research tool

- An **expertly designed taxonomy** with more than 1,400 unique terms for social and behavioral science research methods

- **Visual and hierarchical search tools** to help you discover material and link to related methods

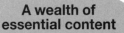

- Easy-to-use navigation tools
- Content organized by complexity
- Tools for citing, printing, and downloading content with ease
- Regularly updated content and features

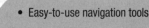

A wealth of essential content

- The most comprehensive picture of quantitative, qualitative, and mixed methods available today

- More than **100,000 pages of SAGE book and reference material** on research methods as well as editorially selected material from SAGE journals

- More than **600 books** available in their entirety online

Launching 2011!

$SAGE research methods online